REBUILDING TRUST

REBUILDING TRUST

CLERGY MORALE IN THE WAKE OF THE ABUSE CRISIS

Edited by

BRANDON VAIDYANATHAN
SARA PERLA
STEPHEN P. WHITE

The Catholic University of America Press
Washington, D.C.

The paper used in this publication meets the minimum requirements of American National Standards for Information Science—Permanence of Paper for Printed Library Materials, ANSI Z39.48-1992.

∞

Cataloging-in-Publication Data is available from the Library of Congress

ISBN (paper): 978-0-8132-4035-0

ISBN (ebook): 978-0-8132-4036-7

CONTENTS

LIST OF FIGURES AND TABLES

ACKNOWLEDGMENTS

A simple comment from Cardinal Timothy Dolan to the then-President of The Catholic University of America, John Garvey, provided the impetus for The Catholic Project's National Study of Catholic Priests, and therefore, of this edited volume. Our thanks to both of them, along with current President Dr. Peter Kilpatrick, who has supported the continuation of our efforts.

This volume would not have been possible without the generous support of the archdioceses of New York and Washington which sponsored our project, and the dedicated contributions of our chapter authors, whose enthusiastic participation made this book a reality. It should go without saying that the ideas expressed in these chapters are the responsibility of the authors and editors alone and not necessarily our generous benefactors.

Several conversations at the beginning of the project were immensely helpful in shaping the scope and direction of the NSCP, including with Dr. Peter Cajka, Dan Cellucci, Dr. Kathleen Cummings, Rev. Carter Griffin, Terry McKiernan, and Rev. Paul Scalia. We are especially grateful for suggestions on survey questions and extensive feedback on drafts of our questionnaires from Dr. Michael Brown, Dr. Michael Kane, Dr. Chelsea Rae Kelly, Rev. Gerard McGlone, Msgr. Steve Rossetti, and Dr. Gary Weaver. We are grateful also to Dr. Tyler VanderWeele and Dr. Matt Bloom for their survey measures on flourishing and burnout respectively.

We were fortunate to have an exceptional team at Gallup with Jenna Levy and Jeff Jones managing our survey. We're especially grateful to Dr. Christopher Jacobi for his masterful quantitative data analysis which served as the basis for much of this volume. Thanks also to Spyridon Kamposoulis for designing the figures in this volume and for Sam Sheng of CompuDesign for typesetting the text.

Many thanks to Dr. Tricia Bruce for leading the qualitative data collection and analysis portion of the study, and our team of collaborators who conducted and analyzed interviews, including Caitlin Fitzgerald, David Flores, Christina

Martinez, Cella Masso-Rivetti, Kate Middleton, Gabrielle Poma, Judith Ramon, Rev. Lucas Sharma SJ, Jennifer Sherman, and Lori Vien.

Thanks to Rev. Thomas Gaunt SJ and team at CARA for developing and conducting the census survey of bishops which was an integral part of our study.

Our gratitude also to Rev. Michael Fuller, General Secretary, and Rev. Jorge Torres, Executive Director for the Secretariat of Clergy, Consecrated Life, and Vocations, of the United States Conference of Catholic Bishops, who have been consistently supportive of our work.

We would also like to thank the two anonymous reviewers for their helpful comments on an earlier version of this volume. We could not have asked for a better editor than John Martino, and we are especially grateful for his meticulous editing which greatly helped clarify our arguments throughout this volume. Sincere thanks to the entire publishing team at CUA Press for their support and guidance.

Closer to home, Brandon is especially grateful to Claire for her support and encouragement of this work, and to Irene, Marta, Mike, Frank, Bernie, and Isaac for putting up with it. Stephen would like to thank Christine, whose loving patience is a balm, and Chiara, Olivia, Leo, and Josephine, who don't know exactly what dad does at work, but who miss him when he's gone. Sara would like to acknowledge her dearly departed father, Dr. Peter Paul Perla III, who was the first author in the family and would be tickled pink to see his daughter's name on this cover.

CHAPTER ONE

INTRODUCTION

Brandon Vaidyanathan, Sara Perla, and Stephen P. White

The clergy sex abuse crisis in the Catholic Church in the United States first came to public attention in the mid-1980s. But it was not until 2002, following a series of investigative reports by *The Boston Globe,* that the true scope of the crisis came to light, causing a national and global scandal. These investigations revealed a widespread pattern of covering up abuse by relocating accused priests rather than removing them or reporting them to law enforcement.

In response, the US Conference of Catholic Bishops (USCCB) met in June 2002 and developed the *Charter for the Protection of Children and Young People* (called the "Dallas Charter" after the city in which the bishops met). The Charter established a zero-tolerance policy for abusive priests, removing them permanently from ministry after one substantiated allegation. Other reforms included: mandatory reporting of allegations against clergy to civil authorities; background checks for all clergy and volunteers; the establishment of victim assistance programs in each diocese; and independent review boards to assist in the implementation of the charter and, on the diocesan level, to assess allegations.

The Charter, however, did nothing to hold bishops accountable for their role in mishandling abuse cases or even for committing abuse themselves. This was highlighted in a particularly dramatic way in 2018, when Cardinal

Theodore McCarrick was credibly accused of abusing a minor, leading to his resignation from the College of Cardinals and eventual laicization. When that particular allegation became public, it also came to light that allegations of sexual harassment of seminarians and young priests had been made against him for years. "Everyone knew," the faithful were told, "It was an open secret." Nothing had been done. In fact, McCarrick had been the spokesman for the US Bishops during the abuse crisis response in 2002, the face of the Dallas Charter reform.

In the same summer that the media was focused on McCarrick's crimes, the state of Pennsylvania released a "Grand Jury Report" exposing how high-ranking church leaders (who were not subject to the Dallas Charter) not only covered up the abuse of children by not reporting it to civil authorities but also allowed abusive priests further access to children.

These developments in the United States, coupled with others worldwide—notably the breakout of an abuse crisis in Chile that involved Pope Francis acknowledging that he made a mistake—led to a global abuse submit at the Vatican in February of 2019. Episcopal accountability was named as a central focus for the meeting. In May 2019, Pope Francis promulgated *Vos estis lux mundi*, establishing new laws for the universal Church. This law established norms for addressing allegations of abuse, and also established how the mishandling of abuse cases by bishops would be investigated and addressed by the Holy See. In the US, the Dallas Charter remains in effect and still represents the global gold standard for national episcopates looking to prevent abuse, respond to victims, and hold abusers accountable. The USCCB is, to date, the only conference of bishops who has been permitted to implement a national "zero-tolerance" policy.

Yet there are continued concerns that the implementation of the Charter has been uneven across dioceses, particularly regarding the definition of "credible accusations" and the due process afforded to accused priests. There is a perception of injustice and a breakdown in trust between clergy and Church leadership. Moreover, as the scope of the Church's anti-abuse policies has expanded, some argue that efforts to strengthen oversight have inadvertently deepened tensions between bishops and priests, particularly regarding trust and transparency.

Today, more than two decades after the implementation of the Dallas Charter, understanding the crisis requires not only acknowledging the pain of abuse survivors and their families, but also examining the charter's broader institutional consequences, particularly how it has reshaped the dynamics of trust and governance within the Church.

These concerns helped to motivate the National Study of Catholic Priests (NSCP), which was conducted in 2022 by The Catholic Project at The Catholic University of America, founded by President John Garvey to be the university's response to the sexual abuse crisis. The three editors of this volume spearheaded this study,[1] which included the largest survey of American priests in more than fifty years. We also conducted in-depth interviews with more than one hundred priests and a census survey of bishops. The study aimed to understand: How has the abuse crisis, and the Church's institutional response to that crisis, affected priests? Are priests flourishing or struggling? How do priests see the Church's efforts to curtail abuse and hold abusers accountable? How has it shaped their relationships with and trust in their bishops? In short, what is the state of the Catholic priesthood in the United States today?

The present volume presents key results of the NSCP alongside a range of interdisciplinary perspectives that address its implications. Our hope is that this work (1) makes a compelling case for the importance of social scientific research in assessing the health of the Church, (2) provides robust empirical data that moves beyond anecdotes and hearsay to document the fears, challenges, and experiences of priests, particularly regarding trust, well-being, and the implementation of the Dallas Charter, and (3) demonstrates the study's value in generating serious reflection on a range of pressing issues. These include the need to improve due process protections for accused priests, initiatives to strengthen clergy well-being, the role of spiritual fatherhood in fostering communion between bishops and priests, and the necessity of structural reforms to rebuild trust and accountability in the Church. Additionally, the volume offers historical, theological, and canonical insights into shifting dynamics within the priesthood, examines generational and ideological differences, and highlights practical efforts within dioceses to renew and support the priesthood in light of these challenges.

1 White (Executive Director) and Perla (Communications Manager) work for The Catholic Project, while Vaidyanathan, Professor of Sociology at Catholic University, led the study's team of researchers. The process and results of the study are described in more detail in chapter 2 and the first appendix.

The Crisis and Its Development

Before turning to the NSCP findings and the contributions of this volume, it is important to first briefly review the clergy sexual abuse crisis—its origins, development, and the Church's response over time. While a more detailed treatment can be found in the works cited below, this section outlines key moments that have shaped the current landscape.[2]

One of the earliest documented warnings about clerical sexual abuse came from Fr. Gerald Fitzgerald, who in 1947 founded the Servants of the Paraclete in New Mexico to provide treatment for priests with behavioral problems, initially focusing on alcoholism but later including sexual misconduct. Fitzgerald repeatedly urged bishops and Vatican officials to remove sexually abusive priests from ministry permanently, arguing that they were incurable and recommending laicization in some cases. However, his warnings went largely unheeded.[3] Many psychologists consulted by the Church hierarchy argued that proclivity to abuse could be held in check with therapy, and that the priests in question could be returned to ministry in a new setting.[4] This practice became a pattern: Priests would take a leave of absence, go to a treatment center, and then be reassigned. The bishops, both in the US and the Vatican, demonstrated a preference for secrecy,

2 For a helpful timeline, see NCR Staff, "Timeline of a Crisis," *National Catholic Reporter*, July 6, 2015, https://www.ncronline.org/blogs/ncr-today/timeline-crisis

3 Thomas G. Plante and Kathleen L. McChesney, eds., *Sexual Abuse in the Catholic Church: A Decade of Crisis, 2002–2012* (Praeger, 2012); Tom Roberts, "Bishops Were Warned of Abusive Priests." *National Catholic Reporter*, March 30, 2009, https://www.ncronline.org/news/accountability/bishops-were-warned-abusive-priests.

4 A window into this therapeutic mindset comes from the document provided to the bishops on October 26, 1995, by Jesuit priest James Gill, MD, with the title "Will Priests Sexually Abuse After Treatment?", which includes the recommendation, "Bishops could be informed that a number of treatment centers have a remarkably low rate of recidivism, especially among ephebophiles [those whose victims were postpubescent children]. This might result in increased hopefulness about the prospect of giving ministerial assignments to priests who have completed treatment in these centers." This recommendation was offered despite Fr. Gill observing in various ways that the data on recidivism was incomplete and unreliable. Available online at https://www.bishop-accountability.org/reports/1995-11-RestoringTrust/rt95-05-after.pdf

reassignment, and internal resolution over transparency and accountability, allowing abuse to persist for decades.[5]

Let us consider just a handful of examples. In the 1960s, James Porter, who was later accused of sexually abusing over 100 children, was quietly reassigned multiple times across dioceses, despite credible allegations, and was not sentenced until 1993. In 1984, Gilbert Gauthe, a priest in the Diocese of Lafayette, Louisiana, was publicly accused of sexually abusing over 30 children. Church officials had been aware of Gauthe's abuse for years and had reassigned him to new parishes rather than removing him from ministry. His case set a precedent for large financial settlements, with the diocese paying more than $4 million in settlements. Many other settlements were later handled confidentially to avoid public trials and scrutiny.[6] In 1985, the Doyle-Mouton-Peterson Report warned US bishops about the growing problem of clerical sexual abuse, predicting severe financial, legal, and moral consequences if decisive action was not taken.[7]

While this report is claimed to have been largely ignored by national Church leadership, some dioceses between 1986–1990 began to improve their personnel policies and training programs to prevent abuse.[8] In 1992, in response to mounting public awareness due to high-profile cases such as that of James Porter, the National Conference of Catholic bishops formulated "Five Principles" to address the issue: (1) respond promptly to abuse allegations, (2) immediately remove credibly accused priests from ministry, (3) comply with civil reporting laws, (4) reach out pastorally to victims and their families,

5 Laurie Goodstein, "Vatican Declined to Defrock U.S. Priest Who Abused Boys," *New York Times*, March 24. 2010, https://www.nytimes.com/2010/03/25/world/europe/25vatican.html

6 Jason Berry, *Lead Us Not Into Temptation: Catholic Priests and the Sexual Abuse of Children*. Doubleday, 1992.

7 Thomas Doyle, Michael Peterson, and Ray Mouton, "The Problem of Sexual Molestation by Roman Catholic Clergy: Meeting the Problem in a Comprehensive and Responsible Manner," Confidential report, 1985, https://www.bishop-accountability.org/reports/1985_06_09_Doyle_Manual/DoyleManual_NCR_combined.pdf

8 See Catholic News Service, "U.S. Church's Response to Sex Abuse Shows Progress, but Questions Remain," August 24, 2018, https://www.ncronline.org/news/us-churchs-response-sex-abuse-shows-progress-questions-remain

and (5) maintain transparency with parish communities and the public while respecting privacy of individuals involved. Between 1993 and 1996, the Conference convened an Ad Hoc Committee on Sexual Abuse, which published three annual volumes under the title "Restoring Trust."[9] The reports offered guidelines for implementing the Five Principles. These guidelines, however, were advisory rather than mandatory; they lacked enforcement mechanisms and relied on voluntary compliance, resulting in inconsistent implementation across dioceses, and thus had limited impact.[10]

In 1997, a jury awarded $119.6 million judgment against the Diocese of Dallas for its mishandling of the abuse committed by former priest Rudolph Kos, though the settlement was later renegotiated and reduced to approximately $23 million.[11] Despite such revelations and legal and financial consequences, patterns of secrecy, reassignment, and institutional protection persisted.[12]

The crisis reached a tipping point in 2002 with *The Boston Globe*'s Spotlight team's investigative series.[13] Their reporting revealed that the Archdiocese of Boston had systematically covered up decades of sexual abuse by dozens of

9 https://www.usccb.org/resources/restoring-trust-vol-i; https://www.usccb.org/resources/restoring-trust-vol-ii; https://www.usccb.org/resources/restoring-trust-vol-iii

10 Michael Merz, "A History of the National Review Board," USCCB, 2011, https://www.usccb.org/resources/nrb-history-5-17-2011

11 Ed Houseright and Brooks Egerton, "Plaintiffs Awarded $119.6 Million in Kos Case." *Dallas Morning News*, July 25, 1997, https://www.dallasnews.com/news/1997/07/25/plaintiffs-awarded-119-6-million-in-kos-case/; Carol Marie Cropper, "A Diocese Settles a Case of Sex Abuse," *New York Times*, July 11, 1998, https://www.nytimes.com/1998/07/11/us/a-diocese-settles-a-case-of-sex-abuse.html

12 For instance, Cardinal Law reinstated Ronald Paquin to ministry in 1998 despite numerous complaints and payouts. See Steven Kurjian, "Records Show Cardinal Reassigned Paquin After Settlements," *Boston Globe*, May 30, 2002, https://www.bostonglobe.com/news/special-reports/2002/05/29/records-show-cardinal-reassigned-paquin-after-settlements/JEaLGAEIYLr2Cyaze6HpRJ/story.html

13 See Jon Henley, "How the Boston Globe Exposed the Abuse Scandal That Rocked the Catholic Church," *The Guardian*, April 21, 2010, https://www.theguardian.com/world/2010/apr/21/boston-globe-abuse-scandal-catholic; Dart Center for Journalism & Trauma, "Abuse in the Catholic Church," *Dart Center*, archived May 18, 2008, https://web.archive.org/web/20080518070854/http://www.dartcenter.org/articles/special_features/church_abuse.php; *Boston Globe*, "Church Allowed Abuse by Priest for Years," *The Boston Globe*, archived at https://archive.is/atjgs

priests. Cardinal Bernard Law and other church officials were shown to have knowingly reassigned abusive priests without informing the new communities of the priests' histories. This exposé shattered the longstanding silence around the issue of sexual abuse, and it highlighted the Church's complicity in protecting the institution over persons, and predators over victims. It showed how Church lawyers quietly settled numerous cases of abuse to avoid public scrutiny. The *Globe's* detailed reporting, which won the Pulitzer Prize for Public Service, sparked national and international outrage, leading to further investigations and revelations in dioceses across the country and, eventually, around the world. The scandal led to the resignation of Cardinal Law as archbishop and fundamentally changed how the general public, many Catholics, and the institutions of the Catholic Church itself understood and responded to clerical abuse. The Spotlight series is credited with breaking the dam of silence and denial that had previously surrounded this issue.

Widespread public outrage forced the bishops to respond decisively. After an April meeting with Pope John Paul II, in which the pope was convinced to allow the conference to establish a "zero-tolerance policy," the USCCB in June 2002 adopted the *Charter for the Protection of Children and Young People* (commonly known as the Dallas Charter, since the General Assembly that year was held in Dallas, Texas). The Charter set forth mandatory policies to address allegations of abuse, prevent future incidents, and provide support to victims.[14] It was, and still is, a landmark reform in the Church's handling of sexual abuse. It mandated that a priest credibly accused of abuse would be relieved "promptly of his ministerial duties," and that if the allegation was substantiated, i.e. "admitted or established" (Article 5), he would be permanently removed from ministry. The Charter also established diocesan review boards to assess allegations as well as a national review board to assess the implementation of the Charter, and it required mandatory reporting of abuse allegations to civil authorities. The Charter further included provisions for safe-environment training programs and background checks for Church employees and volunteers who have contact with children. Victims assistance programs were mandated to provide support. The charter faced

14 USCCB, "Charter for the Protection of Children and Young People," 2002, https://www.usccb.org/offices/child-and-youth-protection/charter-protection-children-and-young-people

near-immediate criticism, however, for failing to apply the same standards to bishops, and for what could be inadequate enforcement mechanisms.[15]

The USCCB also commissioned studies on child sexual abuse by clergy. In 2004, the John Jay College of Criminal Justice published *The Nature and Scope of the Problem of Sexual Abuse of Minors by Catholic Priests and Deacons in the United States.*[16] The report identified 10,667 allegations of abuse involving 4,392 priests between 1950 and 2002, representing about 4% of all priests during that period. The victims were predominantly male (81%), mostly between the ages of 11 and 14 at the time of the abuse. The vast majority of abuse cases were, even by 2002, decades old. Nevertheless, the so-called "John Jay Report" summarized the systemic failures already alluded to, and it highlighted that only 2% of accused clergy received sentences. While the report provided valuable insights, it faced criticism for relying on self-reported diocesan data, potentially underestimating the scale of the abuse.[17] A follow-up report in 2011 examined the underlying factors contributing to the crisis.[18] This time, critics argued that the report's analysis

15 Thomas Green, "Critique of the Dallas Charter," *National Catholic Reporter*, September 19, 2002, https://natcath.org/NCR_Online/documents/Greencritique.htm. For instance, Green notes that "not a word is said about bishops who in the past have failed to behave responsibly in discharging their supervisory responsibilities or who in the future may fail to do so. Is not that neglect precisely one of the major causes of the undercutting of episcopal authority among the faithful?" Green also notes that "With due regard for the aforementioned restoration of an accused cleric's good name, the document should have affirmed a presumption of his innocence until he is proven guilty." This point is further developed by Avery Dulles, "Rights of Accused Priests: Toward a Revision of the Dallas Charter and the Essential Norms," *America,* June 21, 2004, https://www.americamagazine.org/issue/488/article/rights-accused-priests. See chapter 7 by Thomas Guarino for more details about Dulles's critique.

16 John Jay College of Criminal Justice, *The Nature and Scope of the Problem of Sexual Abuse of Minors by Catholic Priests and Deacons in the United States.* 2004, https://www.usccb.org/sites/default/files/issues-and-action/child-and-youth-protection/upload/The-Nature-and-Scope-of-Sexual-Abuse-of-Minors-by-Catholic-Priests-and-Deacons-in-the-United-States-1950-2002.pdf

17 Joe Feuerherd, "Leaked Numbers Provoke Dispute," *National Catholic Reporter*, February 27, 2004, https://www.bishop-accountability.org/news2004_01_06/2004_02_27_Feuerherd_LeakedNumbers.htm

18 John Jay College of Criminal Justice, "The Causes and Context of Sexual

of the causes of abuse focused too much on extrinsic factors such as the sexual revolution, rather than addressing the Church's internal culture of secrecy and clericalism.[19] The John Jay Reports and later studies concluded that most incidents of sexual abuse occurred during the 1960s and 1970s, with the highest rates reported in the late 1970s, followed by a sharp decline after 1985 that has remained low in the years since.[20] Today, the known incidence rate of sexual abuse among Catholic clergy remains low.[21]

In the years following the adoption of the Dallas Charter and the publication of the John Jay Reports, revelations of abuse and cover-ups continued to emerge, demonstrating that the Church's initial measures were insufficient to address the depth of the crisis. The most significant of these developments was the release of the Pennsylvania Grand Jury Report in 2018, which documented more than a thousand cases of abuse by over 300 priests across six dioceses over a 70-year period.[22] The report detailed systemic efforts by Church leaders to shield abusive clergy and avoid public scandal, often at

---

Abuse of Minors by Catholic Priests in the United States, 1950-2010," https://www.usccb.org/sites/default/files/issues-and-action/child-and-youth-protection/upload/The-Causes-and-Context-of-Sexual-Abuse-of-Minors-by-Catholic-Priests-in-the-United-States-1950-2010.pdf

19 Kathleen McChesney, "What Caused the Crisis? Key Findings of the John Jay College Study on Clergy Sexual Abuse," *America,* June 6, 2011, https://www.americamagazine.org/faith/2011/06/06/what-caused-crisis-key-findings-john-jay-college-study-clergy-sexual-abuse-150155

20 John Jay College of Criminal Justice, "The Causes and Context of Sexual Abuse," 32.

21 Jonathan L. Wiggins and Mary L. Gautier, *Summary of 20 Years of Data Collected Annually for the CARA Survey of Allegations and Costs for U.S. Catholic Dioceses, Eparchies, and Religious Communities of Men* (Center for Applied Research in the Apostolate, January 2025), https://static1.squarespace.com/static/629c7d00b33f845b6435b6ab/t/6787e82e7d337b11e27ac467/1736960046969/CARASummary2024.pdf

22 Pennsylvania Office of Attorney General, *Report I of the 40th Statewide Investigating Grand Jury: The Sexual Abuse of Children in the Roman Catholic Church* (Office of Attorney General, 2018), https://www.attorneygeneral.gov/report/ This report prompted a wave of similar investigations by attorneys general in other states, further revealing the systemic scope of the crisis. See, e.g., Maryland (https://www.marylandattorneygeneral.gov/news%20documents/OAG_redacted_Report_on_Child_Sexual_Abuse.pdf) and Illinois (https://clergyreport.illinoisattorneygeneral.gov).

the expense of victims. While the overwhelming majority of cases highlighted in the Pennsylvania Grand Jury Report were, like those in the John Jay Report, decades old, the findings prompted new grand jury investigations in other states and led to legislative efforts to expand statutes of limitations for abuse cases.[23]

The McCarrick scandal also became a pivotal moment for the Church. Once a highly influential cardinal, Theodore McCarrick was laicized in 2019 after a canonical trial found him guilty of solicitation in the context of the Sacrament of Reconciliation and sexual sins with adults and minors with the "aggravating factor of abuse of power."[24] This unprecedented action against a cardinal demonstrated the Church's belated commitment to holding even its most powerful members accountable. Still, the Vatican's own 2020 report on McCarrick revealed deep systemic failures, including missed opportunities to investigate credible allegations and a culture of secrecy that allowed his misconduct to go unchecked.[25] The scandals led to renewed efforts to improve accountability, such as Pope Francis's Motu Propio *Vos estis lux mundi*, which established new procedures for investigating bishops accused of abuse or

23 Brian Clites, "Catholic Church Sex Abuse: The Difference a Pennsylvania Grand Jury Made in the Lives of Survivors," *Pennsylvania Capital-Star*, August 25, 2019, https://penncapital-star.com/commentary/catholic-church-sex-abuse-the-difference-a-pennsylvania-grand-jury-made-in-lives-of-survivors-opinion/; Tara Isabella Burton, "Even More States Have Launched Investigations into Clerical Abuse Since the Pennsylvania Report," *Vox*, October 24, 2018, https://www.vox.com/2018/9/17/17847466/state-investigations-clerical-abuse-dc-virginia-maryland-florida-new-york; Julie Zauzmer Weil, "The Pennsylvania Grand Jury Report Shook the Nation and the Vatican: So Why Didn't It Change Laws at Home?" *The Washington Post*, August 14, 2019, https://www.washingtonpost.com/religion/2019/08/14/pennsylvania-grand-jury-report-shook-nation-vatican-so-why-didnt-it-change-laws-home/.

24 CBS News, ""Former U.S. Cardinal Theodore McCarrick Defrocked over Sexual Abuse," February 16, 2019, https://www.cbsnews.com/news/cardinal-theodore-mccarrick-defrocks-catholic-church-laicization-sexual-abuse-live-updates/

Reuters, "Former U.S. Cardinal McCarrick Defrocked for Sex Crimes," February 16, 2019, https://www.reuters.com/article/world/former-us-cardinal-mccarrick-defrocked-for-sex-crimes-idUSKCN1Q508H/

25 Secretariat of the Holy See, "Report on the Holy See's Institutional Knowledge and Decision-Making Related to Former Cardinal Theodore Edgar McCarrick (1930–2017)," November 10, 2020, https://www.vatican.va/resources/resources_rapporto-card-mccarrick_20201110_en.pdf

cover-ups.[26] Yet these policies have also faced criticism for their inconsistent and opaque application, as well as for the category of "vulnerable persons" which some argue is defined so broadly that it risks being unhelpful.[27] The Vatican routinely declines to disclose whether any bishops are facing *Vos estis* investigations and never releases the details of those investigations, only declaring that a bishop has been exonerated or convicted, and often allowing bishops found guilty of undisclosed infractions to resign rather than be formally removed from office or face canonical charges.[28]

Hence, despite watershed reforms, the Church continues to face significant challenges in addressing sexual abuse, particularly in ensuring consistent implementation of reforms and holding Church leadership accountable for past failures. Survivor advocacy groups like Survivors Network of those Abused by Priests (SNAP) have continued to push for transparency, justice, and changes to legal frameworks. Recent investigations underscore that the crisis is far from over. A 2024 report from the Michigan Attorney General revealed that 56 clergy members, including 48 priests, have been accused of sexual abuse within the Diocese of Lansing since the 1950s.[29] Once again, the large majority of these abuse cases were decades old.

26 Pope Francis, Apostolic Letter issued Motu Proprio *Vos estis lux mundi* (May 5, 2019). Available at vatican.va

27 Ed Condon, "Analysis: '*Vos estis* and "Vulnerability,"' *Catholic News Agency*, May 13, 2019, https://www.catholicnewsagency.com/news/41273/analysis-vos-estis-and-vulnerability

28 For example, Bishop Michael J. Hoeppner of Crookston, Minnesota, was subject to a *Vos estis* inquiry, but the archbishop leading the investigation could not disclose even that the matter was being investigated. Hoepper was allowed to resign, and some observers found it unseemly that he was allowed to preside over a "farewell Mass," during which he offered only a generic apology. See Catholic News Service, "Pope Accepts Resignation of Bishop Who Heads Minnesota's Crookston Diocese," April 13, 2021, https://www.catholicsun.org/2021/04/13/pope-accepts-resignation-of-bishop-who-heads-minnesotas-crookston-diocese/; Marie Wiering, "Hoeppner Apologizes to Crookston Diocese During Farewell Mass," *National Catholic Reporter*, April 19, 2021, https://www.ncronline.org/news/hoeppner-apologizes-crookston-diocese-during-farewell-mass

29 Caitlin McCormack, "56 Clergy, Including 48 Priests, Accused of Sexual Abuse Dating Back to the 1950s in Michigan Catholic Diocese: AG." *New York Post*, December 17, 2024, https://nypost.com/2024/12/17/us-news/56-clergy-including-48-priests-accused-of-sexual-abuse-dating-back-to-the-1950s-in-michigan-catholic-diocese-ag/

Meanwhile, the financial fallout from abuse settlements continues to mount. For instance, the Archdiocese of Los Angeles, which had previously paid more than $700 million to victims, announced an additional $880 million settlement in 2024 to address over 1,300 abuse claims, bringing its total payouts to more than $1.5 billion over the past two decades.[30] By 2025, over 40 dioceses had declared bankruptcy, largely as a result of abuse claims.[31] In some cases, Church leaders have been accused of strategically using bankruptcy filings to limit financial liabilities and delay justice for victims, raising concerns about fairness for survivors.[32] These criticisms reflect the Church's ongoing struggle, decades after the worst of the abuse occurred, to reconcile past failures with its efforts to restore trust and credibility.

Yet as the Church grapples with the priorities of justice for survivors, institutional accountability, and financial stability, another critical question remains: What impact has this ongoing crisis had on the morale and well-being of priests? It may be considered remarkable that any young man would consider the Catholic priesthood in the midst of these scandals, given the lowered public prestige of the priesthood and the ever-constant threat of allegations of abuse. In fact, the numbers of men entering seminary has been remarkably steady since 2000, although not sufficient to replace the numbers of retiring and deceased clergy.[33] Moreover, US dioceses pour significant resources into training young men for the priesthood, such that every

30 Richard Winton and Hannah Fry. "L.A. Catholic Church Payouts for Clergy Abuse Top $1.5 Billion with New Record Settlement," *LA Times*, October 16, 2024, https://www.latimes.com/california/story/2024-10-16/archdiocese-of-los-angeles-to-pay-880-million-in-the-largest-clergy-sexual-abuse-settlement

31 Marie T. Reilly, "Catholic Dioceses in Bankruptcy," *Penn State Law eLibrary*, December 20, 2024, https://elibrary.law.psu.edu/bankruptcy/.

32 Kristina Cooke et al., "Boy Scouts, Catholic Dioceses Find Haven from Sex Abuse Suits in Bankruptcy," *Reuters*, December 30, 2022, https://www.reuters.com/world/us/boy-scouts-catholic-dioceses-find-haven-sex-abuse-suits-bankruptcy-2022-12-30/

33 For a summary of these trends, see Stephen White, "All Vocations Are Local," *The Pillar*, June 20, 2025 (https://www.pillarcatholic.com/p/all-vocations-are-local), drawing on data from the Center for Applied Research in the Apostolate (https://cara.georgetown.edu/).

priest who leaves ministry for whatever reason represents a significant lost investment. While US lay Catholics are notable for both the numbers and energy with which they participate in Church life and activity, priests remain essential to the community, not only for offering sacramental opportunities to the laity but for the parish governing structure. Their well-being is a vital question for the whole US Catholic Church. Are priests flourishing in their vocations, or are they struggling under the weight of suspicion and diminished trust?

In asking this question, the study found that a particular area important to clergy well-being has been adversely affected by the developments of the past two decades: the relationship between priests and their bishop. The abuse scandal has shaped not only how priests are perceived by the laity but also how they relate to their superiors—particularly in an environment where trust in Church leadership has eroded. The burden of navigating this crisis falls on both priests and bishops, and as dioceses face financial strain, structural changes, and shifting public expectations, these challenges become more complex. But while bishops still have a fair amount of leeway in how they respond to these challenges, priests are well aware that they are at the mercy of their bishop's decisions, especially should they face an allegation themselves.

Twenty years after the implementation of the Dallas Charter, we need to understand: How has the crisis, and the Church's institutional response to it, affected priests' relationships with their bishops as well as the laity? How do they perceive the Church's efforts to address abuse and ensure accountability? Similarly, how has the crisis reshaped the role and leadership of bishops? These questions form the basis of the National Study of Catholic Priests. A key motivation for the study was to move beyond anecdotal evidence and collect reliable data on how priests perceive the consequences of the sex abuse crisis and their relationships with their bishops. The findings of this study, and the reflections they have generated, shape the contributions of this volume.

Contributions of the Volume

In Chapter 2, we highlight the main results of the NSCP. We focus in particular on issues of clergy well-being, trust between priests and bishops, priests' views on the implementation of the Dallas Charter, and generational tensions among priests. Some good news for Catholics is that, consistent with past studies, the vast majority of priests report high levels of flourishing.[34] Nevertheless, significant concerns emerge regarding burnout, declining trust in bishops, and the lasting impact of the sexual abuse crisis. Trust in bishops is notably low, with nearly half of diocesan priests expressing little confidence in their bishop's leadership, a sentiment exacerbated by perceptions of inadequate due process protections and fears of false accusations. Trust in bishops turns out to be an important predictor of priestly well-being. Trust in one's bishop is also strongly associated with priests' theological and political alignment with the bishop. The study reveals ideological shifts within the priesthood, with younger priests overwhelmingly identifying as theologically orthodox and politically conservative or moderate in contrast to older priests, many of whom consider themselves more progressive. These findings underscore the need for institutional reforms to rebuild trust, improve clergy well-being, and foster a culture of accountability and pastoral support within the Church. The subsequent chapters include both additional analyses of the study as well as reflections, both theological and practical, on its implications.

In chapters 3 and 4, Maureen Day offers additional analyses of the qualitative data from the NSCP. Chapter 3 focuses on the key supportive factors that contribute to priestly morale. Day identifies the main sources of internal support (i.e., spiritual practices, self-care, and imagination) and external support (i.e., relationships with other priests and with bishops) that impact priestly morale. The subsequent chapter focuses on the signs and implications of burnout among priests. It explores the psychological dimensions of burnout—emotional exhaustion, cynicism, and a sense of ineffectiveness—and discusses six factors that influence burnout (work overload, control, reward, community, fairness, and values). The chapter also suggests practical strategies to shift from merely avoiding burnout to actively cultivating engagement among priests, highlighting the importance of reducing workload, providing adequate training, and fostering supportive relationships.

In chapter 5, Brooke Tranten historically contextualizes the changing levels of priests' trust in their bishops over the past few decades. She focuses

34 See Stephen J. Rossetti, *Why Priests Are Happy: A Study of the Psychological and Spiritual Health of Priests* (Ave Maria Press, 2011) and *Priesthood in a Time of Crisis: A New Study of the Psychological and Spiritual Health of Priests* (Ave Maria Press, 2023).

in particular on the relatively high levels of trust (63%) that American priests had in their bishops just before the sexual abuse scandals of 2002. Tranten argues that such presbyterial trust emerged in a generation of younger, more conservative priests inspired by the stability and longevity of Pope John Paul II's leadership in the 1990s. The chapter demonstrates how John Paul II's pastoral vision influenced the American episcopal conference in their own leadership decisions, resulting in a conference that was at once inspired to teach and lead forthrightly and reluctant to exercise its own authority when it came to enforcing norms in the case of sensitive or controversial matters. The chapter also examines how John Paul II's papacy helped to shape the American episcopate in terms of appointments and discipline, reinforcing orthodoxy and providing a sense of stability in the post-Vatican II Church for young priests. It concludes with reflections on what lessons this era might offer for rebuilding presbyterial trust today.

In chapter 6, Bishop Frederik Hansen provides a theological and canonical analysis of the relationship between bishops and priests in the Church to provide context for the NSCP findings. The chapter explores the theological foundation of priesthood, emphasizing the sacrament of holy orders and its three levels: episcopate, presbyterate, and diaconate. It outlines the role and responsibilities of bishops, rooted in Christ's mission and apostolic succession. Subsequently, it examines the relationship between priests and bishops as co-workers sharing in the apostolic mission of the Church. Finally, it discusses the canonical and pastoral governance of priests by bishops, emphasizing the importance of mutual respect, collaboration, and the spiritual bond between the bishop and his presbyterate. The chapter concludes with suggestions for improving this relationship in the context of Church teaching.

In chapter 7, Msgr. Thomas Guarino offers a trenchant, even controversial, critique of the implementation of the Dallas Charter. He argues that the NSCP confirms Cardinal Dulles's predictions that the implementation of the Charter would severely damage the relationship between American bishops and priests, leading to a widespread lack of trust. The chapter reflects on how the Charter, while aiming to address the sexual abuse crisis, has been implemented in ways that undermine natural justice and the theology of the priesthood. The chapter also explores how the Charter's procedures have created an adversarial relationship between bishops and priests, eroding priestly morale and contributing to a deep-seated distrust in episcopal leadership.

Chapter 8 discusses the crisis of trust and communion between bishops and priests. Fr. David Songy focuses on the NSCP findings which show that most bishops see themselves as spiritual fathers while most priests do not see bishops as fathers but instead as administrators. This divergence in perception has led to a crisis of communion that affects the entire Church. The chapter explores this crisis through a theological reflection on spiritual fatherhood, emphasizing the importance of bishops embodying their role as spiritual fathers in a way that resonates with priests. It identifies the essential qualities of spiritual fatherhood, drawing on theological, psychological, and socio-historical perspectives. It also offers practical recommendations for bridging the gap between bishops and priests, focusing on mutual trust, ongoing formation, and the role of spiritual fatherhood in fostering communion.

Chapter 9 takes a more practical turn and details new efforts to strengthen, support, and renew the priesthood in the Diocese of Fall River (Massachusetts), which were undertaken in light of findings from the NSCP. Acknowledging both the joys and profound challenges of priestly ministry, Bishop Edgar Moreira da Cunha and Matthew Robinson discuss the essential role of bishops in fostering trust, fraternity, and well-being among their clergy. It details practical steps taken within the diocese to address these challenges, including the implementation of targeted initiatives for priestly formation, holistic well-being, and structural reforms to strengthen presbyteral culture. Emphasizing that flourishing priests are key to flourishing parishes, the chapter calls for a renewed commitment—on the part of both clergy and laity—to supporting priests spiritually, emotionally, and institutionally in their vital mission.

Finally in chapter 10, Fr. Anthony Stoeppel together with editor Sara Perla outline key recommendations for strengthening the Catholic priesthood by focusing on both individual priests and the diocesan environment. The chapter calls for improved priestly well-being through structured support systems, enhanced administrative training, renewed camaraderie among clergy, and ways for bishops to better support priests. It also proposes a national commission to reassess the Dallas Charter's impact.

This volume also includes two appendices. Appendix A provides an in-depth overview of the methodology and results of the NSCP, including the nationally representative survey of priests conducted by Gallup, the in-depth qualitative interviews conducted by our research team, and the census survey of bishops conducted by CARA. It also details the sampling techniques, response rates, questionnaire design, data collection, and weighting procedures used in the survey. Appendix B presents highlights from our 2025 longitudinal follow-up survey of priests who participated in the 2022 study, assessing how priests' well-being, morale, and trust in episcopal leadership have changed over time. These results are not discussed elsewhere in the volume, which was completed before the new study was carried out. Nevertheless, we include these preliminary findings since they provide important information on stability and change in priests' experiences and attitudes in relation to the issues raised in this volume. After the publication of this book, we will continue to mine the second survey for additional insights; interested readers should monitor our website at https://catholicproject.catholic.edu.

The clergy sexual abuse crisis in the United States has left a profound and lasting imprint on the Church, not only in its moral and legal dimensions but also through its impact on the relationships that sustain its mission. While significant reforms have been enacted, the crisis is far from over, given the ongoing tensions between accountability, due process, and institutional trust. This volume makes it clear that one of the most pressing and yet underexamined consequences of the crisis is its impact on the priesthood itself—on the well-being of priests, their trust in their bishops, and their ability to carry out their vocations in a context of heightened scrutiny and diminished confidence. By bringing empirical research into conversation with historical, theological, and pastoral perspectives, this volume seeks to better understand present challenges and offer constructive pathways forward for rebuilding trust and strengthening the priesthood as well as the Church in America.

CHAPTER TWO

THE NATIONAL STUDY OF CATHOLIC PRIESTS

Brandon Vaidyanathan and Christopher Jacobi

The National Study of Catholic Priests (NSCP) is the most comprehensive study of the American Catholic priesthood in more than half a century. Conducted between February and June 2022, the study includes (1) a nationally representative survey of 10,000 diocesan and religious priests, conducted by Gallup (with a 36% response rate); (2) a census survey of US bishops, conducted by Georgetown's Center for Applied Research in the Apostolate (CARA) (with a 67% response rate); and (3) 104 in-depth qualitative interviews conducted with priests across various dioceses and religious communities. These methods provide a rare and rigorous examination of the well-being, morale, and challenges facing Catholic clergy today.

Survey-based research on the Catholic priesthood in the United States has a long history, shaped by shifting ecclesial concerns and broader social transformations.[1] Fr. Joseph H. Fichter, SJ, was among the first to apply sociological tools to the Catholic priesthood as a profession. Though not nationally representative, Fichter's studies pioneered the empirical investigation of priestly morale, vocational trajectories, and social location.[2]

1 For an overview, see Bryan T. Froehle, "Research on Catholic Priests in the United States, Since the Council: Modeling the Dialogue Between Theology and Social Science," *U.S. Catholic Historian* 29, no. 4 (2011): 19–46.

2 Joseph Fichter, SJ, *Religion as An Occupation: A Study in The Sociology of*

The first truly national portrait came with Fr. Andrew Greeley's landmark 1970 study, "The Catholic Priest in the United States," conducted through the National Opinion Research Center (NORC). Drawing on responses from 5,155 priests, Greeley offered unprecedented insight into priests' theological outlooks, spiritual lives, and evolving views on authority in the wake of Vatican II.[3]

Building on this foundation, Catholic University of America sociologist Dean Hoge conducted a series of nationally representative surveys that traced generational and ideological shifts within the priesthood over time. These included his "Survey of American Catholic Priests," which in 1985, 1993, and 2001 replicated the Greeley survey (with sample sizes of 1,062, 1,186, and 1,279 respectively).[4] His later work, *The First Five Years of the Priesthood* (2002), surveyed 527 newly ordained priests and 72 resigned priests to assess early vocational satisfaction and burnout. These studies, along with CARA's regular national surveys on priests' and seminarians' attitudes, formation, and parish life—as well as their research on bishops—has helped institutionalize survey research on the clergy within the life of the Church in the US.[5]

Professions (University of Notre Dame Press, 1961); Fichter, *America's Forgotten Priests: What They Are Saying* (Harper and Row, 1968).

3 Andrew Greeley and National Opinion Research Center, *The Catholic Priest in the United States: Sociological Investigations* (United States Catholic Conference, Publications Office, 1972); Greeley, *Priests in the United States: Reflections on a Survey* (Doubleday, 1972).

4 Dean R. Hoge et al., "Changing Age Distribution and Theological Attitudes of Catholic Priests, 1970–1985," *Sociological Analysis* 49, no. 3 (1988): 264–80; Dean R. Hoge et al., "Changes in Satisfaction and Institutional Attitudes of Catholic Priests, 1970–1993," *Sociology of Religion* 56, no. 2 (1995): 195–214; Dean R. Hoge and Jacqueline E. Wenger, *Evolving Visions of the Priesthood: Changes from Vatican II to the Turn of the New Century* (Liturgical Press, 2003).

5 For instance, CARA conducts an annual survey of ordinands to the priesthood (e.g., for the class of 2023 report, see https://www.usccb.org/resources/ordination%20class%202023%20final%20report.pdf). They also conducted a national survey of recently ordained priests in 2020: https://cara.georgetown.edu/store/p/enter-by-the-narrow-gate. CARA's 2016 survey of Catholic bishops also provides valuable insights into the experiences and challenges of bishops. See Stephen J. Fichter et al., *Catholic Bishops in the United States: Church Leadership in the Third Millennium* (Oxford University Press, 2019).

Following the sexual abuse crisis, the 2002 *Los Angeles Times* national survey of 1,854 priests offered additional insights, particularly regarding priests' reactions to the sexual abuse crisis and their trust in episcopal leadership.[6] More recently, the 2021 Survey of American Catholic Priests (SACP), led by sociologists Brad Vermurlen, Stephen Cranney, and Mark Regnerus surveyed 1,036 priests and revealed a growing ideological divide and declining trust in bishops, particularly among younger, more conservative clergy.[7] Other important large-scale studies, though not nationally representative, include Msgr. Stephen Rossetti's surveys of priests about their psychological and spiritual well-being in 2004, 2009, and 2021.[8]

The National Study of Catholic Priests (NSCP) builds on this long tradition, offering the most comprehensive national portrait of the US priesthood since Greeley's 1970 survey and shedding new light on the evolving dynamics of vocation, leadership, and trust in a Church still grappling with the aftershocks of the crisis. Conducted twenty years after the implementation of the *Charter for the Protection of Children and Young People* (Dallas Charter), at a time when the priesthood faces significant scrutiny and cultural shifts, this study offers a crucial data-driven perspective on the realities of contemporary priestly life. It explores questions such as: How do priests perceive their vocation today? What contributes to their well-being or burnout? What factors shape their trust in bishops? How has the clergy sexual abuse crisis and its aftermath impacted their morale and ministry? By combining quantitative survey findings with qualitative insights from priests themselves, this study provides a nuanced and multidimensional understanding of the state of the American priesthood.

This chapter presents key findings from the study, beginning with an examination of priestly flourishing—how priests experience happiness, fulfillment, and meaning in their ministry. It then turns to factors that

6 Jill Darling Richardson, "Poll Analysis: Priests Say Catholic Church Facing Biggest Crisis of the Century," *LA Times*, Oct. 20, 2002, https://www.latimes.com/la-timespollpriests-471pa1an-story.html

7 Brad Vermurlen et al., *Introducing the 2021 Survey of American Catholic Priests: Overview and Selected Findings* (October 28, 2021). Available at SSRN: https://ssrn.com/abstract=3951931 or http://dx.doi.org/10.2139/ssrn.3951931

8 Stephen J. Rossetti, *Why Priests Are Happy: A Study of the Psychological and Spiritual Health of Priests* (Ave Maria Press, 2011); Rossetti, *Priesthood in a Time of Crisis: A New Study of the Psychological and Spiritual Health of Priests* (Ave Maria Press, 2023).

contribute to clergy burnout. The chapter further investigates priests' trust in their bishops, revealing a widening perception gap between priests and episcopal leadership. Finally, it highlights the continued impact of the clergy sexual abuse crisis, both in shaping priests' experiences of ministry and in their concerns about due process and support from their dioceses.

Ultimately, this study seeks to move beyond anecdotal narratives to offer a comprehensive, empirical portrait of the US priesthood today. Its findings provide evidence-based insights into the struggles and strengths of clergy and offer a foundation for meaningful reforms aimed at strengthening the priesthood and fostering a healthier Church in the United States.

Flourishing

To measure priestly well-being, we used a comprehensive quantitative measure that aims to go beyond subjective well-being (which has typically been the focus in the psychological literature) to measure human flourishing. The instrument we used, known as the Harvard Flourishing Measure,[9] includes 10 questions, each of which is measured on a scale from 0–10. The questions cover five dimensions which together can be seen as constitutive of human flourishing, at least as understood in the western philosophical tradition: (1) happiness and life satisfaction, (2) mental and physical health, (3) sense of meaning and purpose, (4) character and virtue, and (5) close social relationships. Each dimension is measured by two items on the survey, and together the 10 items are added to yield a comprehensive flourishing score out of 100. While attempts to quantitatively measure a concept as rich and complex as human flourishing are inherently limited, especially when based on self-reported assessments,[10] this summative measure is nevertheless useful to give us a global sense of the well-being of priests and bishops.

Using this comprehensive measure of flourishing, we find that priests have an average score of 82 out of 100, and bishops score 83 out of 100. These averages are relatively high in comparison to the general population,

9 Tyler J. VanderWeele, "On the Promotion of Human Flourishing," *Proceedings of the National Academy of Sciences* 114, no. 31 (2017): 8148–56.

10 For debates on measures of human flourishing, especially the measure used in our study, see Matthew T., Lee et al., eds., *Measuring Well-Being: Interdisciplinary Perspectives from the Social Sciences and the Humanities* (Oxford University Press, 2021).

whose overall score is around 7 out of 10.[11] To answer the question of what proportion of priests and bishops can actually be classified as flourishing, we used the cutoff threshold of 75 out of 100 recommended by the Harvard team, and using this approach, we found that 77% of priests and 81% of bishops can be categorized as flourishing. Our finding here resonates with other research on clergy which finds generally high levels of well-being in this population.[12] As one diocesan priest told us: "I feel remarkably fulfilled in my life as a priest. I mean, just being able to minister to people, being able to love them. Being able to be Christ for them. It's just, it's such a beautiful life." Another diocesan priest described for us what makes priestly life beautiful:

> I encounter beauty just in [the] kind of the sacred space that the priest occupies and people allowing me into their hearts, into their difficulties, into their relationship with God. So, like in these meetings or in confessions, people choosing to share the really difficult and painful parts of their life where there's a lot of death. And I think the beautiful part comes in entering into that with them and helping facilitate [that] they're going to the resurrection with our Lord. So that would be thc most beautiful part of what I do, I think is just being able to step into people's death and help bring them to life.

Priestly formation today equips priests with regular practices to cultivate closeness with God and healthy relationships in their community. Priestly ministry is often experienced as deeply rewarding—a way to dedicate oneself fully to service, and to be an instrument of God's grace and love. As one religious priest told us:

> I'm happy in my life. I find true joy. I love what I do. I love the people. I feel like I'm firing on all cylinders. I every day remind myself how I am incapable on my own power to do this. I say, "God, this is your Church, you take care

11 The general population scores in other research are reported out of 10 rather than 100. Tyler J. VanderWeele et al., "Measuring Well-Being: A Review of the Flourishing Index and the Secure Flourishing Index," *Social Science & Medicine* 266 (2020): 113302, https://doi.org/10.1016/j.socscimed.2020.113302

12 Rossetti, *Priesthood in a Time of Crisis.*

> of it; where you need me, give me what I need." . . . I have a great healthy community here. Friends outside the community. A structure of healthy self-care, regular prayer routine. And the feeling of a sense of support by my staff, or my brothers, by the parish, the parishioners that I am part of something positive and new and transformative. . . . There's creativity, there's growth, there's opportunity . . . what I do is meaningful and impactful.

We see here multiple indicators of flourishing at work—experiences of happiness and joy, love for one's work, love of others, a sense of humility, a sense of God at work in and through oneself, an ability to entrust oneself to God, healthy community and friendships, regular routines of prayer, self-care, the support of others, and overall a sense that one is making contributions that are deeply meaningful and impactful. Statistical analysis of our data also finds that priests who say that the Eucharist is central to their lives report significantly greater levels of flourishing than others.[13] We also find that theologically conservative priests report higher levels of flourishing than others, and some of this relationship is explained by a higher frequency of prayer.[14]

The deep sense of meaning and purpose that priests find in their vocation emerges as a central pillar of their well-being. This strong vocational commitment is reflected in the fact that 83% of priests "agree" or "strongly agree" with the statement that "My morale as a priest is good," and only 4% report considering leaving the priesthood. However, a profound sense of purpose does not render priests immune to suffering, nor does it prevent their sense of well-being from being challenged over time. While priests widely express contentment and fulfillment in their ministry, our research also reveals the weight of their responsibilities, the emotional and spiritual burdens they carry, and the pressures they navigate daily. These challenges present very real stressors that, when left unaddressed, can contribute to burnout in priestly ministry. In the next section, we turn to these stressors in greater depth, examining the dynamics of burnout and its impact on the well-being of priests.

13 Laura Upenieks, "Occupational Stressors and Flourishing Among Roman Catholic Priests: The Eucharist as the 'Source and Summit'," *Review of Religious Research* 66, no. 4 (2024): 305–31.

14 Stephen Cranney, "Conservatism, Prayer, and Flourishing Among Catholic Priests," *Review of Religious Research* 66, no. 4 (2024): 388–98.

Burnout

We assessed burnout among priests using three indicators from the *Flourishing in Ministry* study developed by Notre Dame psychologist Matt Bloom.[15] These measures capture emotional exhaustion and negative perceptions of ministry, based on priests' responses to the following items: (1) "It happens more and more often that I talk about my ministry in a negative way," (2) "During my ministry work, I often feel emotionally drained," and (3) "I usually feel worn out and weary after my ministry work."

Our findings reveal that 45% of priests report experiencing at least one symptom of ministry burnout, though this burden is not evenly distributed. Diocesan priests are significantly more likely to report burnout (50%) compared to religious priests (33%). However, only 9% of priests overall exhibit signs of severe burnout (i.e., agreeing to all three statements). Many diocesan priests, in particular, spoke of feeling stretched thin, with some expressing a sense of being treated as mere functionaries within their dioceses. As one diocesan priest put it, "Not only is the diocese just looking at me . . . to fill a hole in a parish, just be a cog in a machine, but there's also like, I'm expendable on the level of PR, like, if it's convenient, they will totally throw me under the bus."

Religious priests, while experiencing lower overall levels of burnout, also pointed to the weight of ministry demands. One religious priest described how the unrelenting busyness of ministry made it difficult to engage in essential practices of renewal: "I think a huge part of the crisis is this, you know, this overwhelming sense of need and busyness, which then—not only does it make it a challenge to pray, to get exercise, it also prevents us from being creative."

Age is also a critical factor when it comes to clergy burnout (see Figure 2.1). Younger priests are especially vulnerable, with 60% of diocesan priests and just over 40% of religious priests under the age of 45 reporting at least one symptom of burnout. These disparities underscore the importance of examining the specific pressures faced by younger clergy. Many describe struggling to meet the increasing demands placed on them as vocations decline: "The demands that are being placed on us, as there are fewer of us, can be overwhelming." Others feel the impact of ministering in an increasingly secular world: "The

15 See Matt Bloom, *Flourishing in Ministry: How to Cultivate Clergy Wellbeing* (Rowman & Littlefield, 2019).

secularization of the world has really led the Church to become irrelevant in so many ways in many people's lives.... If we become simply irrelevant, it's hard to help people. That's the biggest crisis." Still others note the cultural stigma around acknowledging burnout; as one religious priest put it: "In our province culture, it's politically incorrect to be burned out."

Figure 2.1: Burnout among priests

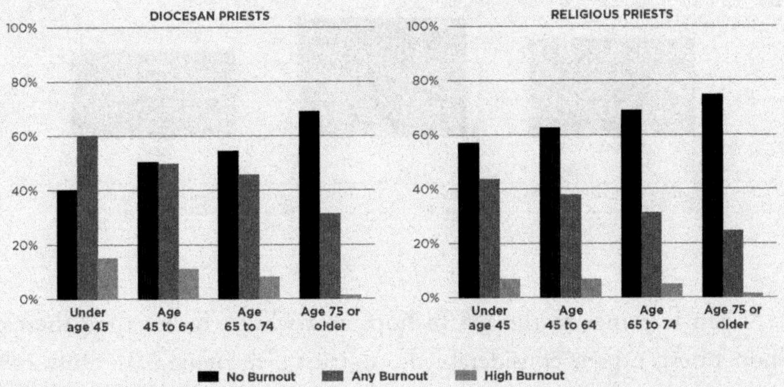

Note: Graph shows the proportion of priests who reported burnout in ministry (cynicism, feeling emotionally drained, or feeling worn out after ministry work). Indicators replicated from the Flourishing in Ministry survey (2018). Please note that "No Burnout" and "Any Burnout" sum to approximately 100%, whereas the "High Burnout" bar represents a subset of the "Any Burnout" bar.

These findings highlight the need for a deeper understanding of the sources of burnout, particularly among younger priests, in order to strengthen priestly formation, improve long-term well-being, and support clergy retention.

As it turns out, a major factor impacting priests' well-being is their relationship with their bishops.

Priests' Trust in Bishops

In our survey, we measured priests' trust in bishops using questions that had been asked in two previous national studies of priests, notably the 1993 and 2001 iterations of the Survey of American Catholic Priests. In these studies, trust in bishops was measured by asking priests "How much confidence do you, yourself, have in the decision-making and leadership of your diocesan bishop?" Replicating this measure in 2022, we found that only 49% of diocesan priests express either "a great deal" or "quite a lot" of confidence in their bishop today, compared to 55% in 1993 and 63% in 2001 (see Figure 2.2). These findings are discussed in greater detail in chapter 5. Meanwhile, if we look at religious priests, 67% of them express such confidence in their major superiors.

Figure 2.2: Trust in diocesan bishops over time

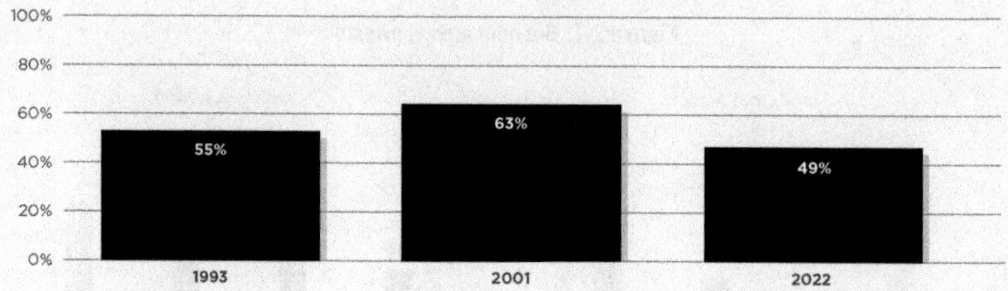

Note: Graph shows percentages of diocesan priests who expressed a "a great deal" or "quite a lot" when asked "How much confidence do you, yourself, have in the decision-making and leadership of your diocesan bishop?" The question was replicated in the Survey of American Catholic Priests (1993), Survey of American Catholic Priests (2001), and National Survey of Catholic Priests (2022).

When it comes to the US bishops as a whole, rather than their own bishop, priests express considerably lower trust (See Figure 2.3). Only 24% of priests today express confidence in the decision-making and leadership of the US bishops in general, which is a considerable drop from previous surveys.[16] As one diocesan priest we interviewed told us:

> I think most priests don't trust "The Bishops." . . . I do think that in general terms, priests don't trust bishops. . . . They can seem imperious, you know, operating from hubris, you know, think they're above the law. And I think that's, I do think there's some validity to those—to those assertions.

Another priest similarly said:

> I don't really trust most of the bishops, to be honest with you. I'll show them all a great amount of respect. And if I was in their diocese, I would really serve them and try. But just looking across the United States and looking across a lot of bishops, . . . I would say I have an overall negative

16 If we look at diocesan priests alone, it is even lower at 22% in 2022, compared to 38% in 1993 and 39% in 2001.

> opinion of bishops, in the United States . . . I just feel like there's a lot of the bishops that are just so like beige, just kind of milquetoast. They're really not leaders or they're just kind of chameleons . . . looking to climb up the ladder.

Figure 2.3: Priests' confidence in their leaders

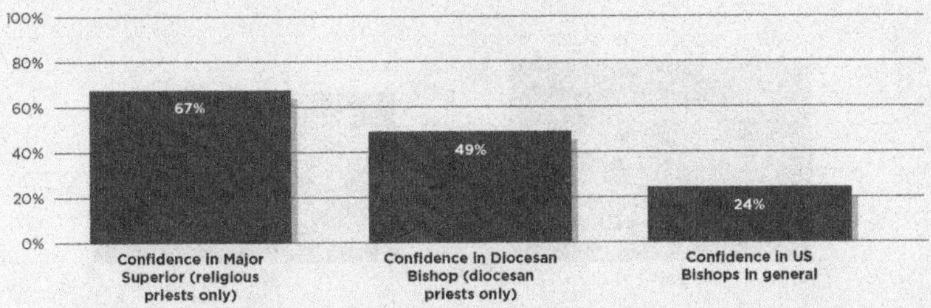

Note: Graph shows the percentages of priests who expressed a "a great deal" or "quite a lot" when asked "How much confidence do you, yourself, have in the decision-making and leadership of the superiors of your religious order/institute" (religious priests only), "... your diocesan bishop" (diocesan priests only) or "... of the US Bishops in general" (all priests).

Such findings should be concerning from the perspective of the health of the Church in the country. We know from previous research that a low-trust organizational climate—i.e., an environment in which most others in one's organization express low trust in organizational leadership—has a negative impact on individuals within an organization, regardless of one's own perception of leadership.[17] In other words, even if a priest is personally content with the bishops, living in an environment in which most of his confreres have a negative perception of the bishops will still affect him.

We also find that trust in one's bishop is statistically associated with a priest's overall well-being. Comparing priests who express "a great deal" of confidence in their bishop to those who express "very little," we find that diocesan priests with greater trust score 87 points on the Harvard Flourishing Measure compared to 77 for those with low trust (see Figure 2.4). This is a substantial difference in personal well-being. We find, further, that trust in one's bishop turns out to be associated with each of the five dimensions of

17 See, for instance: Lixin Jiang and Tahira M. Probst, "Do Your Employees (Collectively) Trust You? The Importance of Trust Climate Beyond Individual Trust," *Scandinavian Journal of Management* 31, no. 4 (2015): 526–35, https://doi.org/10.1016/j.scaman.2015.09.003

the Harvard Flourishing Index: happiness and life-satisfaction, mental and physical health, meaning and purpose, character and virtue, and close social relationships (see Figure 2.5). On each of these dimensions, diocesan priests who trust their bishop more are doing significantly better than those who trust their bishop less.

Figure 2.4: Levels of flourishing by diocesan priests' trust in their bishop

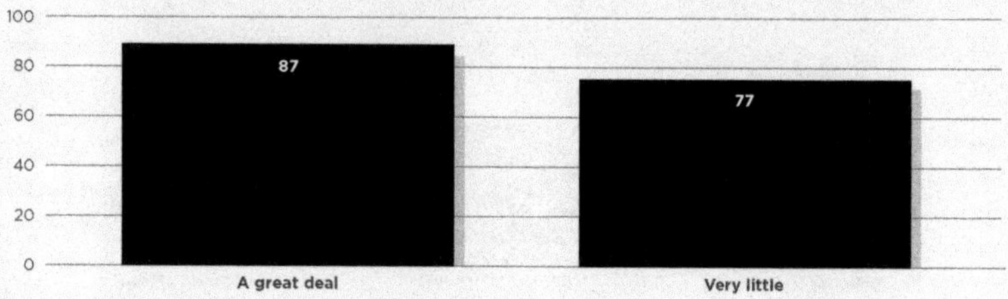

Note: Graph presents differences on the Harvard Flourishing Index (a 0-100 multi-dimensional measure of well-being including mental health, physical health, purpose, character, and social relationships) by extent of trust in one's bishop, among diocesan priests only.

Figure 2.5: Domains of flourishing by diocesan priests' trust in their bishop

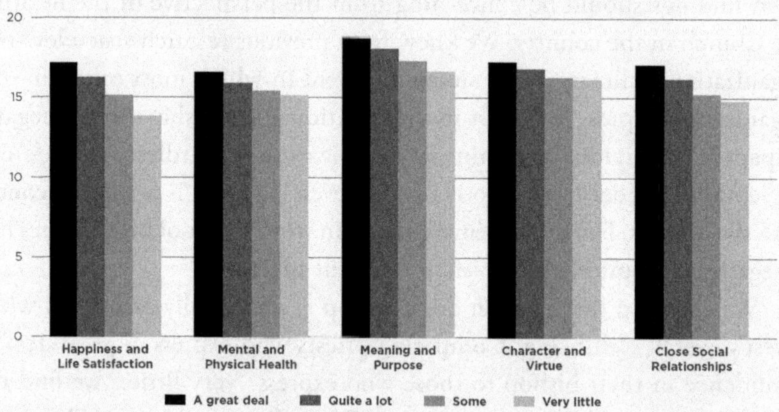

Note: Y-axis presents total score along each of the five dimensions of the Harvard Flourishing Index. The maximum score in each area is 20. X-axis presents diocesan priests' response to the question "How much confidence do you, yourself, have in the decision-making and leadership of your diocesan bishop?"

When we examine the social support systems of priests, we see further evidence of distrust of bishops. Bishops rank lowest among priests' sources of support—only 60% of diocesan priests report experiencing "strong" or "somewhat strong" support from bishops, compared to 87% for parishioners, 88% for family, and 93% for lay friends (see Figure 2.6).

Figure 2.6: Priests' sources of social support

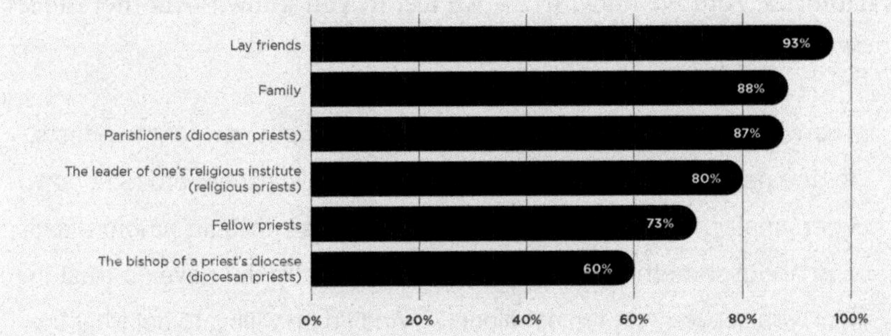

Note: Graph shows the percentages of priests who reported the sense of support from these sources as "strong" or "somewhat."

We also found striking differences between bishops and priests in their perceptions of episcopal support for clergy well-being. When bishops were asked "How well would you help your priests with their personal struggles if they asked for help?" 92% of them claimed "very well"; but when diocesan priests were asked the parallel question—"How well would your bishop help you with your personal struggles if you asked for help?"—only 36% answered "very well" (see Figure 2.7).

Figure 2.7: Differing perceptions of whether bishops would help priests with personal struggles

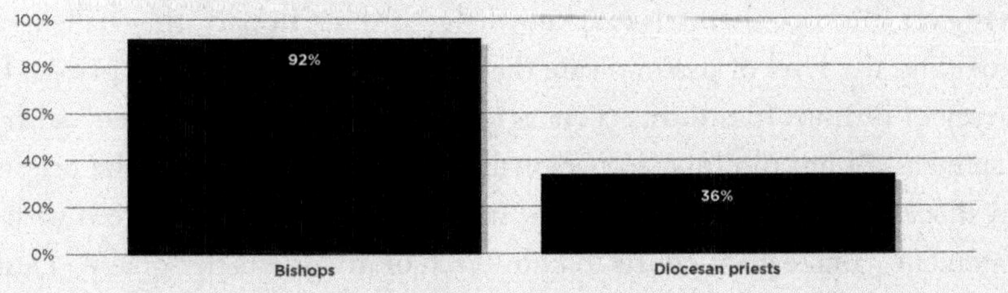

Note: Bishops were asked "How well would you help your priests with their personal struggles if they asked for help?"; Priests were asked "How well would your bishop help you with your personal struggles if you asked for help?" Graph reports percentages who responded, "Very well."

This finding provides concrete statistical evidence of a disconnect that some bishops have heard anecdotally from priests. We also find that 40% of diocesan priests say that priests in their diocese feel like they would be seen as a liability if they approach the bishop with personal struggles. As one diocesan priest put it: "We've been saying for a decade now that bishops see their priests as liabilities. And we know it.... We feel it, you know?" Another diocesan priest echoed this sentiment:

> There is a morale problem in our archdiocese right now for the priests, for the people. I don't think they feel that there's a shepherd right now. I personally have no confidence in [my bishop]. I would no more call him about something than a stranger on the street. I have no trust in him whatsoever. And I'm not alone.... And I'd be willing to bet [that the bishop] doesn't know much about us [priests] at all.

Diocesan priests tend to be more critical of their diocese's policies and practices than religious priests are of their religious communities. They also report lower levels of mutual support among priests and view their bishops as less approachable than religious priests perceive their major superiors. Sixty-eight percent of diocesan priests say that priests in their diocese criticize diocesan policies and practices, compared to just 34% of religious priests who say the same about their communities. Additionally, 38% of diocesan priests report that priests in their diocese appear stressed when they talk about their bishop, whereas only 15% of religious priests say that priests in their community appear stressed when discussing their major superior.

In a time of crisis within the Church, support for priests is more essential than ever. Bishops themselves acknowledge, at least in part, the challenges of providing the level of pastoral care they would like to offer their priests. Our survey of bishops found that 52% agreed "strongly" or "somewhat" with the statement, "I am too busy to personally counsel and pastor all the priests of my diocese." At the same time, 92% "strongly" or "somewhat" agreed with the statement, "I take great efforts to know each of my priests personally." Despite these efforts, many priests feel their bishop is not the spiritual father they wish he were. As we will see below (Figure 2.11), this disconnect is further reflected in priests' images of their bishops. At least some of this mistrust stems from priests' experiences with the implementation of policies introduced in response to the abuse crisis.

Living in Fear

When asked about their views on the Dallas Charter and the zero-tolerance policy, most priests expressed strong support. A full 90% believe their dioceses have a strong culture of child safety and protection, and nearly 70% of diocesan priests see the policy as a positive reflection of the Church's values and an important step in rebuilding public trust. However, 40% feel that the zero-tolerance policy is too harsh (Figure 2.8).

Figure 2.8: Priests' views on the zero-tolerance policy

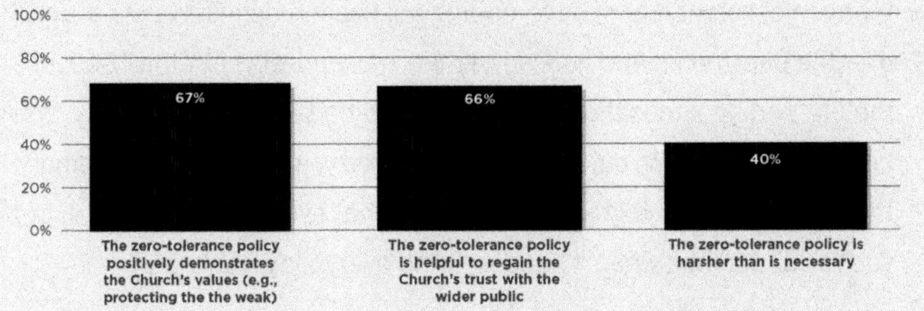

Note: Graph shows the percentages of diocesan priests who "strongly agree" or "agree" with each item.

At the same time, many priests worry that in the current climate, false accusations of abuse are too easily made. A single allegation—even if later proven false—can permanently damage a priest's reputation. Alarmingly, 82% of priests report regularly fearing being falsely accused of sexual abuse (see Figure 2.9).

Figure 2.9: Priests' fear of false accusation of abuse

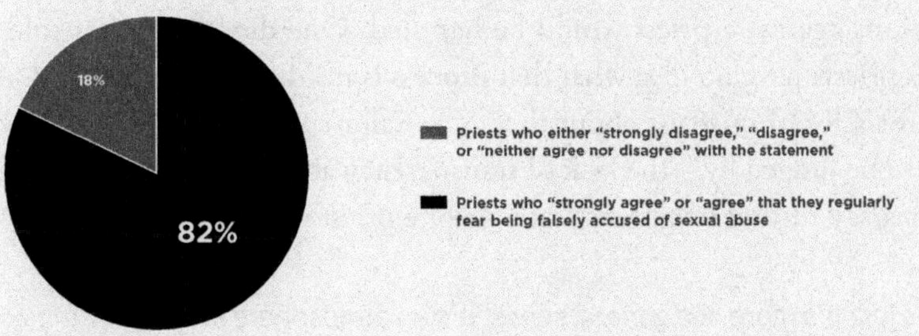

Note: Graph shows percentages of priests' responses to the statement "I regularly fear being falsely accused of sexual abuse."

Fear of false accusations is not confined to specific demographic or religious subgroups. The data do not indicate substantial differences in levels of fear of being false accused of sexual abuse between diocesan and religious priests, or between US-born and foreign-born clergy. Regarding age and cohorts, the highest levels of reported fear are found among priests under the age of 45 and those ordained since 2000, with 85% expressing fear of being falsely accused. Nevertheless, this fear is not limited to younger clergy and spans generations: approximately three-quarters of priests in the oldest age cohort (75 or older) also report this fear. As one diocesan priest told us:

> Living in constant fear of a life-ending accusation definitely puts a cloud over the priesthood. And honestly, I think most priests have that. Because the life-ending accusation doesn't have to be based in any reality. You know, it can just come out of somebody's three years of recovered memory, therapy, and have no ground in anything that ever really happened, but you're still doomed when it happens. And everybody knows that.

Priests' concerns about false accusations being "life-ending" are intertwined with the fear that they will not receive adequate support in the case of an allegation. As one diocesan priest put it, "Among the priests, there is this general sense, first, that the bishops don't have our backs.... There's this sense ... that the bishops are against a priest who's been accused, rather than doing what the bishop must do but still supporting the priest."

Uncertainty about the process once an accusation is made against a priest further compounds this fear. Many priests told us in our interviews they did not have a clear understanding of the process in their diocese for how allegations against a priest would be handled. One diocesan priest told us, "We as priests have no idea what that process is inside that review board. And so there's a lot of mistrust about that ... we don't know what standard we're going to be judged by." The lack of transparency about the process combined with hearsay further heightens fears. As one priest told us:

> It's just it's more of a general sense. It's an atmosphere around the thing that is like, ... you got a text from the vicar general. And, you know, "We need to talk." And ... you call and ask why. And of course, they don't tell

> you, right? So of course, automatically, you know, the cortisol levels start to rise, and all of that.... So you got two options. One, you can either go in hostile and bring a lawyer, or you get screwed and not. Either way, not helpful! You know, and I've known situations where that is, you know, on both ends. It's like, you know, guy went in, you know, fully lawyered up, and the bishop was pissed. Because he wanted it to be over quickly. And it wasn't—because the guy was exercising his rights. And then there was another guy who went in was like, "Okay, nothing to worry about? All right, I'll see you on Tuesday," and goes in and, you know, has to have an escort so he can go get his underwear from his rectory.

Priests also complained about how the policies implemented by the Charter make "a suspect out of everybody," as one priest put it. "How do you prove that something didn't happen?" one priest asked. "How do you get your reputation back?"

Many others, while expressing full support of zero tolerance for abuse of minors, expressed concerns that new procedures to combat the sexual abuse of "vulnerable persons" more broadly, coupled with a perceived absence of due process, amounted to a violation of justice. As one diocesan priest told us: "I get zero tolerance for priests abusing children, okay. But we've got zero tolerance for priests doing anything wrong at this point." Another told us: "This concept of 'vulnerable adults' ... is so, so very broad just to be almost undefined." As a religious priest put it, "Hard and fast rule of zero tolerance, like ... somewhere you're going to have to draw a line! ... Just saying any priest with any whiff of anything is gone, ... that just isn't just!"

The fear of improper application of these policies in a circumstance of alleged abuse deeply worries the majority of priests. Many diocesan priests in particular fear they will not be adequately supported by their dioceses and bishops in the case of a false accusation (See Figure 2.10). In the case of a false allegation, only 36% of diocesan priests think their diocese would provide them with sufficient resources to defend themselves in court, and only 51% think their bishop would support them. By contrast, among religious, priests at least 85% think their religious community would provide them resources and their superior would support them.

Figure 2.10: Priests' expectations in case of false accusations of abuse

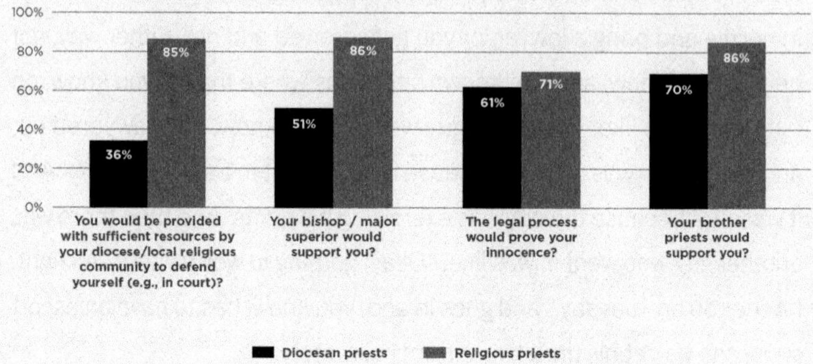

Note: Graph shows percentages of priests who reported being either "very confident" or "moderately confident" on each item.

Diocesan priests, thus, fear being abandoned by their diocese and bishop should they find themselves falsely accused. As one diocesan priest put it:

> You're *persona non grata* when something comes to light in terms of an accusation. I do believe that it should be ... innocent until proven guilty. Lawyers will tell you this, if you have to go to see your bishop about something serious ... you come in with a lawyer. All of a sudden, it's adversarial, ... you're in your corner and they're in their corner. I think that's what the Charter unleashed ... you are guilty until proven innocent in the church.

Religious priests, in contrast, do not have a comparable sense of inevitable abandonment by their community. As one religious priest told us: ""Thank God, you know, if I was accused of some misconduct ... I could stay in the community; I would be taken care of. Well, if you're a diocesan priest, it's like here's your hat.... Have a nice life. Don't call us, we'll call you." Another religious priest put it this way:

> You can't throw these people out on the street. They're still part of your religious order. They can't function as a priest, but you still have to clothe them, house them, and feed them. So, there's all limitations placed on what they can do. You know, where they live, who they interact with, you

> know. Their ability to drive a car or you know, their permission to travel all that. So it's all restricted. You know, they're on a very tight leash . . . [but] we take care of them.

Unfortunately, many bishops appear unaware of the depth of these concerns among their priests. On average, bishops see themselves in a much more positive light than the priests they shepherd see them, reflecting a significant gap in perception that has yet to be bridged.

Misaligned Perceptions

The Rite of Ordination envisions bishops as shepherds, fathers, brothers, and co-workers to their priests. The Catechism of the Catholic Church also states that "the promise of obedience they make to the bishop at the moment of ordination and the kiss of peace from him at the end of the ordination liturgy mean that the bishop considers them his co-workers, his sons, his brothers and his friends, and that they in return owe him love and obedience."[18]

Our study, however, reveals a significant gap between how bishops perceive their relationship with priests and how priests perceive their bishops. While 83% of bishops see themselves as shepherds to their priests, only 54% of priests see their bishops as shepherds. Similarly, although the majority of bishops consider themselves to be brothers (73%) or fathers (70%) to their priests, less than half as many priests (28%) describe their bishops in these terms. Likewise, while 73% of bishops see themselves as co-workers with their priests, only 32% of priests agree (Figure 2.11).

These differences raise important questions. Do bishops see themselves through rose-colored glasses? Are priests—worn down by stress and uncertainty—viewing their bishops with undue cynicism and fear? The truth likely includes elements of both. Many priests believe that policies introduced since the Dallas Charter have depersonalized them and have shifted their perception of their bishops from that of a father or brother to that of a CEO, bureaucrat, or financial administrator. As one diocesan priest observed: "Our Archbishop is a remote figure. Not at all personable. Not approachable. He appears to be a busy CEO and religious functionary."

18 *Catechism of the Catholic Church*, 2nd ed. (Libreria Editrice Vaticana, 1997), §1567, Available at vatican.va

Figure 2.11: Images of the bishop held by bishops and priests

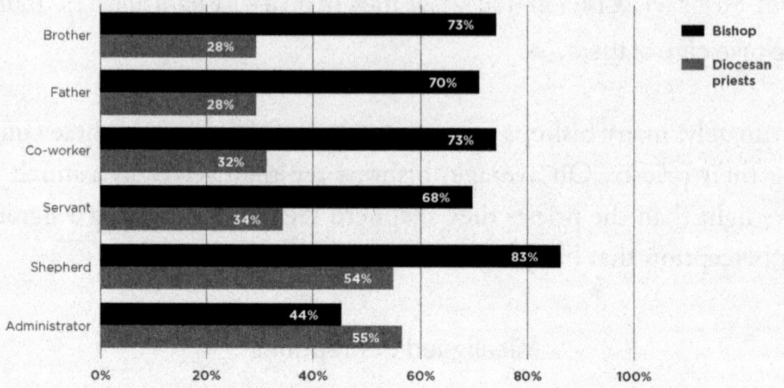

Note: Graph shows percentages of diocesan priests who selected each type for their bishop vs. bishops who saw themselves in that way.

Regardless of whose perception most accurately reflects reality, what matters to our study is the impact these views have on the morale of priests and the health of the presbyterate. To repair trust, improve communication, and restore a sense of fraternity between priests and bishops, intentional efforts must be made to strengthen personal and pastoral bonds. And here, it is important to remember that priests do want to trust their bishops. As one diocesan priest told us: "We want to trust the bishops—that's, you know, we put our hands in the bishops' [hands] at some point and said, I promise respect and obedience to you and your successor. We chose that freely. So we knew that's part of it. And we want that."

A Polarized Clergy

Polarization has been a growing concern in the United States in recent decades, and this is a problem within the Catholic Church as well—not only in terms of political differences but also theology.[19] Our data finds that there is a significant ideological divide between older and younger priests in both

19 Mary Ellen Konieczny et al., eds. *Polarization in the US Catholic Church: Naming the Wounds, Beginning to Heal* (Liturgical Press, 2016); *National Catholic Register*, "Catholic Bishops Warn of Polarization in Church, Urge More Dialogue," May 15, 2024. https://www.ncregister.com/cna/catholic-bishops-warn-of-polarization-in-church-urge-more-dialogue

political and theological self-identification. However, the data also indicates that the American presbyterate is becoming less polarized over time. Simply put, the number of newly ordained priests who identify as politically liberal or theologically progressive has been steadily declining since the Second Vatican Council and has now nearly disappeared.[20]

This shift is particularly pronounced in priests' theological outlook. When asked to describe their views on theology and doctrine on a scale from "very progressive" to "very conservative/orthodox," stark generational differences emerge (See Figure 2.12). More than half of priests ordained since 2010 place themselves on the conservative side of the scale, and notably, none of the surveyed priests ordained after 2020 identified as "very progressive."

Figure 2.12: Self-rated priest theological orthodoxy by ordination year

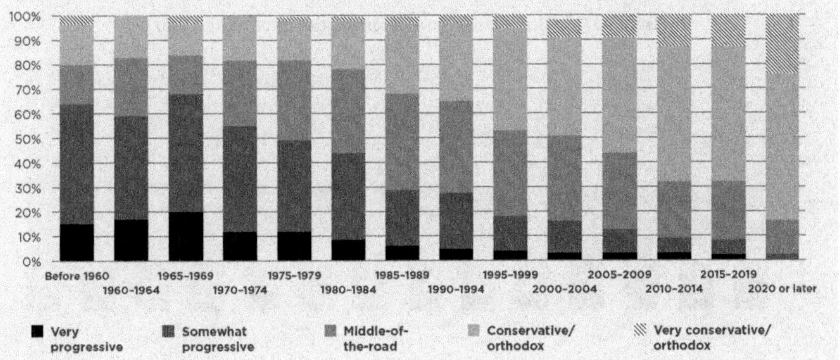

As one priest told us:

> Priests in their 70s and 60s now would be one cohort. And then you have the JPII-generation that would be very orthodox, but still have some, you know, free-flowing-liturgy-stuff. Then you get in the Benedict stuff, which is like, you know, the hard-on-everything-kind-of-guys. And the young

20 Our research here also reflects the findings of another recent national study, the 2020–2021 Survey of American Catholic Priests, which finds that priests have become more conservative over the past two decades when it comes to morality, politics, and theology. See Brad Vermurlen et al., "The Ongoing Conservative Turn in the American Catholic Priesthood," *Sociological Spectrum* 43, no. 2–3 (2023): 72–88, https://doi.org/10.1080/02732173.2023.2215461

guys now, I'd say, you have a lot in common with those last few cohorts, but no one's really—the super-progressive wing really didn't replicate themselves.... While it can look like a generational divide, it's really a theological, philosophical divide.

While both political and theological self-identification among priests have followed a similar trajectory—namely, the near disappearance of liberal or progressive identification—there are noteworthy differences. Politically, the trend appears to have stabilized, with a significant proportion of priests identifying as moderate. While 52% of the most recently ordained cohort describe themselves as either conservative or very conservative, 44%—the highest percentage of any cohort—identify as moderate (Figure 2.13).

Figure 2.13: Self-rated priest political orientation by ordination year

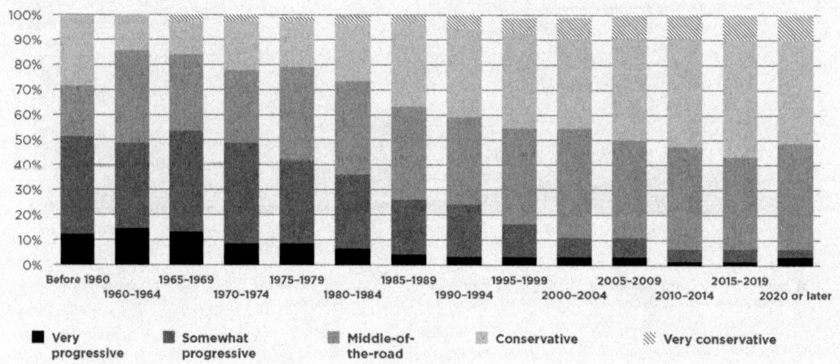

Theological self-identification, however, has followed a different pattern. The once-sizeable middle ground has largely vanished. Among the youngest cohort, 85% identify as either conservative/orthodox or very conservative/orthodox, while only 14% describe themselves as middle-of-the-road—the lowest percentage of any generation. Meanwhile, the share of new ordinands who identify as theologically progressive or very progressive has plummeted from 68% in earlier cohorts to nearly zero today.

One result of these shifts is a perceived lack of respect across generational cohorts. As one older priest put it: "I personally feel, when I'm around the younger priests, that I'm looked down on. It's almost like the attitude, 'I can't wait 'til you guys get out of here so we can run the Church the way it should be run.'" Meanwhile, a younger priest told us: "Then the older priests, I've given up on it. I think a lot of them are really cynical and jaded. And to go hang out with them is to just fall into the same cynicism. There's a lot of gossiping, and it's exhausting. So, I just avoid hanging out with priests because of that."

Polarization and Episcopal Trust

Earlier (in Figure 2.2), we had noted that 49% of diocesan priests express confidence in the leadership and decision-making abilities of their bishop. It is important to note here that the mean levels of trust are not the same across all dioceses but show considerable variation. In some dioceses, 100% of surveyed priests express trust in their bishop, while in others, trust levels drop as low as 9% (Figure 2.14).

Figure 2.14: Differences in average levels of trust in the bishop by individual dioceses

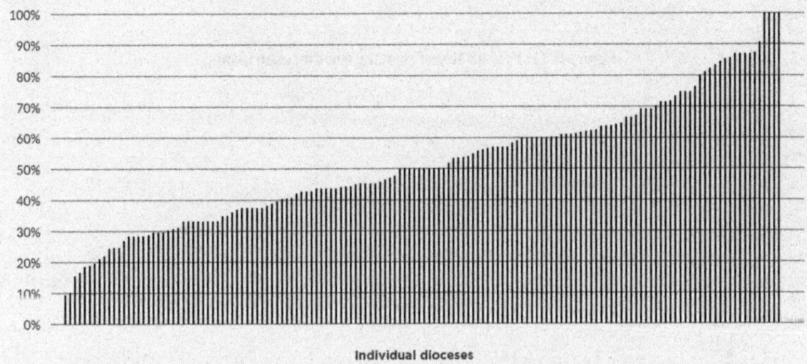

Note: The graph shows the average percentage of diocesan priests who expressed a "great deal" or "quite a lot" of confidence in the decision-making and leadership abilities of their diocesan bishop. 149 dioceses were included; a minimum number of 6 respondents by diocese was set for statistical purposes. Each bar represents a diocese.

One potential explanation for these differences is diocesan size. In large archdioceses, priests are less likely to have personal interactions with their bishop and may feel more depersonalized. Our analysis confirms that diocesan size has some impact on trust: in smaller dioceses (those with 100 or fewer priests), an average of 53% of priests report trusting their bishop, whereas in very large dioceses (with more than 500 priests), that number drops to 38%.

Two factors prove to be even stronger predictors of priests' trust in their bishops than diocesan size: political and theological alignment. A priest's perception of whether his bishop shares his theological and political views strongly influences his level of trust. For example, a theologically conservative priest who believes his bishop is also theologically conservative is likely to report high trust in his leadership. Conversely, priests who perceive a theological disconnect with their bishop tend to report significantly lower levels of trust. The same pattern holds for political alignment: higher perceived alignment on political matters is associated with higher trust in one's bishop, and lower alignment with lower trust.

Figure 2.15 highlights this pattern clearly. Among priests who believe they are "not well at all" aligned with their bishop on theological matters, only 10% express trust in him. For those who feel completely misaligned politically, only 20% express trust in the bishop. By contrast, more than 60% of priests who see themselves as aligned "very well" with their bishop on either front report trusting him. These findings suggest that priests' perceptions of their bishop's theological and political views play a significant role in shaping their confidence in his leadership.

Figure 2.15: Probability of trusting the diocesan bishop

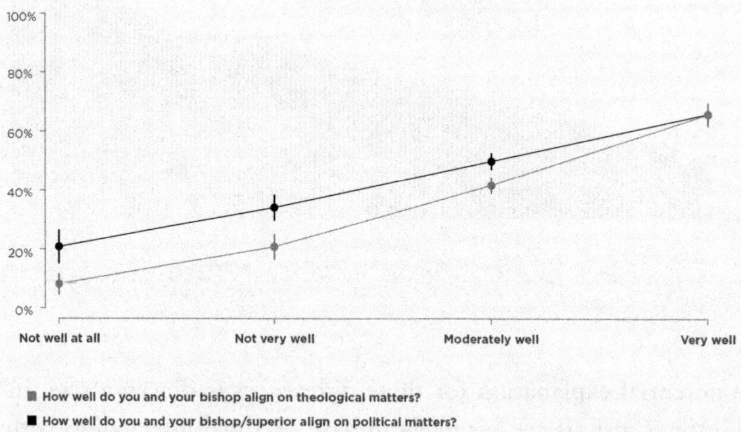

Note: Predicted probabilities with 95% confidence intervals from logistic regressions of trust in bishops (1=agree or strongly agree; 0=else) with controls (age group, size of diocese and an indicator for ordination in the US vs. foreign ordination, theological alignment, political orientation, theological orthodoxy). Diocesan priests only.

Figure 2.16 demonstrates the relative impact of various factors on a priest's trust in his bishop. The odds of trust are nearly 2.5 times higher for priests who perceive themselves as theologically aligned with their bishop, and about 2 times higher for those who feel politically aligned.

Figure 2.16: What predicts trust in diocesan bishops?

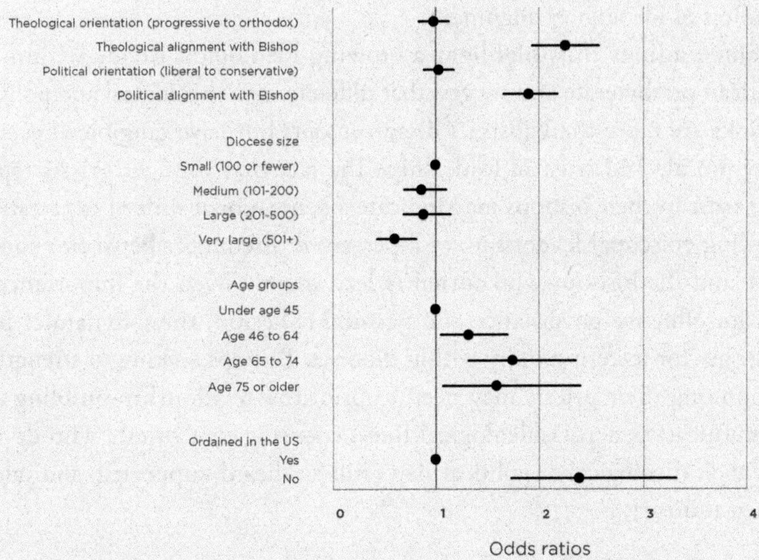

Note: Odds ratios with 95% confidence intervals of trust in bishops; based on logistic regression (1= a "great deal" or "quite a lot" of confidence in the decision-making and leadership abilities of their diocesan bishop; 0=else). Odds ratios less than 1 represent lower odds of trusting the bishop; values greater than 1 represent higher odds. Diocesan priests only. Where no confidence bar is present, that is the reference group in the categorical specification.

In comparison, diocesan size has a much smaller effect—priests in very large dioceses have 50% lower odds of trusting their bishop than those in the smallest dioceses. One of the only other factors with a comparable impact to theological alignment is ordination location: priests ordained outside the US have 2.5 times greater odds of trusting their bishop compared to those ordained here. We also see that older priests have greater odds of trusting their bishop than younger priests. This suggests that personal alignment with a bishop's theological and political views plays a far greater role in shaping trust than structural factors such as diocesan size. While large dioceses may indeed make it harder for priests to form personal relationships with their bishops, or for bishops to see themselves as fathers rather than CEOs in relation to their priests, the data indicates that ideological and formative factors—particularly theological and political alignment—may be stronger determinants of trust. The significant effect of ordination location further underscores the role of formation: priests ordained outside the US may come from cultures with different expectations regarding episcopal authority and hierarchical relationships, making them more inclined to trust their bishop regardless of ideological alignment.

Our findings thus highlight a growing ideological divide within the American presbyterate and suggest that differences in theological and political outlooks are more than abstract disagreements but have tangible effects on clergy morale and trust in leadership. The fact that younger priests report lower trust in their bishops may indicate a generational shift in expectations regarding episcopal leadership, or a perceived disconnect between younger clergy and the bishops who currently lead them. Given the importance of trust for effective governance and pastoral cohesion, these dynamics pose challenges for fostering unity within dioceses. Bishops seeking to strengthen trust among their priests may need to prioritize relationship-building and communication across ideological lines, ensuring that priests who do not share their theological or political views still feel heard, supported, and valued in their ministry.

The Crisis Is Not Over

More than two decades after *The Boston Globe's* Spotlight exposé and the implementation of the Dallas Charter, most priests do not believe the clergy sexual abuse crisis is over. In fact, 61% of priests disagree with the statement that "The sexual abuse crisis in the Church is basically over," while only 20% agree. One reason for this is that priests are often the first responders to abuse disclosures. Clergy abuse survivors are present in parishes, and it is frequently parish priests—not bishops—who hear their stories firsthand and help them navigate their pain. Our data shows that 71% of priests personally know at least one survivor of clergy sexual abuse, and 11% know five or more (Figure 2.17).

Priests on the whole report feeling prepared and actively engaged in ministering to survivors. Sixty-nine percent say they feel well-prepared to minister to a victim of abuse, 54% report that they are already doing so, and 49% have been approached by someone who believes they were a victim of child sexual abuse. These encounters not only shape priests' pastoral work but also reinforce their sense of the gravity of the crimes committed, which should never be forgotten.

Figure 2.17: The number of people priests know who were victims of clergy sex abuse

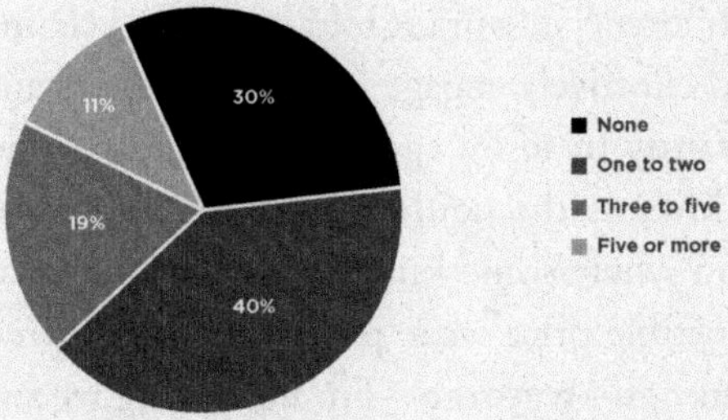

One priest described the heartbreak of these conversations:

> It's a heartbreaking thing. I have had conversations with people who have been victims of sexual abuse in general, but also clergy sexual abuse. And people who are actually serving in the Church as priests who themselves were abused. So it's the sadness of those conversations—and just holding that tragedy in my own heart, for those people who have been affected like that.

Another priest shared how a friend's disclosure changed his perspective: "I had a friend who, unbeknownst to me, had been a victim of abuse from a priest, as a matter of fact. Early on, he revealed that to me. And so that certainly did change my perspective." Such encounters have helped deepen some priests' sense of ministry. As one priest put it: "Sometimes that's all you can really do—just cry with them. And it has been really good for my priesthood and really good for understanding this [crisis]."

It is also crucial to keep in mind that priests have not only been perpetrators of sexual abuse but also victims. When asked whether they had personally experienced sexual harassment, abuse, or misconduct during their seminary formation, 9% of priests reported that they had, while another 6% were unsure or declined to answer—which suggests that some of the latter group likely also experienced abuse. "Personally, I am a victim," one priest admitted to us in an interview. "I was sexually abused while I was in seminary. You have to understand trauma. You've got to understand abuse."

Priests also expressed concerns about the ways in which they have learned to adjust to the reforms implemented through the Dallas Charter. "It's made me very afraid to be around children," one priest told us. Several claimed that they didn't see how they could effectively engage in youth ministry anymore. Others felt they had to constantly tread on eggshells. "There's windows on my office door; there's windows to the confessional," one priest said. "I don't put myself in a situation where something could be misconstrued or misunderstood." "This is a horrible price we're paying," another priest told us. "But we have to pay it. I'm not—trust me—I'm not saying we shouldn't be paying it. We should be paying it. But it's horrible."

What Do Priests Think Would Help?

At the end of the survey, we asked priests: "What is one step that could be taken to improve priests' trust in bishops?" (or major superiors, in the case of religious priests), and offered a textbox in which to write in their responses. From our analysis of these open-ended responses, six key themes emerged.

1. Efforts to Build Relationships with Priests

The most common category among priests' responses (more than 35%) was the desire for open, honest, personal, and regular communication between bishops and priests. Respondents emphasized that trust is built not through programs or policies but through presence, listening, and genuine relationship. Many called for greater pastoral presence, informal connections, and structured opportunities for meaningful conversation. Priests longed for bishops who are approachable, listen well, and are physically and emotionally present in the daily lives of their clergy. For instance, priests said:

- Have bishops actually reach out to priests personally.
- The bishop should be available to his priests. The Bishop should follow the example of Charles Borromeo and visit the priests on "their turf" in the rectories and churches where they serve. The priests NEED to see the bishop entering into the rectory and the parish church to see with his own eyes the well-being of the priests

and faithful. Once priests know the bishop is concerned with their well-being then trust will grow.

- Bishop should meet with his priests more often instead of just with chancery personnel.
- The bishop should plan to visit the priest in his parish or invite the priest to the bishop's house and have dinner together while conversing on a brotherly level on positive experiences he is going through and on challenges he is facing in his ministry and show support to him.
- Bishops need to see priests as their closest collaborators instead of HR, risk management, and other diocesan personnel. They need to make more of an effort to spend meaningful time with their priests so that they can truly know them. One cannot have a relationship with a memo from the bishop.

2. Justice and Structural Reform

More than 25% of priests stressed in their responses the importance of fair treatment, especially in cases of misconduct or accusation. Many called for bishops to be held to the same standards as priests and insisted on due process for clergy accused of wrongdoing.[21] Priests also called for clearer, fairer, and more participatory structures of governance. This included complaints about lack of transparency in decisions, favoritism in assignments, and double standards in disciplinary matters. For instance, priests noted:

- Hold Bishops accountable and to the same standards as priests, especially in regards to the sexual abuse crisis and in other disciplinary matters.
- NOT TREAT ACCUSED AS BEING GUILTY!! THEY FEEL ABANDONED.
- Clear, Consistent, and Stable policies. Changing rules undermine trust.

21 It is worth noting that the survey was conducted almost three years after the promulgation of *Vos estis lux mundi*, which was intended to hold bishops accountable in a way similar to priests.

- A more adversarial judicial process—insisting an accused priest retain canonical and (if need be) civil lawyers. Insist on the presumption of innocence.
- Bishops should be chosen from the priests who have proven themselves to be good pastors, reasonable theologians and competent administrators. It is my hope that the days of choosing brown-nosed climbers and self-referential jerks are behind us.
- Stop choosing bishops from the Roman finishing, MBA schools, and starting looking for those in the trenches. Stop giving universal power and responsibility to bishops as executive, legislative, and judicial. No one is good enough to handle that much power and responsibility.

3. Transparency in Communications

A third category includes more specific emphasis on institutional transparency, clarity in decision-making, and honest dialogue about sensitive or complex issues. Priests wanted more information about how and why decisions are made, especially regarding assignments, diocesan priorities, and the handling of allegations. For instance:

- Open discussion about what happened, mistakes, why they did not take responsibility.
- Clarity and explanation of reasoning in making decisions.
- More transparency on all levels of community life.
- Transparency. I believe that, for much too long, we have hidden beneath euphemisms and vague terms to couch what is really going on, as if the people of God are unable to handle the truth. In order for the Church to regain any sense of credibility, bishops must be forthright and clear in defining issues as they occur. Even to us as priests, I feel that my own diocesan bishop, and the USCCB as a whole, is not forthright in saying why a priest is being removed or leaving ministry.
- The bishop could initiate a discussion seeking the views of his priests on a specific issue.

4. Leadership Formation for Bishops

Many priests expressed frustration with what they perceived as bureaucratic, distant, or managerial leadership styles. They called instead for bishops who are pastoral in spirit and better formed for their leadership roles. This included recommendations for ongoing human and leadership formation, as well as attention to psychological maturity and emotional intelligence. Below are some illustrative responses:

- I think there needs to be more non-business experience required to become a bishop—being a pastor, being close to people.
- Our Archbishop is a remote figure. Not at all personable. Not approachable. He appears to be a busy CEO and religious functionary.
- Bishop must be a devoted man with no strong narcissism.
- Ongoing human and spiritual formation for bishops (nationally-based regional workshops on different topics with mandatory attendance).

5. Spiritual and Moral Integrity Among Bishops

Priests often spoke about the moral authority of bishops as crucial to building trust. They emphasized that bishops must live with visible integrity, humility, and faithfulness to Church teaching. Several highlighted the need for bishops to model spiritual leadership and simplicity of life, particularly in contrast to perceived clerical privilege or image management. For example:

- Get bishop's [sic] who actually love being a priest and aren't just climbing the ladder.
- We need men of genuine and visible prayerfulness to pray with us and to show us their own prayerful weakness. Now is not the time for wasting energy on programs. Programs do not produce healing.
- Many of the bishops with whom I am acquainted practice their own form of clericalism, which assumes that they know better than anyone else. I would like to see a little more authenticity in bishops, and a little less arrogance.

- Simplicity and sincerity of life stemming from a communion and fellowship with God. The major superiors are to be humble and gentle and get rid of bossing. Give a sound spiritual leadership in the Community. They are to be models of religious life. Be spiritual leaders.
- We need to see that they care more about the Gospel than liability. That they are willing to take risks for the sake of saving souls. That they value each and every person more than diocesan assets or worldly notions of success.

6. Empowerment and Recognition

Some priests expressed a longing to feel valued and supported—not just as functionaries but as whole persons and collaborators in mission. They spoke about the need for bishops to recognize their gifts, offer encouragement, and provide emotional and pastoral support. This theme often overlapped with communication but focused specifically on affirmation and personal investment. For instance, priests wrote:

- Mutual respect will enhance the relationships within the community.
- There is no way to atone for the lack of concern that has been evident to priests. No one ever contacted me to see how I was doing. Every time I hear how counselors are available to children every time something negative happens to affect their lives I wonder, why didn't somebody do that for us?
- More fatherly and fraternal support. Sometimes it feels like I'm working for a large corporation.
- Bishops should be fathers to their priests. They should empower their priests to do the right thing, that is what the church asks. Myself and my brother priests feel as though we would be penalized if we do something that is in line with the church but against the so called "spirit" of Vatican II. I am a young priest and my priest friends and I are penalized and held back for the hard work and dedication we pour out into ministry in the Vinyard [sic] of God's church.

- Knowing that major superiors are "on my side" and truly care about my well-being. Saying "thank you" to priests who have weathered difficult assignments.
- For bishops to regularly affirm the work and dedication of their priests. For bishops to actively take steps to reduce the stress and work-load of their priests.

Across these themes, priests express that they want bishops to be fathers, not CEOs; they want bishops to listen to them and be present to them; they want bishops to be visible and accessible; they desire mutuality over hierarchy; and they want to be seen and respected as persons. Beneath the surface of many responses is a shared longing for communion; one could even say "synodality": a Church in which bishops and priests walk together in mutual trust and humility, living out a shared mission.

Conclusion

The NSCP offers an unprecedented look at the realities of priestly life in the United States. It reveals a deep vocational commitment among priests, with high levels of happiness and fulfillment reported across the board. However, it also uncovers pressing challenges: burnout, widening ideological and generational divides, growing mistrust between priests and bishops, and fears surrounding the implementation of abuse prevention policies.

One of the study's most striking findings is the decline in trust between priests and their bishops, which has significant implications for clergy morale and the overall health of the Church. It is alarming that more than 80% of priests live in fear of a false allegation of abuse, and most of them think their bishops and dioceses will not defend them. While most bishops view themselves as spiritual fathers and shepherds to their priests, many priests perceive them instead as bureaucratic administrators or CEOs, disconnected from the realities of daily ministry. This disconnect is further exacerbated by political and theological misalignment, which strongly correlates with lower levels of trust.

The clergy sexual abuse crisis remains a defining issue for priests. While nearly all support efforts to protect minors and restore trust in the Church, many fear that zero-tolerance policies and procedural ambiguities leave them vulnerable to false accusations and inadequate support. At the same time, priests are often first responders for abuse survivors, placing them at the heart of the Church's ongoing efforts toward healing. Many priests also bear their own personal wounds, with not an insignificant proportion having experienced sexual abuse or harassment themselves.

Despite these challenges, the study affirms the resilience and dedication of priests. Their profound sense of mission and service continues to sustain them, even in the face of difficulties. Yet real reforms are needed to support their well-being, rebuild trust, and strengthen fraternity within the presbyterate. Priests are not just asking for better policies—they are asking to be known, supported, and treated with dignity. Underneath many of their concerns is a longing for relationship: for bishops who act as spiritual fathers, not simply institutional managers. Addressing issues of burnout, fostering open communication between bishops and priests, and ensuring fair and transparent policies in handling allegations are essential steps toward a healthier and more unified presbyterate.

By providing a data-driven foundation for understanding these dynamics, this study serves as a call to action for Church leaders, seminary formators, and lay Catholics alike. The future of the priesthood and of the Church as a whole depends on fostering a renewed culture of trust rooted in justice and oriented toward the common good.

PRIESTLY MORALE: INTERNAL AND EXTERNAL SOURCES OF SUPPORT

Maureen K. Day

Priests' vocational morale is a key dimension of the data collected by the National Study of Catholic Priests (NSCP). The data also include responses on the social support that priests receive and their relationship with their bishop, which prove to be particularly correlated with morale. This chapter will explore the ways the NSCP interview data reveal the ways priests' experiences of support affect their morale as reported on the survey. The interviews reveal five major supports that positively affect the morale of priests: spiritual practices, self-care, imagination, a sense that the bishop cares for the priest as a person, and regularly connecting with a supportive community of priests. The more robust all five of these, the greater the self-reported morale of the priests. These also seemed to have a protective effect on burnout; priests who did not report enjoying these generative supports as strongly had lower morale, indicating that they are more susceptible to the risk factors for burnout, which were nearly universally present among the priests. This chapter examines priests' supportive practices and networks; the discussion of burnout and these findings' collective implications follows in the next chapter.

The Ups and Downs of a Vocation

Although the vast majority of Catholic priests are not married, literature from the sociology of marriage and family offer a way to think about commitment and satisfaction to this vocation. Sociology of family has for decades said that there are two marriages in every marriage: a bad marriage and a good marriage. It is not that some marriages are good and others are bad. Rather, every marriage is a mix of both good and bad, and the question for marital happiness and stability is whether the "good marriage" is salient enough and vibrant enough to weather the challenges or idiosyncrasies of the "bad marriage."[1] There was even an effort to quantify this in the literature, with the good marriage needing to be five times better than the bad marriage in order to properly compensate for the negative. As an alternative to this more quantitative approach, one might use the image of a well. Is the water cool, deep, and clear enough to get us through dry spells? If so, the couple will find their marriage happy and satisfying, even when navigating the elements or situations that are difficult.

This can inform the way we understand the quality of a priest's experience of his vocation. When asked about what made for a good or a bad day in ministry, or what sorts of graces and challenges they faced, all readily talked about the positives and negatives. They could also identify areas where they had support, and many could identify where they would like more support. When asked about burnout directly, all the interviews could weigh in, sharing experiences either from their own ministries or from priests they knew. Priestly morale seems to look a lot like the findings on marriage: there are ups and downs in every vocation. For each individual priest the question is whether the good is rich enough to sustain him in moments or seasons of

1 J. M. Gottman and R. W. Levenson, "Marital Processes Predictive of Later Dissolution: Behavior, Psychology and Health," *Journal of Personality and Social Psychology* 63 (1992): 221–33, https://doi.org/10.1037//0022-3514.63.2.221. J. M. Gottman et al., "Predicting Marital Happiness and Stability from Newlywed Interactions," *Journal of Marriage and the Family* 60 (1998): 5–22, https://doi.org/10.2307/353438. Arlene S. Skolnick, "Grounds for Marriage: How Relationships Succeed or Fail," in *Family in Transition*, 15th ed., ed. Arlene S. Skolnick and Jerome H. Skolnick (Pearson, 2009), 192–201. Arlene Skolnick, "Married Lives: Longitudinal Perspectives on Marriage," in *Present and Past in Middle Life*, ed. Dorothy H. Eichorn et al. (Academic Press, 1981).

challenge. Indeed, priestly morale is not about avoiding the challenges (as in marriage, these are often unavoidable), but about pouring himself into positive experiences that deepen his ministerial well, which preserve him when these inevitable challenges arise.

As the next chapter will demonstrate, nearly all priests reported challenge in at least one dimension or domain of burnout, and typically this was connected to the volume of work. Our question for these purposes is whether the positive and meaningful elements of priests' lives and ministry are rich enough to result in an overall positive assessment of their experience of their priestly vocation as captured in the survey question on their morale. In response to the statement "My morale as a priest is good," thirty-six percent strongly agreed, forty-seven percent agreed, nine percent neither agreed nor disagreed, six percent disagreed, and less than two percent strongly disagreed. These numbers are similar to another study that examined priestly morale.[2] With the next chapter exploring the more depleting aspects as well as offering recommendations for increasing priestly morale, this chapter focuses on the internal and external sources of support in a priest's vocation.

Sources of Support

There are two loci of support reported by the priests, which we will call internal and external. Internal sources of support are those over which the priest has more direct control, and we might think of these as generative practices or generative ways of looking at the world. External sources of support for these priests are relational and, because of this, the priests do not have full control over whether or not they receive these, as these supports are dependent, in part, on others. In understanding how both internal and external loci of support contribute to priests' vocational morale, we will want to pay attention to how these correlate in this survey response. If we do not see a dramatic difference in a variable across morale groupings, we cannot determine whether there is any relationship with priestly morale. Similarly, if all the respondents report similar levels of support from a practice or party, we should be reticent to claim that this person or party is either important or unimportant for priestly morale. In other words, we can make the strongest claims about the

2 Stephen J. Rossetti, *Why Priests Are Happy: A Study of the Psychological and Spiritual Health of Priests* (Ave Maria Press, 2011), 87.

connection between morale and support when we see substantial differences across morale groupings when naming their sources of support. To quickly define terms, priests who have a "higher morale" are those who selected "strongly agree" or "agree" when responding to the survey question. Priests who have a "lower morale" are those who responded "neither agree nor disagree," "disagree" or "strongly disagree" for this question.

Table 3.1 Sources of priestly support

Internal Sources of Support	*External Sources of Support*
• Spiritual practices	• Bishop/Superior relationship
• Self-care practices	• Priestly relationships
• Imagination	

Internal Sources of Support

Beginning with the internal sources of support, the priests communicated several generative practices or attitudes: spiritual practices, self-care practices, and having attitudes or imaginations that focused on the blessings in their lives rather than the hardships. Within Catholic moral theology, imagination refers to the particular interpretive lens that a person brings to their reality.[3] This imaginative lens will favor one interpretation of their reality over others in a way that shapes their understanding, moral evaluation, and consequent action. For example, priests might experience a similar reality (e.g., busyness), but—because of their differing imaginations—they may interpret that reality through very different lenses. Some will feel forsaken, overwhelmed, and underappreciated in their busyness, while others will see their many obligations as an abundance of needs in the world that they have the opportunity to help address.

3 Richard M. Gula, *Reason Informed by Faith: Foundations of Catholic Morality* (Paulist Press, 1989). Gula, *The Call to Holiness: Embracing a Fully Christian Life* (Paulist Press, 2003).

Spiritual Practices

Most common among these internal supports—perhaps even universal—were spiritual practices directly connected to the spiritual care of parishioners as well as their own prayer life. Things like presiding at Mass, hearing confessions, and the like were commonly listed items when interviewees were asked about what makes for a "good day" in their life as a priest. Even though priests offer these practices for the benefit of others, clearly these are also intrinsically rewarding and help to sustain them during harder moments. A "good day" was also one that had opportunities for prayer; these were more intentional ways for the priests to deepen their relationship with God. The importance of prayer in sustaining their well-being is underscored as it is a common response to the question that asks priests what "keeps them going."

It is important to note, however, that there is little to no difference in their discussion of prayer across morale groupings. Again, *this is not to say that prayer does not contribute to priestly morale*; in fact, research has found that a priest's prayer life is critical to his well-being.[4] Likely, given the ways priests connected prayer to their ability to do their job with love and fidelity, this is a very important—likely necessary—source of support for them. Given its universality among respondents to the NCSP, however, we cannot distinguish empirically the role it may play. Further complicating this finding, the literature indicates that the amount one prays does not always correlate with positive psychological outcomes. Sometimes people are distressed and turn to prayer;[5] supplicants who perceive their God as cold and distant can actually increase their stress and anxiety in praying.[6] Studies that break down prayer into different types find that some are helpful for well-being and

4 Rossetti, *Why Priests Are Happy.*

5 M. Bradshaw et al., "Prayer, God Imagery, and Symptoms of Psychopathology," *Journal for the Scientific Study of Religion* 47, no. 4 (2008): 644–59, https://doi.org/10.1111/j.1468-906.2008.00432.x.

6 C. G. Ellison et al., "Prayer, Attachment to God, and Symptoms of Anxiety-Related Disorders Among US Adults," *Sociology of Religion* 75, no. 2 (2014): 208–33, https://doi.org/10.1093/socrel/srt079. M. Bradshaw and B. V. Kent, "Prayer, Attachment to God, and Changes in Psychological Well-Being in Later Life," *Journal of Aging and Health* 30, no. 5 (2018): 667–91, https://doi.org/10.1177/0898264316688116

others are not. Prayer efficacy (i.e., prayers that aim to impact our world), prayers for support, and asking God for forgiveness are associated with higher anxiety, while praise of God and prayer expectancies (i.e., surrendering to how and when God answers prayers) correlate with lower anxiety.[7] Another study found that frequency of prayers of supplication and confession were negatively related to well-being, while frequency of prayers of adoration and thanksgiving were positively associated with well-being.[8] All this to say that we only know that all the priests prayed regularly and none said their prayer life was dry. However, we do not know the quality or purpose of their prayer and how this might raise or lower their morale.

A similar observation can be made of sacramental and spiritual care of parishioners. Because ministering to their flock was incredibly meaningful for the vast majority of priests regardless of morale level, the support and generativity this might bring cannot be empirically established based on this survey. Suffice it to say that no priest in the interview sample said they were in any way resentful about providing spiritual or sacramental care (even if some harbored negative attitudes or had a sense they were doing too much that could wear them down).

Self-Care Practices

Turning to self-care practices, this is an area where there are substantial differences between morale groups. According to their interviews, priests who have a higher morale took practices of self-care—such as a weekly day off, seeing friends, or engaging in a hobby—much more seriously than those who were lower. For example, this "strongly agree" priest recognizes the urgency of certain moments, as he missed his day off to help coordinate the transfer cycles of priests, but committed to getting some leisure time soon:

7 Laura Upenieks, "Unpacking the Relationship Between Prayer and Anxiety: A Consideration of Prayer Types and Expectations in the United States," *Journal of Religion and Health* 62 (2023): 1810–31, https://doi.org/10.1007/s10943-022-01708-0

8 David Benjamin Newman, "Within-Person Relationships Among Prayer, Well-Being, and Daily Events," MA thesis (College of William and Mary, 2014).

> [On my day off], I'm on the phone with the current bishop for an hour. I'm on the phone with the retired bishop for a half hour and then I had to call this, then I had to call that. . . But I'm gonna make up for it. I'm going to go up to New York City for the day on Wednesday.

He realizes that both these time-sensitive tasks and his day off are important and shifts his day off to honor both. Another "agree" priest talks about the importance of friendships in keeping the water level high in his ministerial well:

> I had some friends over yesterday after celebrating three Masses in the morning. I had some people over and I thought, "What am I doing? Why am I hosting people?" I'm exhausted and I had another Mass—a fourth Mass—in the evening and I thought, "This is gonna be terrible. I'm gonna be dead." But that time with my friends gave me energy I just felt and then I really, I think my last Mass—my fourth Mass of the day—was actually probably my best or personally like most fulfilling for me.

It is reasonable to think that having friends over on a full day would be chaotic and ultimately depleting, but he found this occasion, instead, to be generative.

This is a clear contrast with the self-care practices of priests with lower morale. Many priests of lower morale had a fatalistic way of talking about the impossibility of self-care, as this "strongly disagree" priest does:

> "[T]here's no one coming to relieve you, you know, like, "Father when you're going to get an associate?" I'm not, I'm not going to get—I'm just going to get more parishes. You guys have been listening for 20 years. Like, "Why don't they send you more priests?" Because there are no more priests.

In his eyes, the workload will only get heavier and there is no relief in sight. Connected to this, another priest who had a diocesan position cautions against a narrative among priests that belittles self-care:

> For five years I served as the full-time director of continuing formation for priests in this diocese. And I can tell you how many priests bragged to me about never taking a vacation.

This interviewee points out a dangerous priestly subculture that valorizes overworking and rejects the need for self-care. Priests with lower morale tend to see self-care as a luxury they cannot afford.

Imagination

A final, and admittedly less common, way that higher morale priests were distinguished from lower morale priests was their imagination, that is, the interpretive lens that they bring to their reality. Priests with higher morale tended to more easily interpret their experiences as a priest through a positive frame, a frame that served to diminish negative aspects of their job. Within the field of positive psychology, Barbara Fredrickson (among others) has demonstrated the efficacy of cultivating positive emotions in cultivating psychological resilience, finding meaning and "undoing" the negative affect after a difficult experience.[9] Cultivating positive emotions widens the possibilities for action that people see before them and helps them to become more flexible, creative, integrative, open to information, and efficient. It is clear how these habits of seeing positivity would act as a support and alleviate burnout and other negative experiences.

To illustrate how a positive imagination can impact priests, this priest who "agrees" that his morale is good discusses his own shift in imagination:

> I used to get frustrated when I was first ordained about the constant interruptions. And then I read an article somewhere where someone was suggesting you need to decide that the interruptions are the job. And once I did that, it was a lot easier to kind of just go with the flow.

As the man lying on the side of the road in the path of the Good Samaritan illustrates, distractions are a part of fruitful ministry. Other high morale priests' imaginations show dispositions of virtue even when not prompted, such as readily seeing beauty or other inspiration in their work:

9 Barbara L. Fredrickson, "The Role of Positive Emotions in Positive Psychology: The Broaden-and-Build Theory of Positive Emotions," *American Psychologist* 56, no. 3 (2001): 218–26, https://doi.org/10.1037/0003-066X.56.3.218

> I say Mass daily, but that's never routine. Like I come to Mass and it's like the first time I'm ever saying Mass, you know? The excitement and the presence that's there with that, so that's never routine either.

This priest echoes the perpetual newness of Christ in his approach to the otherwise routine aspects of his work.

A handful of times those with high morale acknowledged the full schedules they had, but at the same time that they compared these schedules with the much more demanding schedules of some families, especially those with young children, as this "strongly agree" priest does:

> I cannot look at a family coming in here after working a full week and carrying the baby in a bassinet or whatever those baby carriers are. And they're trying to make it through Mass and the baby's trying not to cry. And I'm going to complain about being overworked or burned out? No way. No, I can never compete with the kind of demands that are on the families of my parish, of my parishioners. No way. Do I get tired? Everybody does.

This desire to compare in a way that makes one's own life appear more favorable is similar to the politics of comparison that sociologist Arlie Hochschild discusses. When spouses want to preserve their relationship, they will compare their spouse to others who are clearly below the "market rate" rather than pushing, for example, their husbands to share in half the housework like "Mark" across the street.[10] Similarly, priests who have a high morale compared themselves to their busiest parishioners, not those with ample leisure time. Having an imagination that helped them to joyfully cope with the challenging aspects of their vocation was a real boon for their morale.

10 Arlie Russell Hochschild with Anne Machung, *The Second Shift* (Penguin Books, 2003), 51–57. Hochschild uses the terms "going rate" and "market value" to explain this comparison.

External Sources of Support

Unlike these internal sources of support (i.e., prayer and spiritual care, self-care, and imagination), external sources of support are largely beyond the control of employees. For the priests, both external sources of support were relational and were, therefore, somewhat dependent on another person or group. The two relationships that seemed to have the most impact on priests' vocational morale were those with other priests and with their bishop or religious superior. This section will first examine the quantitative data before turning to the interview data.

There was a clear difference between the morale groups when asked about support they received from other priests, their bishop, and—for religious priests—their religious superior (See Figure 3.1). The priests who agree that they are supported by other priests overwhelmingly come from the high morale group; only minorities of priests with lower morale feel supported by other priests. There is a similar pattern when asked about the support of their bishop, with 76 percent of those who "strongly agree" enjoying support from their bishop and 60 percent of those who "agree" saying the same; those with lower morale report much lower levels of support. Finally, high percentages of religious priests report being supported by their religious superior, with 89 percent who "strongly agree" their morale is good and 81 percent of those who

Figure 3.1: Support (strong and somewhat strong support combined) from priests, bishop, and religious superior, by morale

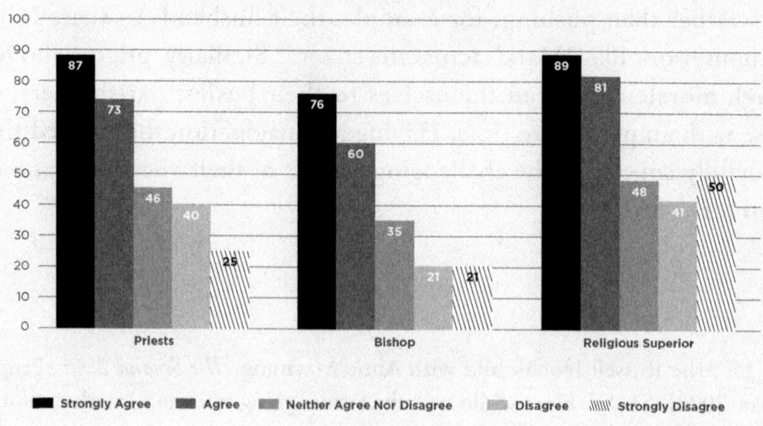

"agree" feeling supported by their religious superior; large minorities of those with lower morale levels report feeling supported here. While not definitively proving causality, these large differences across morale groups indicate there may be a relationship with these sources of support and priestly morale.

In contrast, priests across the various morale groupings reported fairly high levels of support from parishioners, lay friends, and family (see Figure 3.2). It is fortunate that so many have access to these sources of support. Unfortunately, it does not appear that these relationships definitively offer much in the way of morale. While there is a gradual drop in the level of this support across morale groups—from 93 percent among those who "strongly agree" to 63 percent among those who "strongly disagree"—significant majorities of priests of all morale groups report feeling supported by their parishioners. The drop is even less substantial when looking at lay friends; 97 percent of those who "strongly agree" enjoy support from lay friendships and 80 percent of those who "strongly disagree" say the same. Feeling supported by their family shows a similarly undramatic difference across groups, with 94 percent of those who "strongly agree" feeling their family's support and 74 percent of those who "strongly disagree" also experiencing familial support. There are slight differences across morale groupings here, but none that are substantial enough to indicate a real impact on morale.

Figure 3.2: Support (strong and somewhat strong support combined) from parishioners, lay friends, and family, by morale

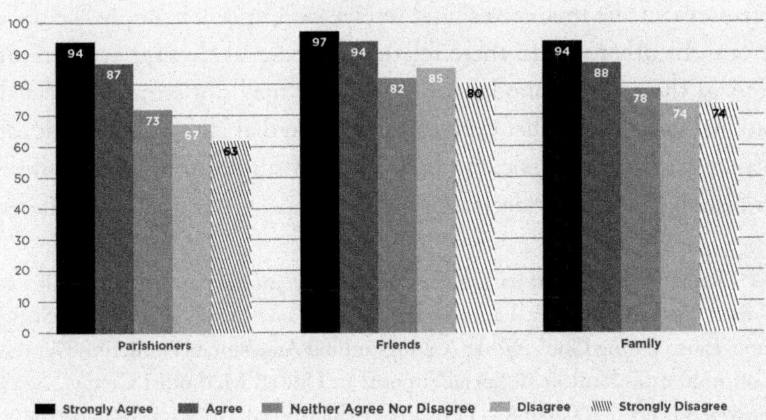

However, as was said of prayer above, this does not mean that parishioners, lay friends, and family do not make an important contribution. Beginning with parishioners, again, majorities of priests of all morale levels felt supported by their parishioners. The disparity of parishioner support between morale groupings is more pronounced than that of friends and family, but not as extreme as the differences across morale groupings when exploring the priest's support from his bishop and fellow priests. Like the relationship with their bishop, a poor "fit" between the priest and the parish may explain some cases of lower morale, but parishioner support could have a lessened impact because the parishioners do not hold a supervisory or corrective role as a bishop does.[11] But most important as to why this survey finding is excluded in this analysis is that the presence or absence of parishioner support was not discussed as an important factor when priests were describing their personal sources of support in the interview portion of the survey.

Turning to friends and family, other studies have found that having close friendships is the single largest predictor of the strength of a priest's relationship to God; clearly when these are explored more deeply, the fruits of these supports become more apparent.[12] This observation, combined with the NSCP data, could signify that this overwhelming support that priests report feeling from their friends and family do touch them on a personal level, but do not translate into priests' vocational morale because their priesthood is not the center of these relationships. Instead, their role as friend, son, uncle, or brother is nourished more than their priesthood. These relationships are likely very important sources of support for priests, providing social contexts where they can "be themselves" and receive care, and not simply "be on" and give care. In other words, these relationships are likely supportive in other aspects of their personhood, even while they may not strongly affect their vocational morale. Another explanation may be that all kinds of relationships can increase priestly morale, but only a lack of support from other priests or their bishop can actually decrease priestly morale. Given the large differences

11 Parishioner support has proven to be important for pastors' morale in a study of United Methodist clergy. Laura Upenieks and David E. Eagle, "Divine Struggles Among Those Doing God's Work: A Longitudinal Assessment Predicting Depression and Burnout and the Role of Social Support in United Methodist Clergy." *Sociology of Religion* 85, no. 1 (2024): 83–111, https://doi.org/10.1093/socrel/srad014

12 Rossetti, *Why Priests Are Happy*, 147–49.

across morale groups we found when it came to support from other priests and their bishop, and how these were amplified in the interviews, the focus of this analysis will be on these two types of relationships.

The qualitative data corroborate these survey findings as well as add some additional insights. The interviewer asked respondents to describe their relationship to their bishop. With this open-ended format, priests shared what was most helpful or damaging in this relationship. When priests felt supported by their bishop, they felt buoyed in their mission. When priests did not feel supported, rarely was this discussed as a simply unfortunate circumstance. Rather, unless the priest was a religious and his community buffered him from negative diocesan experiences, this was usually described as something quite toxic. So it is not simply that episcopal support buoys priests; a lack of support from their bishop seems to actively erode their morale. Finally, even though some reported a lack of support from their religious superior in the survey, religious priests did not seem to be especially concerned if they were not close with their superior. This could be because they are steeped in the charism and fraternity of their order or congregation and are not in need of support from their superior. Or it could be that religious superiors are typically in their role for a short while before a new member is elected to replace them, and so it is easy to adopt a "this too shall pass" attitude toward any tension. Whatever the case, religious priests were rarely troubled by a lack of support from their superior like the diocesan priests were of their bishop, and so the analysis for this subsection is more applicable to diocesan priests.

Relationship with Bishop

An important aspect of bishop support is an affective connection between the priest and the bishop. First and foremost, their reported support was less in the domain of the administrative and more in the realm of informal connection:

> I think I have more interaction with them maybe than priests had in the past. . . . He's been our bishop for several years now and he'll call us on our ordination anniversary. We can text him. I know some guys who've have texted him to talk about sports teams that they root for in common. He's happy to receive that. He has events, gatherings,

> like the Fourth of July picnic at his residence. He's got a big yard for all the priests and a view of the fireworks they set off at the high school. I think he's very available and I think he enjoys meeting us and hanging out with us in social situations and that shows, which makes us comfortable with him.

This basic desire for friendship and to host events that foster quality time affirms to priests that their bishop cares about them. Another mentioned the words of care the bishop offered shortly after his arrival:

> I think when he came, he made it very clear number one, that priests were very much in the forefront of his mind and that he had a goal of unifying the priests and supporting us. And from so from day one, he was just beautiful about that. He was as honest as could be, and he would talk about, you know, the struggles that he had, and I think every priest that I know of anyway, responded very favorably to him because we were, we were very hungry to, to hear that.

Knowing that they were a priority was very heartening for the priests and brought goodwill to the relationship.

These are in stark contrast with a priest who does not feel that affection:

> [W]e know that there's favoritism and I'm a priest fourteen years. I have not been made a pastor, there's guys that are ordained two years and are made pastors because they're young and the bishop likes them. . . . I've tried to contact him in his first year three times and got no response.

The damaging effect of favoritism was a common theme among those who did not have a positive relationship with their bishop. Another discussing the decreasing affect over the tenures of three bishops relates:

> So they'll say [the first bishop] loved his priests, for better or for worse. [The second bishop] respected his priests. [Makes a gesture, alluding to current bishop] uses his priests. That's a big—you go from love to use.

The priests went from feeling loved to feeling instrumentalized; this cannot be good for morale.

A final priest contrasts this reality with the ideals he learned in seminary:

> [I]n seminary, they're like, "All the bishops, your spiritual father, bishops, your spiritual father." No, he's not. He's your CEO. And that's about, you know, you might even have more loyalty from the CEO, just because they value your input more.

Clearly this disillusionment has left him cynical about his relationship with the bishop. Recalling the data that bishops are more likely to describe themselves as shepherds (83%), brother (73%), co-worker (73%), father (70%), and servant (68%) in relation to their priests, while priests are more likely to describe their bishop as an administrator (55%) or shepherd (54%). Given the significant gap in priests' and bishops' assessment of the bishop-priest relationship, bishops should work harder to manifest outwardly the shepherd and brother they imagine themselves to be. For this personal concern and affection to be experienced by priest is not simply important for priests' well-being; it is theologically mandated. The fatherhood and shepherd roles as well as the shared fraternity between priests and bishops—elaborated in the chapters of this book by David Songy and Fredrik Hansen—are teachings that must be revisited.

Availability was another quality that priests appreciated in their bishops. Some spoke of reserved hours each week of which priests could avail themselves if they wanted to speak privately with their bishop. Others said that their bishop made it a habit of regularly reaching out to check in with his priests. Not surprisingly, not getting responses from their bishop or rarely communicating with him was discouraging for the priests:

> I've been ordained now five years and I've never sat down with him personally except when I was first assigned to my first parish, that was a five-minute conversation, and I've been ordained five years. It's sad, unfortunately. It's really sad. It's just not a personal caring for the priests.

This priest longs for greater time with his bishop and, as his last sentence indicates, missing this is taken as a personal misstep, not a professional misstep.

But this emphasis on the personal does not mean that priests ignored the professional. They also wanted a bishop who could competently complete all his expected tasks. They wanted their bishop to have the necessary soft skills, including maturity, good listening, treating the priests as adults, regular communication, taking their perspectives into account when making decisions, and being decisive but not rash. Frequent complaints in the professional realm were that bishops were poor listeners or were too top-down in their decision-making.

Something that particularly upset priests about their bishops was inconsistency. Sometimes this was a perception that they were not applying policies evenly, especially if there was a perception that some priests were favored and others were not. Inconsistency might be a desire to be seen as "one of the guys" in social contexts, but being quite "my way or the highway" when it came to leadership. It might also manifest as reneging on promises, for instance, telling a priest that he could remain the pastor at his parish after his seventieth birthday only to move him to another parish shortly thereafter. Another was told that his mother could live with him in the rectory but then, when he was moved to another parish, his bishop told him that his mother should find alternative accommodations. All these situations dissolved the trust that priests wanted to have in their bishop, leaving them feeling quite unsupported. Although Thomas Guarino's chapter 7 in this book focuses on the lack of trust priests feel due to hypothetical treatment after false accusations, the findings reveal that this lack of trust manifests in more ordinary ways, as well.

Relationship with Other Priests

Camaraderie with other priests was another external source of support that showed a difference across morale groups. Priests who did not enjoy a formal priest support group or more informal relationships of support with other priests talked about the absence of this differently than they spoke about the absence of support from their bishop. With the bishops, a lack of support fomented feelings of anger, resentment, a perception that the bishop does not care or is incompetent, and so forth. When a priest revealed that his relationships with other priests were inadequate, this typically evoked feelings of sadness or disappointment; rare was the priest who said anything negative about priests writ large (even while some said certain "types" of priests were problematic). Because religious priests have this support "built in" to their lives, it was rare for them to say that this was an inadequate area of support. It was much more common to hear dissatisfaction in this area from diocesan priests.

Nearly across the board, priests shared that their relationships with other priests were very important to their sense of well-being. Some priests shared that, although they were very busy, they still managed to get adequate time with other priests, although many of these still wanted more of this:

> [M]ore often now, priests are saying, "We need to get together more often." Every time we get together for continuing education or retreat, that's a major theme that comes out of it, "We need to do this more often." Because we support one another and we complain to one another.

It is worth noting that the fruitfulness of gathering is evident to the priests, but it is hard to carve out the time apart from these mandatory events. He continues, noting the unique positionality of priests that makes this gathering so urgent:

> I don't have a partner go home to and say, "Hey, this is how bad my day was." I think that there's a bubbling need for that to occur, and I think this bishop will pick up on that and I think the guys will keep pushing that, that we have to have that happen more often, we need that.

He closes by noting that he trusts that the diocese will put the structures in place to make this need a reality.

And while there is wisdom in the diocese not regulating everything regarding priests' support, requiring participation in a priests' support group of some kind would force many priests to set aside the time to do that which they already want to do. Mandating groups is especially important when priests report challenges that would vary considerably from one area to another. Some priests in rural parts of the country say that regular gathering is not feasible owing to the geographic spread in their area. Others say the diocesan support would look more like helping them to decrease their workload to allow for more visits; often it was hard to find a window that worked for everyone even in a small group of priests. Is there even time to prioritize priestly fraternity? One priest wonders about this:

> [W]e're so stretched. And as I look at the future, I think that's a great part of the anxiety, is something has to give in a priest's life. We're not going to be able to, something of our calendar has to be lined out, x-ed, "Nope, you don't do this." And I hope it's not that. I hope it's not fraternity or leisure time spent with each other, dinners or lunch, you know, and so forth.

In thinking about his overly-full schedule, his concern that he will be asked to sacrifice time with other priests is palpable.

As far as taking lessons from religious life or even American Catholicism historically—when it was common to have multiple priests in a parish—having multiple priests in a rectory was a desire for some, but certainly not all. Some very much liked their alone time at the end of the day, but it was not uncommon for some to profess loneliness or a desire for shared experiences, that is, someone who could talk through problems with you and personally knew all the people involved and the issues at stake, but could offer a different set of eyes and a partner to address any concerns. There was also diversity in the desired composition of the group. Some preferred the same four priests they had been meeting for a weekly dinner with for the last thirty years; others preferred an open invitation for whomever was free. Some preferred to meet with "like-minded" or similarly experienced priests; others wanted things to be more mixed up. Some liked larger groups, while others found these draining and preferred groups of three or four. Figuring out both what each priest *wants* and what each priest *needs* could be very helpful in structuring generative as well as formative support groups.

However, there is a double-edged sword to support groups. Many spoke of these as a great place to vent or let off steam with other people who, because they were also priests, were really the only ones who could understand what these experiences were like. The flip side of this approach to the priest support groups is that some priests found them so profoundly negative that they completely avoided them. They described these priests as cynical and jaded and found themselves falling into the same patterns of negativity. Other research has found that support groups can lead to either positive or negative mental health outcomes.[13] These studies and the priests' mixed experiences

13 For positive outcomes in the sharing of problems, see Christopher Justin Jacobi et al., "Mental Health Correlates of Sharing Private Problems in

suggest that support groups may need to be more reflective and self-critical to ensure that even in their venting they are actually bringing generativity—and not cynicism, factionalism or schadenfreude—to the participants.

The complicated nature of relationships among priests is noted elsewhere in the data as there is an important gap between older and younger priests and their animating theologies. Not all priests reported a cleavage within their own diocese and some reported a good deal of unity, "I think our presbyterate has a good sense of togetherness. That there's not a real sense of divide between liberals and conservatives or antagonism between young and old." As this quote demonstrates, even though priests may not have personally experienced these rifts, they still knew the typical dividing lines.

This feeling of bifurcation among the presbytery can be hard on priests when it is present and can lead to a sense of isolation, entrenchment, or factionalism, as this older priest offers:

> I think there is a great divide between the older priests and the younger priests. And the archbishop denies that's there. And, quite frankly, it's there. And he's not doing anything about it. So I think that, you know, I personally feel when I'm around the younger priests that I'm looked down on, and it's almost like the attitude "I can't wait til you guys get out of here so we can run the church the way it should be run." So that's the feeling I get around a lot of the younger guys.

That "you guys get out of here" refers to their retirement or death and is perceived as a "can't wait til" moment among younger priests is clearly going to decrease fraternity and morale. Younger priests also had complaints about their older counterparts:

Congregations During the COVID-19 Pandemic," *Journal for the Scientific Study of Religion* 61 (2022): 553–63, https://doi.org/10.1111/jssr.12780. For negative outcomes, especially in the long-term, see Justin P. Boren, "The Relationships Between Co-Rumination, Social Support, Stress, and Burnout Among Working Adults," *Management Communication Quarterly* 28 (2014): 3–25, https://doi.org/10.1177/0893318913509283. J. Byrd-Craven et al., "Co-Ruminating Increases Stress Hormone Levels in Women," *Hormones and Behavior* 53, no. 3 (2008): 489–92, doi: 10.1016/j.yhbeh.2007.12.002

> Then the older priests, I've given up on it. I think a lot of them are really cynical and it's jaded and to go hang out with them is to just fall into the same cynicism. And there's a lot of gossiping and it's exhausting and so I just avoid hanging out with priests because of that.

Needing to avoid other priests because you find them depleting and *facilitating* burnout is disheartening for newer priests looking for support. Again, group culture should be monitored for the well-being of all involved.

Finally, there were a handful of priests who had assignments that put them into regular contact with other priests; these few circumstances are telling. Perhaps they needed to be at the chancery twenty hours per week or maybe they were one of several priests teaching and ministering at a large high school. This formal obligation ended up affording them considerable formal and informal time with other priests:

> Yeah, we're pretty blessed here at the at high school, we've got seven priests that teach. . . So we see a lot of priests every day and those that don't teach, we get together about once a month for a meeting and just on a topic that the diocese gives us and then we have a holy hour together, social dinner and just a couple of hours to hang out and visit.

They see one another regularly during the day and also take intentional time each month to support and enjoy one another. Long-term positions were not required for fraternity, though. There were a number who shared in a several-session professional development or a project that also helped them connect to other priests in a meaningful way. As the foregoing demonstrates, the more a diocese can foster stronger relationships between priests and their bishop as well as collegiality and fraternity among priests, the better the morale of the presbyterate.

Implications

To briefly summarize, the major sources of support for priests have both internal and external loci. There are three primary internal sources of support. The first is spiritual practices, which include both their own prayer and devotional practices as well as the ministerial care they offer others, such as offering grief support to parishioners or presiding at Mass. The second is to honor their self-care practices; high morale priests are aware of their needs, and they prioritize these in a way that still honors their ministerial tasks. Finally, a handful demonstrated imagination or attitudes that emphasized the blessings in their role; these included a sense of newness in pieces of their job that could become routine or comparing their schedules to that of working parents. The external sources of support which showed up as most consequential to morale in the data were relationships with other priests and their relationship with their bishop. The quality of both of these types of relationships seemed to have a direct correlation with priestly morale. The next chapter discusses the implications of the above in greater depth, but there remain some implications worth touching on here.

Priests have nearly full control and responsibility for their internal sources of support. Beginning with spiritual practices, their days are full of opportunity to touch the lives of others in ministry, and the most fulfilled priests seem to take great joy in and formation from these encounters. Carving out time to cultivate their own spiritual lives—whether through the examen, formal prayer, adoration, spiritual reading, or others—seems to also be key for their well-being. They should take time each day to care for themselves, no matter how busy they are; they need to know that they are a priority to God and deserving of care just as much as those to whom they minister. If they do not make their self-care a priority, countless other things will crowd this out. Of course, a day off might have to be moved due to pressing matters, but this should be postponed, not cancelled. Finally, imagination seems to be an under-utilized gift for priests. How we choose to interpret an event or a person's actions affects our attitude and related actions toward that person or event and sometimes even beyond these. Being mindful of the ways God might be inviting us to see things differently—perhaps through a lens of beauty, humility, or newness—should result in greater wholeness as the priests who employ this practice demonstrate.

Priests also, while not having full control, do have the ability to initiate and prioritize their relationships with their bishop and other priests. Among the priests for whom support from their bishop was lacking, on the one hand, there were some priests who said they reached out to their bishop and felt rejected when they did not get the relationship they were looking for. This is very unfortunate and perhaps serves as a powerful reminder to bishops that their priests need their care. On the other hand, there were a larger number who seemed to be waiting for the bishop to prioritize them. Taking initiative personally or as a deanery to have formal and informal conversations with their bishop might better serve priests' vocational morale than hoping that the bishop reaches out first. There was a very clear consensus that priests wanted more time with other priests. The problem seems to be that they do not have time to gather, but some of them make solving this problem a priority. Going back to the marriage analogy at the start of the chapter: marriage takes work. A vocation of any kind takes work. In this case, the resource that needs to be prioritized is the priests' time. They need to connect regularly, whether in large, formal groups, more fluid "whoever is available" settings, as pairs for lunch, or whatever might work for them and their many obligations. Perhaps they can only gather their closest four priest friends for breakfast at 6am or for a late dinner at 8pm, but they need to make this a priority. Again, they owe it to themselves and one another to enjoy and support one another in their vocations. The next chapter will go into greater depth on these implications, especially in light of the priests' discussion of burnout.

CHAPTER FOUR

CLERGY BURNOUT AND IMPLICATIONS FOR WELL-BEING

Maureen K. Day

The previous chapter opened with findings from the sociology of marriage asserting that every marriage is a mixture of good and bad; the question was whether the good aspects of the marriage were generative enough to get the couple through the inevitable challenges. Hypothesizing that priests might have a similar experience within their priesthood—that there are both depleting and life-giving aspects within their vocation—the chapter then outlined the most pivotal external and internal supports that surfaced in the interview data. This chapter begins by examining the ways priests may experience challenges and even burnout in their work and closes by discussing implications that consider both the support findings of the previous chapter as well as these burnout findings.

Burnout

Psychologists Christina Maslach and Michael Leiter define and elaborate burnout as "a psychological syndrome emerging as a prolonged response to chronic interpersonal stressors on the job. The three key dimensions of this response are an emotional exhaustion, feelings of cynicism and detachment from the job, and a sense of ineffectiveness and lack of accomplishment."[1] These dimensions might appear alone or together and may vary in degree, but collectively comprise the characteristics of burnout.

Emotional Exhaustion

This first dimension—*emotional exhaustion*—seemed to potentially loom the largest for priests. It is very important to distinguish having a heavy workload from being emotionally exhausted by it; people working part-time might still experience burnout while those working sixty-hour weeks could find their work very fulfilling. Although very few seemed to be treading into this realm of emotional exhaustion, nearly all interviewees were concerned about overwork, like this priest who "agrees" that his vocational morale is good, "Burnout, no. Fatigue and sometimes exhaustion." When asked how he distinguishes burnout from fatigue or exhaustion, he touches on elements from Maslach and Leiter, claiming that burnout is "Not wanting to go on and feeling like I didn't have the energy to go on that wouldn't be replenished by a good night's sleep or a day off or a couple of light days." He acknowledges that he has a lot on his plate, but he can keep burnout at bay by being self-aware and taking some free time as needed. Priests nearly universally said that their workloads were very challenging, and many also said there are pieces of the job (e.g., administration, mediating conflict) that they find draining, but many still maintained high morale.[2]

It was typically only those with lower vocational morale who showed signs or voiced feelings connected to the second and third dimensions of burnout. Beginning with *cynicism*, detachment, and other experiences of depersonalization of work, the priests tended not to voice a cynicism towards

1 Christina Maslach and Michael P. Leiter, "Understanding the Burnout Experience: Recent Research and Its Implications for Psychiatry," *World Psychiatry* 15, no. 2 (June 2016): 103–11, https://doi.org/10.1002/wps.20311. In his survey of priests, Stephen Rossetti found that 11 percent of priests suffered from significant levels of emotional exhaustion, 6 percent from cynicism, and 19 percent from inefficacy, with 1.5 percent of his sample struggling with all three of these dimensions. Stephen J. Rossetti, *Why Priests Are Happy: A Study of the Psychological and Spiritual Health of Priests* (Ave Maria Press, 2011), 71.

2 Rossetti likewise found that 42 percent of priests were overwhelmed by their workload. Rossetti, *Why Priests Are Happy*, 32.

the typical tasks of shepherding a parish. Even those with very low morale found a good deal of meaning and solace in celebrating the sacraments, accompanying those who are grieving, and so on. Instead, cynicism among priests appeared more as a hostility toward or disillusionment with the bishop or diocese, as this "strongly disagree" priest offers:

> Do you know the previous bishop—and again, like, you don't say this to your gathered presbytery—he's like, "Every priest is an interchangeable cog. So I can take out any piece from any parish and put them anywhere else and it's fine." Like, that's the dumbest thing I've ever heard.

Although this bishop could have meant that all the priests were competent, well-trained, and capable of running any parish in the diocese, this priest heard a message of depersonalization and instrumentalism, which demonstrates his perception that diocesan leadership is out of touch with the priests.

The third dimension of burnout is a *lack of efficacy*, that is, feeling ineffective or lacking in accomplishment. A priest who "strongly disagrees" that he has good morale stated:

> I don't have a clue what the Church will look like in 20 years, and will we still be here in 20 years? I don't mean that universally. I don't know about the universal church. But the United States, I'm not sure we have a future here.

It must make much of a man's work seem utterly pointless when he wonders whether there will be a substantial Catholic presence in the United States in a generation.

A lack of accomplishment also arose in the context of wanting to be affirmed more often by the bishop, rather than only receiving a phone call when something goes wrong, as this priest who "disagrees" that his morale is good comments:

> And lack of affirmation. You get a general email that that's just "Oh, thank you all for all the hard work that you're doing as you navigate to COVID pandemic. Here's a list of updated restrictions." And okay that that sounds nice. But you know, like, something a bit more personal every

> now and then would be. Like even just to check in, like "Hey, how's it going?" You know, "Hey, I put you in the parish eight months ago. Uh, how's it going?" You know, I think a lot of us feel because it's easy to get the "you're not" message. But the affirmation of "Hey, you're really trying here, we appreciate that" at an individual level would be nice.

Although many of the priests with higher morale also mentioned they would like to hear more words of gratitude from their bishop, it did not seem to be so urgent or "make-or-break" for them.

There is also literature that compares clergy burnout with other helping professions.[3] Part of the susceptibility to burnout that clergy experience is attributable to their position requiring a number of diverse roles. Clergy roles regularly include that of preacher, presider at rites and sacraments, provider of pastoral care, teacher, organizer, and administrator. Seen globally, these roles each require distinct competencies and come with their own unique stressors. Clergy regularly transition between these roles many times during a single day. This can lead to role overload, which can contribute to burnout. There is also an intensity to clergy work that takes an additional toll on priests. To name a few examples, there can be high emotions among those they minister to in the contexts of funerals, bereavement, and other contexts of suffering or grief. There can be conflict within their staff or parishioners that they must manage. When making leadership decisions, situations often have no clear right or wrong answers, and pastors' choices inevitably give rise to criticism. Other comparative studies have found that clergy burnout is positively correlated with interpersonal conflict among parishioners, lacking a space to process feelings, exposure to people in crisis, criticism, lacking help, and excessive paperwork.[4] External, systemic factors leading to clergy burnout include too much work, poor social support, difficult parishioners, denominational structures, and needing to be radically available at all times.[5]

3 C. J. Adams et al., "Clergy Burnout: A Comparison Study with Other Helping Professions," *Pastoral Psychology* 66, no. 2 (2016): 147–75, https://doi.org/10.1007/s11089-016-0722-4

4 Richard W. Foss, "Burnout Among Clergy and Helping Professionals: Situational and Personality Correlates" (PhD diss., Fuller Theological Seminary, 2002), 63.

5 William N. Grosch and David C. Olsen, "Clergy Burnout: An Integrative

Maslach and Leiter also note that burnout can be contagious, such that we should treat it not just as a personal phenomenon, but also as a social one. This is corroborated in the interview data. First, there were some who were low in morale who, because of their own social circles, assumed that most priests' morale was low, as this "disagree" priest demonstrates:

> They come out with these studies that [say] "Hello, priestly morale is so good." I'm like, "What? Where are you getting that from? None of the people that I talk to." They don't talk well about the bishops and about what they're doing. It's just not the reality amongst the guys on the front lines. None that I really know.

If a priest's morale is low, it can affect his social circle, or at least his perceptions of that social circle; or the social circle's low morale can reinforce his own. A few of the higher morale priests observed that priest support groups can become complaining sessions that breed negativity; this is why some priests choose to avoid these groups. In referring to one of the groups in his diocese, this "agree" priest observes:

> I'd be happy to go, but I feel like a lot of it just, it tends to just devolve into gossiping—usually about the bishop—and so [if] it's just exhausting, then what's the point. So, I have a small group of priest friends and we go to the movies together, we'll go have dinner.

He saw negativity in one group but finds community and renewal with a different group of priests.

Domains of Burnout

Maslach and Leiter also discuss six domains that—when not aligned with workplace well-being—can be depleting of workers. These are work overload, control, reward, community, fairness, and values. Each of these were seen in varying degrees among the interviewees. Work overload was the most

Approach," *Journal of Clinical Psychology* 56, no. 5 (2000): 619–32. https://doi.org/10.1002/(sici)1097-4679(200005)56:5<619::aid-jclp4>3.0.co;2-2

common among priests of all morale levels; even though few reported the *dimension* of emotional exhaustion, work overload seemed to be the most high-risk *domain* for the priests. Lack of control, insufficient reward, and poor community were fairly common among those with lower morale. Finally, concern with fairness or a conflict of values were present in the data, but were not especially common.

Beginning with *work overload*, this experience seemed to be nearly universal among the priests. The vast majority said their days were consistently full and that there were weeks or even longer stretches that were especially demanding. For instance, one talked about a Saturday full of baptisms, a wedding, confessions, and two Masses. Another spoke of a few times that he had gone two or three weeks without a day off. A key difference between those who had a higher morale and those whose morale was lower was that those with higher morale said they made the effort to carve out or make up days off while those with lower morale tended to describe days off or other forms of self-care as a luxury they could not afford.

Second, there is a link between the lack of *control* one feels in their work and burnout. When employees do not feel they have the capacity to influence decisions that affect their work, that they lack autonomy or that they lack the resources to do a job well, they are more likely to experience burnout. While priests might be seen as fairly autonomous to their parishioners, and canonically the pastor has much authority within his parish, there are elements that can be beyond priests' control. When bishops assign priests to tasks that they find draining, or when priests find themselves in circumstances that require competencies they do not have, this can be very depleting. Priests regularly said they did not get adequate or even any training in administration, and yet this was a major component of their job. A work overload issue that overlaps with control is the priest being told to delegate so that he can find better work-life balance, but not having the volunteers or personnel to do this, as this priest who "neither agrees nor disagrees" that he has good vocational morale demonstrates, "It's easy for us to be taught or otherwise told, you gotta have balance in your life. But then support that, with the role expectations that come along with what we're asking you to do." Priests cognitively understand that they need to avoid burnout, but if a diocese states this without providing the practical support to make it happen, the concern can appear to be insincere lip service.

The third domain, *reward*, refers to positive reinforcement for a job well done. This recognition and affirmation could take material forms in other occupational contexts, but the priests wanted relational rewards, such as a personal (not a generic template) note of thanks, especially from their bishop. Those with lower morale tended to report a dearth of these acknowledgments. While they may have personally felt that they were accomplishing much, not hearing affirmations from those higher up seemed to devalue the work, especially if their contact with their bishop only occurred when something went wrong. It is tiring when interactions with the bishop are limited to corrective conversations or impersonal contact.

Community is the fourth domain and has to do with the relationships connected to their priesthood. When these relationships lack support, trust, and good feelings, there is more likely to be burnout. As the previous chapter elaborated, this is seen easily in the survey data, with bishops imagining themselves to be very relational with their priests, while priests see their bishop more as an administrator or—more warmly—as a shepherd; in other words, bishops imagine themselves to be more affectively close to their priests than the priests experience. Further, just under half (49%) of diocesan priests say they trust their bishop. But another area of community that can be lacking for priests, especially those with low morale, is camaraderie with other priests. Priests with higher morale tended to meet with other priests regularly. Those with lower morale were more likely to not have this, even if they wanted it, saying that finding the time to make this happen was often a challenge because of workload.

Fifth, *fairness* refers to equity, respect, just procedures, and the like. Perhaps because of the focus on sex abuse for this study, it was voiced by many that they did not believe that they would be supported if they were unjustly accused; this lack of trust is discussed in depth in Thomas Guarino's chapter. But looking beyond this topic at the more day-to-day issues, fairness was not a common complaint for many. If it were to come up, it had considerable overlap with community: concerns about fairness were voiced by priests who also expressed a desire for more relational care from their bishop as this was seen as proper to the priest-bishop relationship.

The final domain is *values*. Values can refer to the ideas and motivations that helped them to discern a priestly vocation to begin with. It was very rare that a priest expressed a real conflict of values between themselves and their parish or diocese.[6] Typically disagreements were about strategy rather than core concerns. However, values can also refer to the tasks themselves, as in the tasks priests find intrinsically valuable. Priests usually find preaching, sacraments, and pastoral care to be intrinsically valuable, but many see administration as a tedious part of their job. This administrative work they must do pulls them from the work they want to do, which can lead to burnout.

There are a few additional observations on burnout worth noting. First, although there were priests of both high and low morale who were more concerned with lazy priests than with burnout, there were a handful of priests who implied that burnout is overblown; most of these had low morale, as in the case of this priest who "disagrees" that his morale is good:

> Now, if a guy wants to bother, yeah, he's gonna get all, quote, "burnout," you know [clicks tongue], "I'm going to take my day off," . . . So yeah, burnout is real. But I mean honestly, I don't buy any priest dying of overwork.

This priest, although he self-reports that he has lower morale, is more dismissive of the idea of burnout and may not recognize that he is experiencing this himself.

Second, as far as getting to the point of being overwhelmed, only those seriously thinking about leaving the priesthood voiced helplessness in the face of challenges. Those with higher morale had more of a surrender or "this is what is mine to do" attitude; the big challenges were not theirs alone to solve. A sense of being isolated, not belonging, or feeling disempowered seems to lead to burnout.

Implications

There are many practical implications for these findings on burnout and the previous chapter's exploration of support. The two main clusters of implications in these findings are, first, moving from "avoiding burnout" to "cultivating engagement." There were priests who told us that their ongoing professional development included helpful workshops on recognizing the signs

6 A notable, but relatively rare, exception to this were priests who saw themselves as more conservative or traditional and thought that their bishop or Pope Francis was undermining a more authentically Catholic approach to parish life and the world.

of burnout and avoiding this by scaling back, taking a day off, and so forth. However, there are reasons to think that a strategy of "cultivating engagement" rather than simply avoiding burnout will be more fruitful. Second, this section will also provide a more practical and structural examination of support, specifically reducing workload and creating structures of accountability for priests and bishops.

Cultivating Engagement

There are several analogous examples that demonstrate that cultivating engagement may be a more effective strategy in promoting morale than simply avoiding burnout. We can see it in the numerous parenting books that encourage mothers and fathers to redirect a child's behavior toward something more appropriate when possible rather than simply telling the child to stop the undesirable behavior. We know that behavior is more quickly modified through positive reinforcement rather than punishment.[7] This wisdom is in the title alone of St. Francis's Admonition XXVII, "Virtue Puts Vice to Flight"; in this he elaborates, for example, "Where there is charity and wisdom, there is neither fear nor ignorance."[8] With each of these we see a belief that if the good is proactively fostered and attended to, that which is not good becomes less of a concern. Similarly, scholars of burnout sometimes turn readers' attention to *engagement*, which is defined as the opposite of burnout: "a state of high energy (rather than exhaustion), strong involvement (rather than cynicism), and a sense of efficacy (rather than inefficacy)."[9] People concerned with the morale of priests would be wise to consider the ways they might help priests to increase their engagement, rather than simply to avoid burnout.

Returning to our six domains of burnout discussed earlier in the chapter, we can see what these tell us about engagement. First, just as work overload

7 H. K. Scott et al., "Behavior Modification," in *StatPearls* (StatPearls Publishing, July 10, 2023), https://pubmed.ncbi.nlm.nih.gov/29083709

8 Regis J. Armstrong, J. A. Wayne Hellman, and William J. Short, eds., *Francis of Assisi: Early Documents—The Saint* (New City Press, 2001), 136.

9 C. Maslach and M. P. Leiter, "Burnout and Engagement in the Workplace: A Contextual Analysis," in *Advances in Motivation and Achievement,* vol. 11, ed. T. Urdan (JAI Press, 1999), 278.

contributes to burnout, a manageable workload increases engagement. It was nearly universal for priests to say there was too much on their plate or they were spread too thin. Ensuring that they have the personnel—whether these be paid or volunteer—to whom to delegate tasks is key. A priest with a sustainable workload can start new initiatives and hone new skills that creatively meet ministerial needs. Second, having professional autonomy and the skills necessary to complete a job well increases engagement. Having insufficient training to do additional work (e.g., roles within the diocese, managing parish finances) was very discouraging to priests and left them feeling unsupported. When proper training is given, efficacy (and engagement) increase. Third, recognition and reward were most desired or appreciated in their relational forms. Being appreciated or acknowledged in their efforts helped them to see both themselves and their work as worthwhile.

Fourth, relationships can make or break a job. There is a saying that one doesn't quit a job, they quit a boss; while this is of course not always the case, it speaks to the importance of relationships in promoting engagement. For a healthy morale, priests need a sense of care, support, and fraternity most from their bishop and other priests. The fifth domain of fairness is closely related to relationships for priests. When priests do not feel they are being treated fairly by people, especially diocesan officials, or that they are getting caught in what they see as unreasonable protocols, they can experience cynicism and anger. Conversely, when they feel that they are being treated justly, they feel like they are part of the team. Finally, experiencing the values of what it means to be a priest (e.g., one-on-one accompaniment, offering sacraments) greatly deepens engagement. The freer they are to perform these duties or to expand their imagination to see undesirable tasks (for example, administration) as core to their priestly identity, the more they will resonate with their work.

Related to this notion of cultivating that which is good is practicing self-care. As discussed in the last chapter, the priests with the higher levels of morale were typically those who held themselves accountable to practices of self-care, such as exercise, visiting friends, and making up missed days off. But some practices of self-care are more generative than others and will have a greater impact on morale. Examining different understandings of self-care and their merits will help priests to be more mindful of their value, or lack of value, as a regenerative practice. I argue that self-care is more helpfully phrased as self-responsibility rather than as simply "time off." That is, self-care is responsibility for the things that only one can do for oneself—such as hygiene, exercise, prayerful practices, connecting with good friends, spiritual reading, adequate sleep and nutrition, a tidy home—and whether these are being appropriately prioritized.

First, it is important to note that some ways of unwinding or unplugging are actually harmful to the self. A good number of the priests mentioned in their interviews that some of their fellow priests struggled with alcoholism; unhealthy coping behaviors are, sadly, not uncommon among priests.[10] Often they were not describing a diagnosed condition, but they noted that a fellow priest drank too much as a way of dealing with stress or to relax. Less often, priests alluded to the easy availability of pornography for lonely priests as another unhealthy outlet. Unlike alcoholism, none of the interviewees said they knew of priests struggling with this, but because of the handful of times it came up, it is obviously a potential pitfall for some.

Second, simply because something is not overtly harmful does not mean that it is actually going to be generative or reinvigorating. We might think of these as "not unhealthy" practices. For instance, we might like to unwind at the end of a workday by watching an episode of a favorite sitcom or courtroom drama. These are, possibly, good transitions from the intensity of the day to something that has more levity or distance. Usually these escapes are not necessarily going to replenish the well of care the typical priest offers those under his care, but in some cases, they might. For instance, perhaps a priest's siblings or nieces and nephews also watch this show, and he can connect with them over the latest episodes. "Not unhealthy" practices may indeed foster joy and connection in important relationships and actually be "healthy," that is, life-giving. The same can be said for a number of other "not unhealthy" practices, such as pet ownership, painting, practicing musical instruments, gardening, or video games. Discernment is needed to determine whether something is a life-giving hobby, a helpful transition from work to personal time, or a distraction from needed self-responsibility, such as prayer or calling a loved one. Discernment can involve a number of different questions, but must include how much time an interest requires and how much goodness it fosters within the priest.

10 Twenty-four percent of priests in Rossetti's study admitted that they dealt with stress by consuming excessive food or alcohol. Rossetti, *Why Priests Are Happy*, 32.

Finally, self-responsibility at its core should involve several objectively healthy practices. Acknowledging that any practice can be misused toward unhealthy ends (e.g., someone may use prayer to avoid having a difficult conversation), this analysis assumes a balanced and properly ordered use of these practices, not escapism or other inappropriate use. Some healthy practices would include prayer and other devotional practices, professional development, exercise and physiological care, and intentionally maintaining important relationships, as well as practicing virtues, such as practicing gratitude or contemplating the beauty in one's day. These practices often impact the well-being of the individual, but some are also likely to positively impact others. Gratitude, for instance, not only helps people acknowledge the many blessings in their lives, but as they express that gratitude through notes, words, and gestures, they also create a more grateful community. As a priest thanks his staff and volunteers for their hard work, he creates a culture of gratitude as well as engagement. This discussion of engagement as well as self-care as self-responsibility helps point to a more life-giving way for priests to engender meaning in and connection to their work than an approach simply aimed at "avoiding burnout."

Support

There are three areas of support that are most pressing for priestly morale: reducing workload, creating structures of accountability to ensure they are fostering their internal sources of support, and considerations for seminaries and dioceses to help facilitate the external sources of support. Each of these areas fall, in some way, on dioceses to ensure priests are getting the support they need.

Reducing workload was an obvious need voiced by many of the interviewees. There are several ways to do this. There are priests who live in areas of the country where the Catholic population is shrinking or is quite thin. Some priests were very resentful that—from their perspective—wealthy but very small parishes were kept open to keep those donors happy. This strategy meant that they said Mass for a small group of parishioners while only a few blocks away there was another Mass going on. It did not make sense to them that the diocese would pile the responsibilities of two parishes onto two priests in this situation when the smaller church could be closed, and then two priests could share the workload of running a parish. More often, there was no second priest, so the pastor would simply run himself ragged caring for the needs of both parishes instead of the bishop choosing to consolidate these. While the move to close parishes is fraught with all sorts of feelings and concerns, the priests in these situations sometimes felt that their needs were not considered. Ultimately, priests need a way to reduce their current workload.

Beyond parish consolidation, there is also the possibility of reducing workload by reducing certain types of work. One of the most disliked tasks named by the priests in the survey was the bookkeeping and administrative aspect of their work. If funds were available to hire a staff person—perhaps shared with another parish—this could free priests from an aspect of their job they do not enjoy (or do not feel they do well). This psychological burden would be mitigated, and they would likely feel more freedom to creatively engage the ministerial aspects of their work.

A second area of support needed are structures of accountability. Priests are often told to gather with one another, to honor their day off and the like, but they are quite likely to cut out these enjoyable—yet necessary—practices when work gets busy. And things are nearly always busy. Priests need check ins: Have you ever taken a sabbatical? How often do you take a full day off? Are you having monthly spiritual direction? Are you meeting with a mentor? Have you been on your annual retreat? Are you in a priest support group? How often are you scheduled to meet? How often do you go? In what ways are these fulfilling/not fulfilling? What sort of diocesan workshops or support groups or discussion topics would be helpful for you? Do you think you would do better living alone in a rectory or with another priest? These and other questions would help priests hold themselves accountable to the most important practices for thriving in their ministries.

Many of these issues are more of a concern for diocesan secular priests than priests in a religious order. This is not to say that religious priests are not also spread thin, but religious communities have many supportive aspects built into them. Religious communities require priests to spend time with others with whom they live. Also, the communities' independent structure acts as a buffer between the priest and the diocese if their relationship with the bishop is not especially positive. Often religious priests said that they know their religious superior quite well, which tends to generate positive feelings; the importance of trust in leadership and its various outcomes is amplified in the next chapter by Brooke Tranten. Their religious community also holds them accountable to prayer practices and moments of leisure, whether that is a walk after dinner, a board game, or simply a set cocktail hour. Many sources of support—both internal and external—are more accessible for those living in religious communities. And religious priests reported higher levels of well-being than diocesan priests. Dioceses should consider whether and how they can replicate some of the structures of religious life for diocesan priests in a way that still respects their secular vocation.

Internal sources of support—spiritual practices, self-care, and imagination—primarily fall to the priests' responsibility, but there are still structural ways these can be supported. Some priests can be better equipped to manage these. Prayer seems to be a solid practice across interviewees, such that it is not a distinguishing factor between low and high morale groups (as was explained in the last chapter), but it is still a necessary one. How to better support priests in this area is not obvious, but workshops on the benefits of some types of prayer as well as the mental liabilities of other types may help them to be more self-aware and not fall into spiritual pitfalls. Perhaps ensuring that every priest is receiving monthly spiritual direction or mentorship and also meets with other priests for monthly prayer and fellowship is an important first step.

For self-care, those who make personnel choices for the diocese need to be in regular conversation with priests to make sure their workload is not perpetually too high to allow for days off as well as regular afternoons or evenings off; workdays that regularly break ten or eleven hours leave little time for self-care, much less relationships and leisure. Self-care must include a recognition of their own finitude and the necessity of drawing boundaries; for every time they say yes to an invitation, they are saying no to something else, whether that is dinner with a friend or time for contemplation. If self-care is one of the first things a busy priest takes off his plate, and we know eschewing this is a deleterious practice, priests need to be held accountable to organizing their workload to include self-care. One way to do this that ties into external support as well is to mandate priest support groups that include check-ins and protocols for managing self-care. Priests need to be honest when their workload is so high that they begin to neglect their relationships, hobbies, or health. In having a semi-public forum to come together and discuss their workloads and self-care practices, they can ensure that they are managing their time and finding balance.

Finally, recalling the findings from positive psychology, formation—both in seminary and ongoing—must shift imaginations so that priests are not only offered preparation for the signs of burnout and the challenges of priestly life, but are helped to develop a sense of beauty, reverence, and gratitude for their everyday tasks. Clearly, administration is not perceived as pastoral care by many of the priests; helping them to see the theological model of the Good Steward in their vocation as well as the administrative savvy of St. Paul may help them to gain a greater appreciation of the spiritual nature of this aspect of their work.

The ways the diocese can offer structures of accountability for external sources of support are more obvious. Although it can be a helpful mechanism to monitor and reinforce self-care, the primary purpose of a mandated priest support group is to foster connection and support among priests. As noted above, priests are looking for a variety of things from these groups. Some want a place to let off steam or just be themselves with others who understand their vocation from the inside. Others want to socialize and share a meal. Still others are looking for prayer groups. And some want these to be small and intimate. Some are struggling with depression and want priests who are in their same boat to lean on. Others enjoyed monthly overnights at one another's rectories. In order for these groups to be fruitful, dioceses must ask their priests what they are looking for so that the different needs are being met. And a priest might join a few of these, depending on what he is looking for. Schedules are tight, but these sorts of supports prove to be very important and must be prioritized. A strategy for groups with busy people might be to meet as a group monthly and rotate people to have one-on-ones for the other weeks. So a group might meet on the first Wednesday for lunch, and then the second, third and fourth weeks they will all pair off with different priests and meet at their own convenience.

The importance of a sense of connection to their bishop also cannot be overstated. Priests yearn for a relationship with their bishop that goes beyond utility, governance, or supervisory roles and that has real meaning on the personal level. Whether they had a great relationship with their bishop or found it lacking, they described the ideal bishop in the same way, using words like avuncular, shepherd, brother, pastor, and father. They wanted the same sort of relationship with their bishop that they were expected to offer their own parishioners, a relationship that is marked by care for the particularities of the person before them. This is why they had an aversion to a bishop who treated them like a cog in a machine and was more of a supervisor or administrator.

Similarly to the priest support groups, having regular contact with their bishop on a human level is important. Thinking about the various suggestions or appreciated practices named by priests, there are a few ways to do this, even given both bishops' and priests' immense demands. The priests did not expect weekly dinners, but regular opportunities and signals of care went a long way. Getting a phone call on their birthday was a practice was appreciated by many. Regular drop-in office hours that were reserved for priests (especially hours that rotated days and times so that various schedules could be accommodated) signaled that the priests were an episcopal priority and that the bishop was available to hear their needs or just check in. Another bishop had regular lunches with just two of his priests at a time; one priest would arrive an hour prior to the lunch start time for an undivided one-on-one hour with the bishop, the second priest would arrive for an hour-long lunch all three shared, and after lunch the first priest would leave so that the second priest could enjoy an hour with the bishop. Another practice, although not mentioned in the interviews, would be to hold quarterly Masses for priests at the chancery (rotating days and times) followed by light refreshments and an hour of socializing. Each of these ways of fostering connection—with different scales and forums—signals that the bishop cares about his priests. While some of these practices show the availability of the bishop and others require more initiative of the bishop, it is important to have both. Some priests, for whatever reason, did not seem comfortable reaching out to the bishop for relational time; it is important that bishops take this first step of invitation regularly.

Content also matters. Priests want to have this connection with their bishop for the sake of both human care and professional care. That is, they want to know that they as a person matter to their bishop, but they also want to know that their professional struggles and needs matter. Having forums (whether these are individual, small group, or large gatherings) where priests can voice their concerns for the sake of supportive changes—not just to feel heard—are also important. The more bishops solicit the priests to hear their concerns and needs and find ways to address these, the more priests will feel supported in their ministry.

Some final considerations are the ways that seminaries and continuing education can support these findings. First, all priests seemed to know what burnout was; they gave appropriate responses and did not ask for clarification when we asked about their burnout. Some said they learned about this in either seminary or diocesan workshops, knew the signs, and felt comfortable self-monitoring for it. While some said they had experienced burnout at some point, none said they were currently experiencing this (even the one interviewee who was taking a leave of absence and did not anticipate remaining a priest). However, many of the priests with lower morale showed two or all three of the dimensions of burnout—emotional exhaustion, cynicism, or a lack of efficacy—in discussing their work. Education on burnout must include not just self-monitoring, but also a sense that priests need to "embrace" their burnout. Some priests talked about a culture of shame or denial (e.g., that good priests don't experience burnout) or implied that burnout is an excuse to be lazy. If these sorts of attitudes overtly or even tacitly linger, priests will be very reticent to admit to their burnout, much less ask for help from others. If priests can recognize burnout as a common feature of caring professions, rather than as something that happens to weak priests, they will better stave this off when it begins to creep into their lives. But, again, "avoiding burnout" is the not necessarily as vital to priestly morale as "cultivating engagement." Although recognizing the symptoms of burnout is important, providing practices that will help them cultivate engagement is even better.

There is also quite a rupture between seminary life and parish life. Seminary life is relationally dense with a tremendous amount of oversight and accountability. Parish life, by contrast, is relatively solitary with little oversight and much independence. To help build these structures of support in priestly life, seminaries should know the support expectations of the seminarians' home diocese and model these practices in seminary. In other words, if a diocese expects their priests to attend a three-hour gathering monthly to have Mass, a meal, and discuss a specific question provided by the diocese, the seminarians from that diocese should set aside time each month to do this. While some seminarians may find this gathering to be "overkill" as their lives are so intertwined with one another in seminary, this creates more of a warm handoff that will facilitate a supportive transition into their priesthood.

This chapter provides a broad overview of burnout, priestly morale, and implications connected to both burnout and support, but these suggested practices should by no means be considered exhaustive or comprehensive. Each diocese has its own unique culture, and each priest and bishop has his own personalities, quirks, gifts, and frailties that must be taken into account when considering how to best support morale. Communication with priests in this regard should not just be "open," but should be actively solicited. With this in mind, this chapter offers some initial considerations in providing more robust support to priests. (The final chapter of this book by Stoeppel and Perla also provides recommendations.) Discovering the particularities of the ways this might look in each diocese—that is, between each priest and bishop and within each priest support group—must be discerned at the individual level.

CHAPTER FIVE

THE JOHN PAUL GENERATION AND THE BISHOPS: A HISTORICAL ACCOUNT OF THE HIGHWATER MARK OF PRESBYTERIAL TRUST IN THE EPISCOPATE

Brooke Tranten

This chapter explores the self-reported high levels of trust (63%) that American priests had in their bishops just before the sexual abuse scandals of 2002. Taking an episodic and historical point of view, it argues that this high presbyterial trust emerged in a generation of younger, more conservative priests inspired by the stability and longevity of Pope John Paul II's leadership in the 1990s. In addition, it demonstrates how John Paul II's pastoral vision influenced the American episcopal conference in their own leadership decisions, resulting in a conference that was at once inspired to teach and lead forthrightly and reluctant to exercise its own authority. The chapter also examines John Paul II's papacy helped to shape the American episcopate in terms of archepiscopal appointments and occasional discipline, reinforcing orthodoxy and providing a sense of stability in the post-Vatican II Church for young priests. It concludes with reflections on how this era of high levels of presbyterial trust can help rebuild presbyterial trust in bishops in the contemporary Church.

In 2022, the National Study on Catholic Priests (NSCP) recorded that 49% of diocesan American Catholic priests "... expressed a 'great deal' or 'quite a lot' of confidence in the decision-making and leadership abilities of their diocesan bishop."[1] This finding of the study highlights an unfortunate and damaging reality of the relationship between bishops and their priests twenty years after the Boston sex abuse scandal and five after the Theodore McCarrick scandal. From that historical context, lack of trust between priest and bishop is perhaps to be expected.

However, it is helpful to compare priests' confidence in their bishops today with previous survey findings, which is possible because a similar question was asked in three previous studies of the American presbyterate. These numbers rose throughout the papacy of John Paul II, from 53% in 1985 (four years into his pontificate), to 55% in 1992, to 63%.[2] When we look at these numbers, we discover that 49% is still the lowest recorded.

Figure 4.1: Priests' trust in their bishop

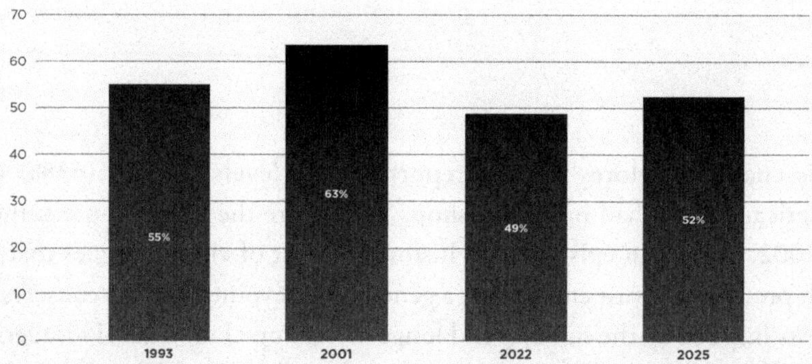

Note: Graph shows percentages of diocesan priests who expressed a "a great deal" or "quite a lot" when asked "How much confidence do you, yourself, have in the decision-making and leadership of your diocesan bishop?" The question was replicated in the Survey of American Catholic Priests (1993), Survey of American Catholic Priests (2001), National Survey of Catholic Priests (2022), and follow-up survey for the NSCP (2025). For the latter, see Appendix B.

1 Brandon Vaidyanathan et al., *Well-Being, Trust, and Policy in a Time of Crisis: Highlights from the National Study of Catholic Priests* (The Catholic University of America, 2022), 6. The percentage is even lower for "confidence in US bishops in general" (24%)

2 Vaidyanathan et al., *Well-Being, Trust, and Policy in a Time of Crisis*. These numbers refer to those who trusted their bishop "a great deal" or "quite a lot," in the wording of the 1992 survey. The prior studies were carried out by Dean Hoge of The Catholic University of America and are described in chapter two of this book. See Dean R. Hoge and Jacqueline E. Wenger, *Evolving Visions of the Priesthood: Changes from Vatican II to the Turn of the New Century*, 2nd ed. (Liturgical Press, 2017).

The largest outlier among the results is actually the high level of trust observed in 2011. In less than ten years (from 1992 to 2001), trust on the part of priests in their diocesan bishops rose precipitously by statistical standards. The 2001 study finds also noted how enthused younger priests (those ordained in the later 1980s to early 1990s) were with the papacy of John Paul II. This chapter intends to provide a historical account of the contextual factors that contributed to this high point of US presbyterial trust in individual bishops by focusing on the events in the American Church that connect most closely to the leadership of Pope John Paul II. It argues that the presbyterial trust in one's bishop in the 1990s has its root in priests' perceptions of the leadership of John Paul II and major events in the American Church, and even society at large.

The first section of this chapter explains the pope's relationship with the American church, and in particular, the pope's disciplinary actions and personal leadership in the 1980s and 1990s gave younger American priests a sense of stability and permanence in their episcopal leadership. The second section presents the findings of the 2001 study, examining the rising generation of younger priests (ordained within ten years or less before the time of the study) who identified with the dynamic conservatism of John Paul II. The final section uses archival evidence to demonstrate how the American bishops perceived the effect John Paul's papacy on their priests and their own renewed priority to affirm unity with the pope. In addition, it summarizes the archepiscopal appointments in the United States made by John Paul II in the 1990s as an example of the pope's concern for stability and longevity in leadership, namely appointments that assured metropolitan archbishops would serve in their archdioceses for more than ten years.

Before the argument can proceed however, a couple caveats are necessary. Within both prior surveys and the NSCP there is a difference between a priest's trust in an individual bishop and his confidence in the US bishops as a whole. Trust in the "US bishops in general" category has been consistently low in all three surveys. However, the NSCP data also show that the trust question regarding individual bishops varied in up to seventeen percentage points depending upon the size of the diocese, with the largest archdioceses reporting the lowest rates of presbyterial trust.[3] The examples in these chapters

3 Brandon Vaidyanathan et al., *Polarization, Generational Dynamics, and the Ongoing Impact of the Abuse Crisis: Further Insights from the National Study of Catholic Priests* (The Catholic University of America, 2023), 10.

demonstrate that younger, more conservative priests had multiple occasions for trust in the hierarchy of the Church and the leadership of Pope John Paul II, but their trust in the episcopal conference was consistently low. The dynamic of stability and longevity that was so important to younger priests in the person of John Paul II had more complex implications for the episcopal conference, but the key to clarifying this matrix is examining the historical expressions of John Paul's pastoral vision and how it was came to be embodied by particular bishops.

John Paul II and the American Church

Elected in 1978, John Paul II quickly identified the American Church and its bishops as a major priority of his pontificate. One of his first major pastoral visits had been to the United States in October of 1979, when he was first pope to visit the White House, among other historic moments.[4] The popular stories, epitomized by the famous "JOHN PAUL, SUPERSTAR" *Time* magazine cover, established the pope as an American celebrity.[5] He was sure to establish relationships with the American hierarchy immediately through the Apostolic Delegate Jean Jadot and later Pio Laghi. Laghi was instrumental in cultivating the pope's relationship with the American government and the Reagan administration. John Paul and Laghi formalized the diplomatic relationship between the Holy See and the United States with the establishment of the Apostolic Nunciature in January of 1984.[6] The pope famously cultivated a close relationship with President Reagan himself, though he disagreed publicly on various aspects of Reagan's policies.[7] As for the bishops, they noticed an immediate and unique enthusiasm on the part of their young priests and seminarians for the new pope. A preparatory document for the 1985 Extraordinary Synod of Bishops noted, "The loyalty of the Church in the United States to the Holy See is unique in recent Church history. This is evident by its support for the successor of Peter and his various needs. Such

4 George Weigel, *Witness to Hope: The Biography of Pope John Paul II*, 1st Perennial ed. (Harper Perennial, 2001), 352.

5 Charles Gati, *Zbig: The Strategy and Statecraft of Zbigniew Brzezinski* (Johns Hopkins University Press, 2013), 129.

6 Weigel, *Witness to Hope*, 378.

7 Paul Kengor, *A Pope and a President: John Paul II, Ronald Reagan, and the Extraordinary Untold Story of the 20th Century* (Regnery Publishing, 2017), 33, 458.

is due in great measure to the devotion and loyalty of our priests who have taught and inspired our Catholic people to make such a response."[8] The pope's preference for the United States from the beginning of his papacy set the stage for the enthusiasm of America's younger presbyterate.

The new pope was serious about reestablishing priestly and episcopal discipline, though the success of his solutions were ambiguous. In 1980, the Holy See threatened Robert Drinan, SJ, with suspension from the clerical state if he ran for another term as a House Representative in Massachusetts. Drinan had been a congressman for a decade and a reliable pro-abortion vote.[9] The American episcopate were put on notice in 1983 when the Archdiocese of Seattle was placed under apostolic visitation after the Holy See received complaints about irregular sacramental and pastoral practices in the archdiocese, including distributing Communion to non-Catholics and Catholics in irregular marriages and allowing Catholic hospitals to provide sterilization procedures. While longtime archbishop Raymond Hunthausen was not deposed, another bishop was appointed an auxiliary bishop of Seattle with special authority over certain aspects of episcopal ministry including liturgy.[10] While Hunthausen and other US bishops successfully pushed back against this unusual arrangement, the message was clear: religious orders and bishops alike were to conduct their competencies in accord with the wishes of the Holy See and the dictates of the documents of the Second Vatican Council, not an open-ended "spirit" of the Council. Subsequent events reinforced that young priests could count on Rome as an active corrective to wayward religious and bishops, assuring the firmness of the Church's clerical discipline.

8 Monsignor Colin McDonald, "An Assessment," n.d., Box 150: Synod, Extraordinary Assembly, 2d, 1985 Folder: 1985 Synod, Briefing Book, National Conference of Catholic Bishops, American Catholic History Research Center and University Archives, The Catholic University of America, Washington, DC (herein ACHRC), 4.

9 Paul V. Mankowski, SJ, *Jesuit at Large: Essays and Reviews by Paul V. Mankowski, S.J.*, ed. George Weigel (Ignatius Press, 2021), 15.

10 John A. McCoy, *A Still and Quiet Conscience: The Archbishop Who Challenged a Pope, a President, and a Church* (Orbis Books, 2015), 217. See also, Raymond Hunthausen, "Seattle Archbishop Rebuts Laghi Chronology: Hunthausen Says Vatican Version Is Far from Correct," *National Catholic Reporter* (Kansas City), November 21, 1986. Ari Goldman, "Prelates Endorse Steps by Vatican on Seattle Bishop," *The New York Times*, November 13, 1986, sec. A1, 11–13.

The charismatic aspect of the John Paul effect perhaps peaked in the early 1990s when the Polish pope enjoyed a surprise triumph with World Youth Day in Denver in 1993. The American bishops were unenthused by the prospect of holding John Paul II's signature event in the United States, worrying about the expense, logistics, and the possibility of a flop in a city chosen precisely for its secular, modern reputation. Organized by associate general secretary of the NCCB Father Dennis Schnurr (later Archbishop of Cincinnati), registration for all three days of the event exceeded planned allowances by 150% at minimum. The closing Mass attracted around 600,000 people.[11] Denver's archbishop, J. Francis Stafford, was pleasantly surprised by the energy of the youth despite his earlier reluctance. The pope's gamble did not merely produce immediate returns; it inspired a wave of vocations and the establishment of lay apostolates like the Fellowship of Catholic University Students (FOCUS) and the Augustine Institute.[12] The boldness of John Paul's choice resonated with young priests and seemed to affirm the viability of what the pope called "the New Evangelization."[13] The rising generation of priests saw the fruit of the pope's dynamic conservatism in their own country with the triumph of Denver World Youth Day and its aftershocks.

This local event reinforced in the United States the resonance of the pope's magisterial corpus, which reached broader levels of recognition in the 1990s. John Paul's tenth encyclical, *Veritatis Splendor* (1993), found wide readership in the US presbyterate for its stalwart defense of traditional understandings of moral theology and its critique of moral relativism. It also reaffirmed the crucial role of the Church's magisterium in its ability to authoritatively define

11 Weigel, *Witness to Hope,* 680–83.

12 Roxanne King, "30 Years Later, World Youth Day '93 Remains a Spiritual Revolution," Around the Archdiocese, *Denver Catholic,* September 7, 2023, https://denvercatholic.org/30-years-later-world-youth-day-93-remains-a-spiritual-revolution/.

13 "Evangelization"—the sharing of the Good News of Jesus Christ—is as old as the Catholic Church itself. "New Evangelization" refers to attempts to spread Catholicism in secularizing, formerly Christian societies; John Paul II began using this term in 1983, when he called for a "commitment, not to re-evangelize but to a New Evangelization, new in its ardor, methods and expression." John Paul II, "Address to CELAM" (Opening Address of the 19th General Assembly of CELAM, March 9, 1983, Port-au Prince, Haiti), *L'Osservatore Romano* English Edition 16, no. 780 (April 18, 1983), no. 9.

and declare on moral questions.[14] The encyclical was exemplary of the learned and constructive pastoral outlook that characterized the pope's public ministry, alongside an embrace of Vatican II that was at the same time wary of what the pope saw as injurious formulations of the Church's moral theology.[15] Many felt that the pope's magisterial intervention in matters of moral theology, which had been a great source of controversy in the postconciliar Church, was long overdue.[16]

Around the same time, John Paul's project established a new baseline of Catholic orthodoxy through a new universal catechism—the first since the Catechism of the Council of Trent published in 1566—came to fruition in 1992 with the release of the *Catechism of the Catholic Church*. The English translation was released in 1994.[17] Also in 1994, John Paul reaffirmed the Church's teaching on priestly ordination with the apostolic letter *Ordinatio Sacerdotalis*. Despite the hopes of some segments of Vatican II-era liberals, *Ordinatio Sacerdotalis* and its later clarifications by the Congregation for the Doctrine of the Faith put a definitive end to any official theological backing for even a theological debate about women's ordination to the priesthood.[18]

14 Lisa Sowle Cahill, "Accent on the Masculine," in *Understanding Veritatis Splendor: The Encyclical Letter of Pope John Paul II on the Church's Moral Teaching*, ed. John Wilkins (SPCK, 1994), 53–54.

15 Matthew L. Lamb and Matthew Levering, eds., *The Reception of Vatican II* (Oxford University Press, 2017), 243.

16 Richard McCormick, SJ, "Some Early Reactions to 'Veritatis Splendor.' (Encyclical Letter Signed August 6, 1993)," *Theological Studies* 55, no. 3 (1994): 481–507 at 489.

17 Weigel, *Witness to Hope*, 662–63.

18 Avery Cardinal Dulles, *Church and Society: The Laurence J. McGinley Lectures, 1988–2007* (Fordham University Press, 2009), 214–15:

> Regarding the argument from magisterial teaching, some maintain that in spite of the recent emphatic statements of John Paul II and Cardinal Ratzinger, the question remains an open one for Catholics. To this it must be answered that the highest doctrinal authorities in the Church, the pope and the prefect of the Congregation for the Doctrine of the Faith, have made it clear that in their judgment the question is irrevocably settled. As I have mentioned, the pope, invoking his authority as successor of Peter, declared that the Church has no authority whatsoever to confer priestly ordination on women and that this judgment is to be definitively held by all the faithful. The term "definitively held," as used the documents of Vatican

While John Paul II continued to travel as much as his aging body allowed, it has been said that his papacy was more active and charismatic in the 1980s, whereas the 1990s saw an emphasis on the magisterial teaching office.[19] This teaching with authority further solidified young priests' perception of the pope as a true rock in the Petrine sense. Rome and the pope would clarify but would not compromise on the doctrine of the Church and would do so in a learned manner. The pope was seemingly putting to rest as many contested questions of doctrine as he could.

John Paul II's Effect on A New Generation of Priests

All of this papal attention on the United States made an impact on the American presbyterate that was immediate and measurable. According to the data collected by Dean Hoge and others, men entered seminaries in the United States in the largest numbers since the end of the Second Vatican Council in the middle part of the 1980s.[20] Those who entered formation in the 1980s would be young priests in the 1990s, answering the 2001 Hoge

---

> II and in several official statements of the Congregation for the Doctrine of the Faith, is reserved to the kind of assent to be given to infallible teaching." Any doubt about the equivalence of the two terms is removed by the response of the Congregation for the Doctrine of the Faith, which explained the pope's term "definitively held" as implying infallibility. . . .
>
> Whether the decision of *Ordinatio sacerdotalis* is to be accepted on a motive of faith can still be legitimately discussed. The pope and the cardinal have not called for an act of divine or theological faith but simply for a firm assent. But inasmuch as this assent is to be given to a teaching contained in the deposit of faith, it seems hardly distinguishable from an act of faith. The *de fide* status of the doctrine, however, has not been so clearly taught that one may accuse those who fail to accept it of heresy. As yet no canonical penalties have been applied against dissenters, but if they "pertinaciously reject" the teaching, they would no doubt make themselves liable to a "just penalty" by virtue of canon law (can. 1371, §1).

19 George Weigel, *The End and the Beginning: Pope John Paul II—The Victory of Freedom, the Last Years, the Legacy* (Random House Publishing Group, 2011), 468.

20 These numbers pale in comparison to the numbers of men in formation and ordained before and during the council, but they still represent a statistical increase based on numbers from the 1970s. Hoge and Wenger, *Evolving Visions of the Priesthood*, 59.

study reporting 63% of all priests would say that they trusted their bishops.[21] To say that the young priests affected this outcome is not just conjecture; Hoge noted that those recently ordained priests (those under 40) made up the greatest percentage of those who said they trusted their bishop, though they represented the smallest numerical group overall.[22] This gave rise to a noticeable generational rift.[23] Many older priests, especially those in their sixties, saw the zeal of the younger generation and the episcopate for John Paul II as a withdrawal from the modernizing changes of the Council, thereby decreasing their own trust in their bishops.[24] The effect was partially the person of the pope, who by himself was a magnetic media and geopolitical event, and partially what young priests thought he represented.

The pope himself was important to these young men. A 2000 CARA study featured the striking statistic that a majority of seminarians in formation at the time were inspired in their vocation in large part due to the personal example of John Paul II.[25] Dean Hoge noted that these young men perceived a sense of self-sacrifice and assertiveness around their vocation gleaned from the pope. The pope offered a public version of Catholicism that emphasized the aforementioned New Evangelization, including an unapologetic reassertion of doctrine.[26] John Paul II offered an emphasis on the distinctiveness of Catholicism that reminded young men of the sacramental importance of the priesthood and its role in the Church.

The Second Vatican Council was the seminal ecclesiastical event of the twentieth century, but to these younger priests the years after Vatican II also represented a collapse of Catholic practice. In their view, doctrine and discipline was in desperate need of reassertion. The immediate post-Vatican II era was plagued not only by large-scale defections from the priesthood and religious orders but also by public dissent from Church teaching and unprecedented liturgical exploration. There were attempts at discipline—for

21 Vaidyanathan et al., *Well-Being, Trust, and Policy in a Time of Crisis*, 6.

22 Dean R. Hoge and Jacqueline E. Wenger, "Survey of American Catholic Priests," 2001. https://www.thearda.com/data-archive?fid=PRIEST01

23 In some of the results of the NCSP on the differences between ideology across generations of priests, this divide appears to still exist.

24 Hoge and Wenger, *Evolving Visions of the Priesthood*, 144.

25 Center for Applied Research in the Apostolate, "New Seminarians Bring Graces and Challenges," *The CARA Report* 5, no. 4 (2000): 1, 11.

26 Weigel, *Witness to Hope*, xx–xxi.

instance, Patrick Cardinal O'Boyle of Washington, DC, removed faculties from dozens of his priests in 1968 after the Washington Association of Priests published a statement that priests should respect use of birth control if individual conscience demanded it.[27] However, most bishops did not follow O'Boyle's example.

Societal context also had an effect, as one of Hoge's interviewees noted, "It was the Council and the changes liturgically that it brought in. Also you had the Vietnam War and a kind of spirit of rebellion, a sexual revolution…"[28] Hoge was clear that younger priests did not disparage the actual teachings of Vatican II, but they were skeptical of the implementation of the Council's teachings.[29] They saw themselves, as well as the pope, as the beginning of an authentic and dynamic postconciliar Catholicism that was conservative in nature but always outward facing. If Hoge labelled this younger generation of priests "conservative," then they tended to identify themselves according to the survey data with "conservative" bishops appointed by John Paul II. The 2022 NSCP showed a similar dynamic in that priests tended to report the highest levels of confidence in their bishops if they also considered their bishop to be ideologically on the same page.[30] Though younger priests formed during the papacy of John Paul II trusted "the Church," their most immediate, personal iterations of the Church, their own bishops and the pope, but not the general ecclesiastic class of their elders.

Clerical morale among younger men with respect to the pope remained high as time went on, as the Hoge study revealed. John Paul II had been pope for nearly twenty years by the late 1990s and showed no sign of vacating the papal office, even after two assassination attempts and the beginning stages of Parkinson's Disease.[31] Having been raised in a tumultuous post-Vatican II Church, younger priests and seminarians found the stability and placidity of the middle John Paul years comforting, as if the upheaval of the previous

27 Peter Cajka, *Follow Your Conscience: The Catholic Church and the Spirit of the Sixties* (University of Chicago Press, 2021), 93.

28 Hoge and Wenger, *Evolving Visions of the Priesthood*, 75, 67.

29 Hoge and Wenger, *Evolving Visions of the Priesthood*, 65.

30 Vaidyanathan et al., *Polarization, Generational Dynamics, and the Ongoing Impact of the Abuse Crisis*, 11. The data shows that "conservative" alignment tracks even when modified to "theological" or "political" conservative identification.

31 Weigel, *Witness to Hope*, 782.

decades in ecclesiastical life was finally settling down. That said, at a time in which priests reported trust in their bishops at an all-time high and idolized their pope, this trust did not extend to the bishops of the National Conference of Catholic Bishops. Trust in the NCCB (rebranded as the USCCB in 2001) barely rose, with Hoge's study reporting the trust bishops in general question as 8% for a "great deal of trust" and "29% for quite a lot." Still, even as priests reported with confidence, "I trust the Church."[32] Trust in the Church, then, among younger priests in the 2000 study was not synonymous with trust in the hierarchy or superiors in general. The pope's initiatives often affected these seminarians more personally than has been acknowledged previously. These young men were in formation when John Paul ordered an apostolic visitation of all seminaries in the United States in 1981.[33] For them, Rome was a benchmark of both belief and identity, centered on the person of the pope. The younger generation of American priests believed that the Church and Catholic culture in the United States was being regularized, despite its problems, and the postconciliar authority vacuum, which the bishops felt most keenly, was being filled.[34] The American Church seemed poised to reassert itself via authoritative teachings from a fearless pope and bishops who had the trust of their priests. This wellspring of confidence grew even as the festering problem of clerical sexual abuse and coverup continued to escalate alongside, only to break into the open in the early 2000s.

This sense of stability these young men had within the Church mirrored the larger societal context, which was the most stable it had been since the 1960s. The nation had fully recovered from the economic recession of the early 1980s and commodity prices had stabilized as the middle class made historic gains in Reagan's second term.[35] The Reagan years passed peacefully into the first Bush administration, capped off with a resounding American victory in the Gulf War that proved well for American pride at home.[36] The watershed

32 Hoge and Wenger, *Evolving Visions of the Priesthood.*

33 Katarina Schuth, *Seminaries, Theologates, and the Future of Church Ministry: An Analysis of Trends and Transitions* (Liturgical Press, 1999), 25.

34 Michael J. Lacey and Francis Oakley, eds., *The Crisis of Authority in Catholic Modernity* (Oxford University Press, 2011), 106.

35 Nina Esperanza Serrianne, *America in the Nineties* (Syracuse University Press, 2015), 124–25.

36 Michael F. Cairo, *The Gulf: The Bush Presidencies and the Middle East* (University Press of Kentucky, 2012), 78.

moment, however, was the fall of the Soviet Union in 1991, thanks in no small part to the work of John Paul II.[37] With external enemies seemingly vanquished and prosperity, American religious conservatives (including Catholics) turned increasingly to the culture wars, which intensified through the 1990s, in part due to John Paul II's interventions. He memorably described the West as a "culture of death" in his 1995 encyclical letter *Evangelium Vitae*, which likely had a profound impact on the political views of these young priests. By the time of the 2001 survey, fresh after the contested presidential victory of George W. Bush with the help of the pro-life movement, young Catholic priests saw themselves as John Paul II's spiritual foot soldiers on behalf of a "civilization of love" against a "culture of death."[38]

John Paul II's American Bishops

Background: The Episcopal Conference in the US

As enthusiastic as young priests were for their pope, many US bishops shared their sentiments, albeit in a more circumscribed fashion. After John Paul II's election, the episcopal conference, consisting of the bishops in assembly and associated bureaucracy, watched how the new pope would handle the nunciature and appointments to the American episcopate. They were intent to maintain their own identity as the leadership of the US Catholic Church and a force in American life, but they experienced transformation over a long papacy.

In 1966, John Cardinal Dearden of Detroit had spearheaded efforts to rework the American episcopal conference in line with Vatican II's emphasis on openness to modernity and the importance of episcopal collegiality.[39] To that end, the conference was spilt into the National Conference of Catholic Bishops (NCCB) and its public policy arm, the United States Catholic Conference (USCC). The NCCB dealt with the theological and ecclesiastical duties that are more traditionally associated

37 Weigel, *Witness to Hope*, 651.

38 John Paul II used "civilization of love" coined by Paul VI, many times, including as a section title within his 1994 *Letter to Families*. For "culture of death," see John Paul II, *Evangelium Vitae* (Liberia Editrice Vaticana, 1995), sec. 12.

39 "Christus Dominus," in *Vatican Council II: Constitutions, Decrees, Declarations* (Costello, 1996), sec. 38.

with episcopal conferences (such as parsing doctrine on a given issue or issuing disciplinary norms). The USCC was home to the conference's various offices and initiatives that dealt with public outreach, including publishing and contact with universities and social organizations.[40] A 1980 Executive Committee report reads, "We want to go from the bishop as bishop to the 'Conference' as a pure bureaucratic body."[41] In other words, from a collection of individuals to the power of a collective. The new pope, however, had signaled that he wanted his bishops and episcopal conferences to focus on evangelization.

In 1980, the NCCB began a years-long study of their internal priorities and engagement with its members and with the aptly-named Planning Committee. A regular NCCB committee, it included Archbishop John Quinn of San Francisco, then the president of the conference, and Archbishop Joseph Bernardin of Chicago, a former president and episcopal conference fixture.[42] In 1981, the Planning Committee surveyed every voting member bishop of the NCCB on long-term goals for the conference. It asked the bishops to rate the importance of a particular goal on a scale of one to five, with five being, "... a strong need for staff activity at 1312 [1312 Massachusetts Avenue NW, Washington, DC, the conference's office] to achieve that objective."[43] The first

40 Thomas J. Reese, SJ, *A Flock of Shepherds: The National Conference of Catholic Bishops* (Rowman & Littlefield, 1992), 41–44.

41 NCCB Committee on Research, Plans and Programs, "Supplementary Document #1, NCCB/USCC Committee on Research, Plans and Programs, Action: Does the Administrative Committee/Board Approve the Model/Process for Definition of Conference-Wide Priorities for 1982 and Beyond?" February 12–14, 1980, Box 300, Special Committee to Study the Procedure of the Committee on Research, Plans and Programs and the Committee on Budget and Finance, 1978–1979, Folder: Nov. 1980, National Conference of Catholic Bishops, ACHRC, 2.

42 Memo, Bishop Thomas Kelly, OP, to NCCB Committee on Research, Plans and Programs, "Supplementary Document #1, NCCB/USCC Committee on Research, Plans and Programs, Action: Does the Administrative Committee/Board Approve the Model/Process for Definition of Conference-Wide Priorities for 1982 and Beyond?" February 12–14, 1980, Box 300, Special Committee to Study the Procedure of the Committee on Research, Plans and Programs and the Committee on Budget and Finance, 1978–1979, Folder: Feb. 1980, National Conference of Catholic Bishops, ACHRC, 1.

43 "Appendix A: Report on Profile Vote on Specific Objectives," NCCB/USCC, November 1981 Box 300, Ad Hoc Committee: Conference Wide Priorities,

objective on the survey (labelled Major Goal 1) reads: "To support, spread and defend the Pope's universal teaching authority and leadership."[44] 120 bishops at the 1981 plenary meeting voted "five" for this Major Goal out a total of around 250 voting members of the NCCB, the most "five" votes of any Major Goal in the same survey.[45] Nearly half of the NCCB held that defending Church doctrine and evangelizing along the wishes of the new pope was a preeminent priority of the episcopal conference for years to come.[46] While it is routine for an episcopal conference to rally around Rome upon the election of a new pope, this numeral majority being willing to identify the pope's priorities as their own is notable in light of the generational differences found in the priest surveys during his pontificate.[47] It demonstrates at least a general alignment of the bishops with the majority of the younger presbyterate's enthusiasm for the still-new pope in 1981. Indeed, Hoge suggests that the bishops were ascertaining the contours of the new papacy, noticing its effect on their priests, and pledging themselves to it in their episcopal conference early on, despite the generational friction that was present.[48]

As John Paul II's papacy unfolded, so did a split within the NCCB itself. The leadership of the NCCB saw their work as a corporatized endeavor, a national coordinating body. A growing portion of the membership of the NCCB, however, wanted the NCCB to assist them, the bishops, in

---

1980–1990, Special Committee to Study the Procedure of the Committee on Research, Plans and Programs and the Committee on Budget and Finance, 1978–1979, Folder: Nov. 1980, National Conference of Catholic Bishops, ACHRC, 1.

44 "Appendix A: Report on Profile Vote on Specific Objectives," 2.

45 "Appendix A: Report on Profile Vote on Specific Objectives," 2–10.

46 The membership numbers of the episcopal conference fluctuate from year to year, but only active (not retired) bishops are permitted to vote in conference proceedings. 250 is a general number from the early 1980s. Jim Castelli, *The Bishops and the Bomb: Waging Peace in a Nuclear Age*, 1st ed. (Image Books, 1983), 21.

47 Reese, *A Flock of Shepherds*. 182. On the other hand, the vast majority of the bishops were lukewarm at best about the prospect of the then-upcoming Extraordinary Synod of Bishops. "Appendix A: Report on Profile Vote on Specific Objectives," NCCB/USCC, November 1981 Box 300, Ad Hoc Committee: Conference Wide Priorities, 1980–1990, Special Committee to Study the Procedure of the Committee on Research, Plans and Programs and the Committee on Budget and Finance, 1978–1979, Folder: Nov. 1980, National Conference of Catholic Bishops, ACHRC, 1.

48 Hoge and Wenger, *Evolving Visions of the Priesthood*, 66.

organizing themselves around John Paul's priorities in evangelization. These two impulses did not preclude each other, but the tension is apparent in the conference records. In 1983, they hired Booz Allen Hamilton to assist in trimming the administrative and planning bloat of the episcopal conference.[49] This firm, best known for its role in reconstructing the American auto industry after the 1970s wave of auto giant bankruptcies, had also handled the episcopal conference's post-Vatican II reorganization in 1967.[50] Now the firm was employed for the opposite purpose—not to grow a bureaucracy to maximize social impact, but to streamline operations and clarity of function.[51]

Nowhere was the changing face of the NCCB more evident than the way that universities and wayward theologians became the primary targets for the NCCB Committee on Doctrine in the 1990s. As detailed above, the new pope was serious about a renewed sense of discipline in the Church, and it seems likely that this papal emphasis influenced US bishops to do the same. There is no evidence that Rome directly pressured the Doctrine Committee, though the committee's more aggressive stance towards clerics dissenting from papal teaching on hot-button theological issues can scarcely be a coincidence. Historically one of the most important of the permanent episcopal conference committees, the Committee on Doctrine took up some longstanding cases of public dissent.[52] In 1996, the Doctrine Committee heavily criticized Notre Dame theology department chair Father Richard McBrien's *Catholicism*, which was a standard reference work in parishes, schools, and universities across the county. The committee found that the book contained "… an overemphasis on the plurality of opinion within the Catholic theological tradition that makes it difficult at times for the reader to discern the normative core of that

49 "Select Committee of Bishops: Meeting of the Executive Committee for Long Range Planning," December 17, 1982, Box 300, NCCB: Ad Hoc Committee: Conference-Wide Priorities, Folder: Planning Committee, Oct.–Dec. 1982, National Conference of Catholic Bishops, ACHRC, 1.

50 Reese, *A Flock of Shepherds*, 81–82.

51 Memo, Monsignor Daniel Hoye to Executive Committee for Long Range Planning, "Subject: 1983–1985 Planning Proposals-Cutback Potential," Box 300, NCCB: Ad Hoc Committee: Conference-Wide Priorities 1980–1985, Folder: Planning Committee, Oct.–Dec. 1982, National Conference of Catholic Bishops, ACHRC, 3–4.

52 Reese, *A Flock of Shepherds*, 259.

tradition."[53] While the committee could impose no penalty on McBrien and not every member of the committee agreed to target McBrien, an exemplar of a Vatican II theological liberal and a major figure in American academic theology, this public censure demonstrated that the hierarchy was aware of the output of Catholic theologians and would offer correction when needed no matter how prominent the target.[54] As young priests admired what they saw as the definitive pronouncements of Rome and the pope, so too could they be consoled by their own episcopal conference's vigilance of academic theology.

But this new zeal for doctrine and discipline at the NCCB only went so far. The committee's pronouncement on McBrien's text came a few years after John Paul II's *Ex Corde Ecclesiae,* an apostolic constitution that treated Catholic higher education in general and reaffirmed the bishops' responsibility for maintaining the doctrinal integrity of Catholic universities.[55] Most bishops were not eager to implement *Ex Corde* at the universities under their purview. Compared with issuing a note on this or that theologian, it was a heavy task to attempt the reform of universities that in many cases had not had formal oversight or direction from the local ordinary since Vatican II. The reasons it did not happen are manifold, but some of the most prominent included potential conflict with religious orders, hostile university faculty or governing boards, and a concern for academic freedom.[56] Pledging public support of the pope was one thing, but enforcing on the local level the acts of his magisterium was another. The pope's reaffirmation of the bishops' teaching office in *Ex Corde* stood out as yet another affirmation for young priests that the pope was serious about reinvigorating the authoritative aspect of clerical ministry. The bishops themselves, however, had a more nuanced perspective that highlighted difficulties with the pope's more assertive style. This reluctance to follow John Paul's leadership could also assist in explaining why young priests still had little trust in the episcopal conference.

53 National Conference of Catholic Bishops, "A Review of Father Richard McBrien's Catholicism," *Origins*, April 18, 1996, 738–44 at 740.

54 Reese, *A Flock of Shepherds*, 264–65.

55 Lamb and Levering, *The Reception of Vatican II*, 424.

56 John P. Langan, ed., *Catholic Universities in Church and Society: A Dialogue on Ex Corde Ecclesiae* (Georgetown University Press, 1993), 6–7.

Episcopal Appointments

Examining Pope John Paul's pattern of metropolitan archepiscopal appointments in the 1990s offers insight into how longevity and stability may have contributed to high levels of presbyteral trust. Archbishop Pio Laghi oversaw the first phase of this process in the 1980s, serving as Apostolic Delegate and later Pro-Nuncio from 1980 to 1990. Archbishop Agostino Cacciavillan succeeded Laghi and served until 1998.[57] The nearly-even time in office for the nuncios also points to the longevity pattern. Each nuncio had time to learn the American Catholic landscape and its episcopate over time. The pattern of episcopal appointments during this time period portrays the two major priorities of John Paul II for the American episcopate as longevity and stability. Of the 25 metropolitan sees in the United States, all but ten of the archbishops appointed between 1990–1999 were in office for more than ten years.[58] This majority includes all of the American cardinals who were also metropolitans, dating back to 1984, beginning with Joseph Cardinal Bernardin in February of 1984.[59] The pattern for longevity in office holds despite the theological perspective of the office-holder and the age of the appointee.[60]

This stability may have contributed to rising numbers of trust during this period. Priests in the 2022 NSCP study expressed that it takes years for bishops to get to know their priests, if they care to get to know them at all.[61] A longer archepiscopal term in office tends to breed more familiarity with the presbyterate, for better or worse. It provides the most opportune environment for a bishop to build a relationship with his priests, which NSCP has found to be an absolute necessity to clerical well-being. John

57 Reese, *A Flock of Shepherds*, 6.

58 "Structured View of Dioceses in North America," Catholic Hierarchy, https://www.catholic-hierarchy.org/diocese/qview1.html#us.

59 Castelli, *The Bishops and the Bomb: Waging Peace in a Nuclear Age*, 134.

60 "Structured View of Bishops—United States of America," Catholic Hierarchy, https://www.catholic-hierarchy.org/country/busqv.html. John Paul's 1983 Code of Canon Law canonically required bishops to offer their resignation to the pope upon their 75th birthday, though this had been a customary practice in the Church since Vatican II's 1965 *Christus Dominus*.

61 Vaidyanathan et al., *Polarization, Generational Dynamics, and the Ongoing Impact of the Abuse Crisis*, 9–10.

Paul's archepiscopal policy made that possible in the largest sees, where it is most difficult for bishops to get to know their many priests.

Despite the pope's appointment of ideologically diverse metropolitans, some stand out for their commitment to the pope's strong brand of public Catholicism preferred by the younger priests.[62] John Cardinal O'Connor of New York established himself as one of the most prominent bishops in America through his media savvy and outspoken advancement of Catholic moral teachings. Beginning his tenure as archbishop of New York in 1984 with a public battle over abortion with vice-presidential candidate Geraldine Ferraro.[63] O'Connor was the leading episcopal voice in the American Church against abortion and insisted that abortion remain the highest priority of Catholic political activity.[64] O'Connor's influence was arguably even greater in Rome. He was named to the Congregation for Bishops in 1987, thereby influencing episcopal appointments around the world, including the United States.[65] Although his NCCB and archdiocesan record showed a man who was more than merely a firebrand culture warrior, O'Connor's public profile as a bishop who adhered closely to John Paul II's version of public Catholicism

62 The Polish pope named Joseph Bernardin as Archbishop of Chicago and created him a cardinal in midst of serious personal disagreement with Bernardin on Bernardin's perspective on nuclear deterrence. Memo, Archbishop Joseph Bernardin to Ad Hoc Committee on War and Peace, "Talks with Pope John Paul II, Cardinal Casaroli, and Cardinal Ratzinger Concerning the 2nd Draft of the Pastoral Letter on War and Peace," February 9, 1983, Box 152, NCCB: Ad Hoc Committee: War and Peace Pastoral, 1980–1983, "February 1983," National Conference of Catholic Bishops, ACHRC. Roger Cardinal Mahony of Los Angeles was never known as an adherent to John Paul's theological outlook, yet he was named to the major see of the West Coast in 1985, where he remained until 2011. Peter Steinfels, *A People Adrift: The Crisis of the Roman Catholic Church in America* (Simon and Schuster, 2013), 26–27.

63 Nat Hentoff, *John Cardinal O'Connor: At the Storm Center of a Changing American Catholic Church* (Scribner, 1988), 81, 76.

64 Richard Doerflinger, "Cardinal John O'Connor, Pro-Life Leader," *First Things* August/September 2022, no. 325 (2022), https://www.firstthings.com/web-exclusives/2022/07/cardinal-john-oconnor-pro-life-leader.

65 A public disagreement with New York Governor Mario Cuomo followed. Hentoff, *John Cardinal O'Connor*. 75.

resonated with many younger priests.[66] Even if they still could not trust the bishops in general, they could trust men like John O'Connor who embodied John Paul II's style in an American fashion. As more bishops who resembled O'Connor were chosen throughout the Polish pope's pontificate, it stands to reason that the ascending cohort of priests would trust them more. In short, the John Paul II-inspired presbyterate was more likely to trust in the John Paul II-inspired episcopate.

Conclusion

The findings of this chapter complement the findings of the 2022 NSCP by elucidating the contours of the "John Paul II effect" on both priests and the episcopate. Even if priests themselves reported having little trust in the episcopal conference, their bishops trusted in the leadership of John Paul II, while the American episcopate was sometimes on the receiving end of Rome's criticism. After initial enthusiasm, the bishops had difficulty adjusting to John Paul's outspoken pastoral vision as they attempted to concretize their own operations in the NCCB in the early 1980s. By the late 1990s, however, the episcopate had been remade by the pope and a more assertive NCCB in discipline and doctrine was the result. Faultlines still remained, for example as bishops were reluctant to implement the authority left to them in documents like *Ex Corde Ecclesiae.* As positive as many bishops felt about John Paul II's pastoral vision, the contours of conference business and the pope's directives were sometimes difficult.

Nevertheless, a long papacy and corresponding long terms for bishops, appointed by John Paul, correlate with a growing trust in the episcopate by the American presbyterate. Younger, more conservative American priests saw more reason for confidence in their bishops in the 1990s, because they were already confident in the pope who was appointing them. They also had a fairly stable (if publicly hostile) cultural and political context in which they were exercising their ministry. John Paul II had remade the American episcopate and made serious attempts to rein in what many perceived as the excesses of

66 George J. Marlin and Brad Miner, *Sons of Saint Patrick: A History of the Archbishops of New York, from Dagger John to Timmytown* (Ignatius Press, 2017), 300.

the postconciliar period, from the Drinan affair to apostolic visitations of seminaries and entire archdioceses like Seattle.

The papacy of John Paul II and the first post-Vatican II generation of American priests arose at a unique historical movement, but lessons surrounding trust, clerical identity, and the bishops persist for today's American Church. The salient point is the importance of the pope in the cultivation and formation of clerical identity, especially as we begin the pontificate of the first pope born and raised in the United Sates. Despite the decentralizing tendencies of some aspects of governance of the post-Vatican II Church, priests derive considerable security in ministry and personal identity from the person of the pope if they perceive him in a positive manner. A strong hierarchy bolsters the security of clerical identity, which in turn enriches the evangelization efforts of the Church. In Hoge's conversations during the John Paul II pontificate, young priests expressed a sense of relief in their enthusiasm for their pope, centering on the considerable difficulties in the Church and pastoral ministry since the Council. They believed that the Church had been reinvigorated in its evangelization through the charismatic pope and was turning the corner from a period of tumult. Some observers have similar hopes at the beginning of the Leonine pontificate, and the American pope's relatively young age at election (69) suggests a longer pontificate than his two predecessors'.

Trust, in this context, is crucial, and constitutes the second major lesson of the John Paul II-era. The 2001 Hoge study shows a presbyterate not obsessed with the old models of the ministry or authority, but on a dynamic and creative conservatism in evangelization and renewal of the Christian life. These young priests trusted in "the Church," even when they expressed their disapproval of some aspects of the leadership of their bishops.[67] Hoge did not define what his interviewees meant by "the Church," but given their appreciation for more traditional trappings of Catholic life and culture, they likely meant the visible, hierarchical structure of the Church in conjunction with its teachings and theology. At minimum, they trusted their leadership to not lead them astray. Trust in the Church, then, is necessary to revive trust between priests and bishops. Early perceptions of Pope Leo XIV as a stabilizing figure, and as a trained canon lawyer dedicated especially to proper procedure in governance, bode well in this regard if they prove to be the case.

67 Hoge and Wenger, *Evolving Visions of the Priesthood*, 68.

The third lesson of the John Paul II era lies in the decisive actions in the papacy that told priests that Rome was doing what it said it was going to do. The examples in this chapter are numerous as they are diverse. Rome attempted to correct what it saw as improper seminary formation in the United States and even questionable diocesan management. The pope reestablished the vigor of the Church's teaching and disciplinary authority in an age that Catholics perceived as theologically and culturally adrift. Young priests were comfortable with Rome determining the direction of the American Church; bishops were naturally less so, but they often had no choice but to respect that Rome's word was final. This sort of institutional stability in the Holy See had a tangible effect in how priests thought of their Church according to Hoge's study. Part of rebuilding presbyteral trust in bishops must translate to the Holy See. For trust to be rebuilt, it must start from the highest levels of the Church. Unfortunately, cases like the McCarrick and Rupnik scandals destabilize the already fractured trust of the American presbyterate.

The John Paul generation of priests, now middle-aged to nearing their sixties, are still a sizeable portion of the American presbyterate and trust is at a historic low. The high levels of trust observed during the John Paul II era stand in stark contrast to the crisis discussed in the NSCP as seen in chapter 1, where the current state of priest-bishop relationships by marked by deep mistrust and disillusionment. Many priests do not trust in their bishops, nor do they trust the Church at large to be focused on spreading the Gospel. The solution is paradoxical. Given the importance of trust in papal and episcopal leadership in the lives of priests, this chapter points to the need for renewal at the level of the hierarchy. The bishops need to act in ways that increase the trust of their presbyterate and not just ask for trust out of the priest's proper obedience to his bishop. The tragedy of the sex abuse crises of the past twenty years are even more disheartening when considered from this vantage point. The trust priests had for their bishops was in many cases unwarranted when it came to sexual abuse. The John Paul II effect on the clergy had a horrific dark side that masked presbyterial and episcopal dysfunction alike. The emphasis on institutional stability contributed to a fear of properly addressing sex abuse. Presbyterial trust must be restored through concrete steps at the diocesan and chancery level.

This chapter juxtaposed the American episcopate's measured but faithful reception of the Polish pope with the dynamic conservatism of a generation of American priests inspired by John Paul. Examining key episodes of American

Church life in the 1990s, we see that the magisterial acts and leadership of John Paul II had a generational effect on American priests and their bishops specifically in regard to the question of presbyteral trust in the diocesan bishop. The chapter has provided historical context for the 2022 National Study on Catholic Priests in the sociological findings of the 2001 Hoge study. It provides a modest historical explanation for a consistent question in the priest studies (namely, presbyteral trust) by exploring the ecclesiastical and societal factors at play during a time when presbyteral trust in bishops was at its highest point. It is good and healthy for priests to be able to trust their bishops, and the NSCP makes the cases that trust is measurably crucial to the well-being of the American presbyterate. The lessons of this chapter imply that bishops should bear the burden of rebuilding presbyteral trust, and they must work toward this task for the sake of the Church in the United States.

CHAPTER SIX

THE ROLE OF BISHOPS IN GOVERNING PRIESTS: THEOLOGICAL AND CANONICAL CONSIDERATIONS

Most Rev. Fredrik Hansen

The National Study of Catholic Priests brought to the fore significant data concerning the relationship between bishops and priests in the United States. Many aspects of the survey's results are to be welcomed, notably the shared zeal for and flourishing in ministry on the part of both bishops and priests. These positive indicators from the survey significantly outweigh the more challenging indicators, such as the lack of trust and a diverging understanding of the episcopal ministry.

Other chapters in this book provide helpful guidance in reading the data of the survey, including from contextual, historical, sociological, and ecclesial perspectives. However, the impact and context of both theology and canon law must also be considered as the NSCP simply cannot be fully—and correctly—understood without firmly grasping what the Church teaches about bishops and priests. To provide the NSCP with this kind of theological and canonical contextualization, this chapter presents four sections: The first

---

At the time the research group on the NSCP was formed (2023) and this chapter drafted (2023–2024), then-Msgr. Fredrik Hansen, JCD, served as Professor of Pastoral Studies at St. Mary's Seminary and University in Baltimore, MD. On November 1, 2024, Pope Francis appointed Hansen as the Coadjutor Bishop of Oslo, Norway, where he now serves as Bishop of Oslo.

section provides an overview of the Church's understanding of priesthood and the sacrament of holy orders. In the second section, the teaching of the Church on the role and governance of the diocesan bishop is outlined. The third section explores the Church's understanding of the diocesan presbyter as a co-worker of the bishop. The fourth and final section covers the diocesan bishop's governance of—leadership of and authority over—his priests.

Priesthood and Holy Orders

The NSCP comprises separate surveys of bishops and of priests. Including a survey of bishops was important to provide scope for comparison and to identify clearly how the two groups approach some of the challenges facing the Church in the United States. It remains important also, however, to recognize the deep bonds that exist among the two—bishops and priests—and that these bonds are theological and, therefore, find their source in Jesus Christ. A reading of the survey primarily in terms of contrasts between two groups could easily lead to further opposition. Framing the reading of the survey through the theology of priesthood will assist the Church in using the NSCP outcomes constructively. This begins with a solid grasp of the sacrament of holy orders.

The priestly ordination rite, in addition to the various prayers and rubrical instructions, includes the text of a homily that the ordaining bishop may pronounce as part of the liturgy. It speaks in clear and theologically precise terms about priesthood, stating that

> . . . the entire holy People of God is made a royal priesthood in Christ. Nevertheless, our great High Priest, Jesus Christ, chose certain of his disciples to exercise in his name, on behalf of the human race, a public priestly office in the Church; for Christ, who was sent from the Father, himself in turn sent the Apostles into the world, that through them and their successors, the Bishops, he might exercise without ceasing his own office of Teacher, Priest, and Shepherd. In addition, Priests are established as co-workers of the Order of Bishops with whom they are joined in the priestly office and with whom they are called to the service of the People of God.[1]

1 *The Roman Pontifical: Ordination of a Bishop, of Priests, and of Deacons* (United States Conference of Catholic Bishops, 2021), 123.

Priesthood comes from Jesus Christ, the "high priest of our faith" (Heb 3:1), and any exercise of priesthood in the Church is exercised in the name of and as a participation in the priesthood of Our Lord (*CCC* no. 1545)—every priest is a minister (a servant) of Christ and the Church. A share in the priesthood of Christ belongs first to the entire People of God that in baptism has been consecrated to Christ and incorporated into the Church (*CCC* no. 1213, *CIC* can. 849). In the words of *Lumen gentium*: "Christ the Lord . . . has made the new people 'a kingdom, priests to his God and Father' (Acts 1:6, see 5:9–10). For by regeneration and anointing of the holy Spirit the baptized are consecrated as a spiritual dwelling and a holy priesthood" (*LG* 10).[2]

In the priestly People of God, participation in the priesthood of Christ takes two forms: i) the common priesthood of the faithful and ii) the ministerial or hierarchical priesthood. These two forms, even though they "differ in essence and not simply in degree, are nevertheless interrelated: each in its own particular way shares in the one priesthood of Christ" (*LG* 10). The affirmation of the Council that the difference between the two forms is both of essence and of degree underscores—in close adherence to the Council of Trent—that the distinction between the ordained priest and the lay faithful is both ontological and hierarchical.

For its part, the common priesthood of the faithful is "exercised by the unfolding of baptismal grace" (*CCC* no. 1547) in a life of Christian discipleship—"the witness of a holy life, by self-denial and by active charity" (*LG* 10).[3] It is to be noted here that Council holds together—to the detriment

2 All conciliar texts in the chapter are from *Decrees of the Ecumenical Councils*, ed. Norman Tanner, 2 vols. (Georgetown University Press, 1990). All quotations from the Code of Canon Law are from *Code of Canon Law, Latin-English Edition: New English Translation*, 4th Printing (Canon Law Society of America, 2023). All quotations from the Catechism are from *Catechism of the Catholic Church*, 2nd ed. (USCCB, 2019).

3 The conciliar decree on the apostolate of the laity, *Apostololicam actuositatem* (November 18, 1965; hereafter *AA*), being one of the Council's documents that further elaborated the teaching of *Lumen gentium* spoke of the common priesthood of the baptized as follows: "[Laypeople] are brought into the mystical body of Christ by baptism, strengthened by the power of the Spirit in confirmation, and assigned to apostleship by the Lord himself. They are consecrated as a royal priesthood and a holy people, so as to offer spiritual sacrifices in all their works ad bear witness to Christ throughout the world" (*AA* 3). Pope John Paul II, in his post-synodal apostolic exhortation *Christifideles laici* (December 30, 1988; hereafter *CL*), would again make

of neither—that just as the ordained priest shares in the priesthood of Christ (rooted in ordination) and has been entrusted with a particular mission because of this priesthood, so does the lay faithful share in the priesthood of Christ (rooted in baptism) that calls for its expression in discipleship.

Jesus Christ, for the "nourishment and continual growth of the people of God ... instituted a variety of ministries which are directed towards the good of the whole body" (*LG* 18). The episcopate and the presbyterate are—together with the diaconate—the three ministries that are conferred by the sacrament of 'holy orders,' one of the seven sacraments of the New Covenant, the outward signs "instituted by Christ to give grace"[4] and entrusted to the Church (*CCC* nos. 1117–18). In more precise terms, the three holy orders are the episcopal order (comprised of bishops), the presbyteral order (comprised of presbyters), and the diaconal order (comprised of deacons).[5] The three orders are sequential. To be ordained a presbyter, one must have been ordained a deacon (*CIC* can. 1031 §1); to be ordained a bishop, one must have been ordained a presbyter (*CIC* can. 378 §1, 4°), having previously been ordained a deacon. They are also continuative. A presbyter remains a deacon; a bishop is still both a presbyter and a deacon. Those that are ordained are enrolled among the sacred ministers of the Church (those belonging to a holy—or sacred—order) and are defined as 'clerics' in the Church's legal norms.[6]

The introductory doctrinal canon on the sacrament of holy orders in the Code of Canon Law is highly instructive and defines it as follows: "By

---

the connections between Christ, baptism, the common priesthood, and the specific evangelizing vocation of the lay faithful. See *CL* 8–17.

4 Baltimore Catechism, Vol. I, 136. In terms of the sacramentality of holy orders, see also Pius XII, Apostolic Constitution *Sacramentum Ordinis* (November 13, 1947), *Acta Apostolicae Sedis* 40 (1948), 5–7.

5 For the historical development of ministry in the Church, from the manifold functions given in the books of the New Testament to the consolidated teaching of the Latin Church on three major orders, see Aidan Nichols, *Holy Order: Apostolic Priesthood from the New Testament to the Second Vatican Council* (Wipf and Stock Publishers, 1990), and David Bohr, *The Diocesan Priest: Consecrated and Sent* (Liturgical Press, 2009), 13–66.

6 Can. 207 §1 states that "there are among the Christian faithful in the Church sacred ministers who in law are called clerics." See further the commentary of Juan Fornés, "Part I: Christian Faithful," in *Exegetical Commentary on the Code of Canon Law*, ed. Ernest Caparros (Wilson & Lafleur/ Midwest Theological Forum, 2004), 2/1:29–34.

divine institution, some of the Christian faithful are marked with an indelible character and constituted as sacred ministers by the sacrament of holy orders. They are thus consecrated and deputed so that, each according to his own grade, they may serve the people of God by a new and specific title" (*CIC* can. 1008). As instituted by Jesus Christ, the sacrament is of divine will and, therefore, configured *to* and *by* Christ. The very purpose of the sacrament is to ensure that the mission entrusted by Christ to the apostles, that of serving and shepherding the faithful, endures to the end of time—the sacrament is to "perpetuate the apostolic office."[7] Like the sacraments of baptism and confirmation, the sacrament of holy orders confers on the priest a sacramental character that is permanent—an ontological bond "unites the priesthood to Christ the high priest and good shepherd."[8] Those who receive the sacrament do so through ordination—the external-liturgical act that consecrates one into an *ordo*.

The ministerial priesthood—through which "the presence of Christ as head of the Church is made visible in the midst of the community of believers" (*CCC* no. 1549)—belongs to and is exercised by those who have been ordained as bishops and presbyters.[9] While presbyters "do not possess the highest honor of the pontificate and depend on the bishops for the exercise of their power, priests nevertheless are united with them in priestly honour, and by virtue of the sacrament of order they are consecrated in the image of Christ, the high and eternal priest" (*LG* 28). Reinforcing the point that both bishops and presbyters share in the ministerial priesthood, the Code of Canon Law uses the term 'presbyter' for the second rank of clerics and 'priest' for both bishops and presbyters.[10] Following common and well-established

7 Congregation for Bishops, *Directory for the Pastoral Ministry of Bishops: Apostolorum successores* (February 22, 2024), 10. Hereafter *AS*, available at vatican.va.

8 John Paul II, Post-Synodal Apostolic Exhortation *Pastores dabo vobis* (March 15, 1992), 1. Hereafter *PDV*, available at vatican.va.

9 The Catechism explains the terms 'order' (Lat. 'ordo') and 'ordination' in this manner: "The word *order* in Roman antiquity designated an established civil body, especially a governing body. *Ordinatio* means incorporation into an *ordo*. In the Church there are established bodies which Tradition, not without a basis in Sacred Scripture, has since ancient times called *taxeis* (Greek) or *ordines*. And so the liturgy speaks of the *ordo episcoporum*, the *ordo presbyterorum*, the *ordo diaconorum*" (*CCC* no. 1537).

10 The Code specifies, for example, that the minister "who is able to confect

practice and the approach taken by the NSCP, this paper uses 'priest' as synonymous for 'presbyter.' Further, it uses the canonically distinct terms 'bishop' (for all who have been ordained to the episcopacy) and 'diocesan bishop' for the bishop entrusted with the care—as the proper pastor—of a particular Church.[11] These distinctions were further stressed by the changes made by Pope Benedict XVI in the Code of Canon Law in his apostolic letter *Omnium et mentem*, wherein canons 1008 and 1009 were amended in order that "the essential distinction between the common priesthood of the faithful and the ministerial priesthood is reaffirmed, while the difference between the episcopate, the presbyterate, and the diaconate is made clear."[12]

A final point on the sacrament of holy orders is the assertion made by *Lumen gentium*: "the fullness of the sacrament of order is conferred in episcopal consecration" (*LG* 21). This point is important for three reasons. First, the conciliar point offered a clear integration of the scriptural and patristic teaching on the sacrament of holy orders—a testament to the breath of theological teaching and learning that the dogmatic constitution incorporated into its exposition of the ecclesiology of the Church. Second, it corrected an understanding that the episcopacy was largely an administrative

---

the sacrament of the Eucharist in the person of Christ is a validly ordained priest (*sacerdos*) alone" (can. 900 §1). It is clear that the canon is not only referring to presbyters but to those who exercise the priesthood in the person of Christ the head of the Church (presbyters and bishops). Similarly, the canon on the minister of the sacrament of anointing of the sick (can. 965) and the canon of the sacrament of penance (can. 1003 §1) speak of the "priest" (*sacerdos*). Unlike these canons, which speak about the priests as both bishops and presbyters, canon 521 §1—on who may validly become the pastor of a parish—speaks of one "in the sacred order of the presbyterate" (*in sacro presbyteratus ordine*). Canon 1031 §1, on the requirements required in a transitional deacon to be advanced to the higher holy order, identifies that order as the "presbyterate" (*presbyteratus*), not the priesthood.

11 The Code defines a "diocesan Bishop" as a bishop "to whom the care of some diocese is entrusted" (can. 377 §1). The diocese (defined in can. 396) is only one of several types of "particular churches" (defined in can. 368) in the Code of Canon Law, and canon 381 §2 explicitly specifies that the head of another type of particular Church is "equivalent in law to a diocesan bishop." For simplicity's sake, in the remainder of this essay this author will refer simply to "diocesan bishop" without mentioning those "equivalent in law" to whom statements might also apply.

12 Benedict XVI, Apostolic Letter *Omnium in mentem* (October 26, 2009), in *Acta Apostolicae Sedis* 102 (2010), 8–10.

office within the Church, one to which certain priests—themselves possessing the totality of sacramental authority—were called to govern a diocese. And finally, it made the episcopacy the foundation—the starting point—of the sacrament of holy orders: the "episcopacy is not regarded in the light of [the presbyterate] but envisaged in itself as the full priesthood in all regards, while the [presbyterate] is to be explained as a limited share of the full priesthood: episcopal consecration is the primary and comprehensive instance of sacramental ordination to office."[13] This is articulated by the fact that it is a bishop who ordains both presbyters and deacons (*CIC* can. 1012).

The Bishops

The results from the NSCP confirm that priests look for and bishops aspire to be the kind of bishop that the Church calls for in the dogmatic constitution of the Church, *Lumen gentium*, the signature document of the Second Vatican Council. That document rooted the episcopal office in the Apostles and their ministerial office.

'Apostolicity' is the fourth mark of the Church as defined by the Nicene-Constantinopolitan creed. This apostolicity begins with the commission and sending of the Son by the Father. The Letter to the Hebrews refer to Jesus as "apostle and high priest" who was "faithful to the one who appointed him" (Heb 3:1, 3). This is the first part of a "continuous 'chain' of commissions and missions: the Father sends Christ; Christ sends the apostles with his own authority (*exousia*) to proclaim the good news . . . the apostles in turn appoint or approve successors who will succeed and represent the

13 Karl Rahner, "Chapter III. The Hierarchical Structure of the Church, with Special Reference to the Episcopate," in *Commentary on the Documents of Vatican II*, ed. Herbert Vorgrimler (Burns and Oates, 1967), I:193. Despite the clarity by which *Lumen gentium* articulated this teaching, Gabriel Richi Alberti has noted that "si può rilevare che il Codice di Diritto Canonico del 1983 non cita espicitamente il n. 21 di *Lumen gentium* per quanto riguarda l*a pienezza del sacramento dell'ordine* o *sommo sacerdozio* o *realtà totale del sacro ministero*, limitandiso nel c. 375 §1 ad un riferimento al 'dono dello Spirito Santo è stato loro danoto,' preso letteralmente dal n. 2 del decreto conciliare *Christus Dominus*." Gabriel Richi Alberti, "L'episcopato: Pienezza del sacramento dell'ordine," in *L'esercizio dell'autorità nella Chiesa: Riflessioni a partire dell'esortazione apostolica "Pastores gregis,"* ed. Arturo Cattaneo (Maricanum Press 2005), 109.

apostolic college until the end of times."[14] The Second Vatican Council—having invoked the teaching of the First Vatican Council—affirms that "Jesus Christ, the eternal shepherd, built holy church by sending apostles just as he himself had been sent by the Father; it was his will that their successors, namely the bishops, should be shepherds in his church right to the end of the world" (*LG* 18). The words of Our Lord, spoken to the apostles after his resurrection: "Peace be with you. As the Father has sent me, so I send you" (John 20:21), were therefore not only an instruction to carry out a particular charge. Rather, having been entrusted by Christ with his sending and authority, the apostles were to both continue his ministry and "guarantee fidelity to Christ, . . . teach with authority . . . guide the community and safeguard its unity. In this way, the Church . . . possesses the mark of apostolicity, inasmuch as it preserves and hands on whole and entire the deposit received through the Apostles from Christ himself" (*AS* 10).

To ensure that the apostolic ministry would continue beyond their lifetimes, the apostles appointed successors—the bishops—who would "take the place of the apostles as pastors of souls, and together with the supreme pontiff and under his authority are sent to carry on the never-ending work of Christ, the eternal pastor."[15] This was expressed more solemnly by *Lumen gentium*, which states that "by divine institution the bishops have succeeded to the place of the apostles" (*LG* 20).[16] The foundation of the episcopal office is, therefore, two-fold: the express will of Christ for the continuation of his mission and the necessary apostolic ordering of the Church.[17]

14 Roch A. Kereszty, *The Church of God in Jesus Christ: A Catholic Ecclesiology* (The Catholic University of America Press, 2019), 166–67.

15 Vatican Council II, Decree *Christus Dominus* (October 28, 1965), 2. Hereafter *CD*.

16 As I have noted elsewhere: "It is noteworthy that in both this case and in the statement on bishops as successors of the apostles, the Council employed more formal language to introduce its doctrinal points: "docet sacra synodus" (*LG* 20); "Docet . . . sancta synodus" (*LG* 21)." Fredrik Hansen, "Sound Decentralization and Institutional Synodality," *The Jurist* 79 (2023): 378, https://dx.doi.org/10.1353/jur.2023.a915493

17 Commenting on *Lumen gentium* 20, Peter Hünermann argues that the handing over of the apostolic office "die doppelte Verankerung des Dienstes in der Kirche, nämlich im Stiftungswillen Jesu Christi und in der Erfordernissen der kirchlichen Gemeinschaft, fortgeschrieben: Beim Übergang in die nachapostolische Zeit wird zunächst die Notwendigkeit und das Bedürfnis der Kirche angeführt

Turning to the ministry of bishops, *Lumen gentium* described it as "the service of the community, presiding in the place of God over the flock, whose shepherds [bishops] are, as teachers of doctrine, priests of sacred worship and ministers of government" (*LG* 20). This episcopal ministry is what the Church designates as the *pastorale munus* (the pastoral office)—"the habitual and daily care of their sheep" (*LG* 27)—by which the diocesan bishops "feed their sheep in the name of the Lord by fulfilling their office of teaching, sanctifying, and governing them" (*CD* 11).[18] That the Council—and the postconciliar magisterium (notably the directory *Apostolores successores*)—adopted the *tria munera Christi* (the threefold office of the Lord as priest, prophet, and king)

---

und als zweites der ausdrückliche Wille der Apostel. Das Amt ist damit als eine relationale Größe charakterisiert." Peter Hünermann, "Theologischer Kommentar zur dogmatischen Konstitution über die Kirche, Lumen Gentium," in *Herders Theologischer Kommentar zum Zweiten Vatikanischen Konzil*, ed. Peter Hünermann and Bernd Jochen Hilberath (Herder, 2009), 2: 411. It is further important to note that apostolic succession is

> a corporate reality. As Saint Peter and the other apostles "constitute one apostolic college, so in a similar way the Roman Pontiff, Saint Peter's successor, and the bishops, successors of the apostles, are joined together" (*LG* 22). The college of bishops (the pope and all the bishops in communion with him) is the successor-college of the apostolic college (Saint Peter and the apostles). The profoundly collegial reality that is the college of bishops, reflecting the apostolic college, is stressed further in one becoming a member of the college of bishops not only through the sacramental act of episcopal consecration but through episcopal consecration and "hierarchical communion with the head and members of the college" (*LG* 22).

Fredrik Hansen, "Sound Decentralization," 376–77.

18 In his post-synodal apostolic exhortation *Pastores gregis* (October 16, 2003), Pope John Paul II would further articulate the inherent unity between the *tria munera* and the pastoral office of the bishop: "These three functions (*triplex munus*) and the powers that derive from them express on the level of action the pastoral ministry (*munus pastorale*) that every Bishop receives with episcopal consecration.... These three functions are, in fact, deeply interconnected; they explain, influence and clarify one another. For this reason, then, when the Bishop teaches, he also sanctifies and governs the People of God; when he sanctifies, he also teaches and governs; when he governs, he teaches and sanctifies. Saint Augustine defines the entirety of this episcopal ministry as an office of love: *amoris officium*." *PG* 9, available at vatican.va.

as the key to explain the ministry of the diocesan bishop[19] echoes the teaching of the Council of Trent.[20] The Church understands the three *munera* as one whole, all three interlinked and never in competition or opposition. For example: when the diocesan bishop issues a pastoral letter to his diocese on the Eucharist, he expresses his office of teacher (by expounding the faith) and shepherd (by bringing—by leading—his people in the direction he considers advantageous to their salvation, in this case through the Eucharist) and high priest (by pointing to and encouraging the eucharistic celebration).

As noted above, the NSCP confirms that both bishops and priests have an understanding of the episcopal ministry that is rooted in and echoes the teaching of the Church outlined above. In both the terminology employed (notably the word "shepherd" and pastoral concepts) and in the aspirational view of a bishop's ministry expressed, the responses and interviews point to adherence to the Church's magisterium and a desire to see that teaching be reflected in the day-to-day ministry of bishops. This is among the most important outputs of the survey as it points to how the teaching of Vatican II on the bishop's office has been absorbed by bishops and priests.

Much like the apostolicity of the Church, invoking the threefold office of Christ roots the entirety of the episcopal ministry in Him who said "I am the good shepherd. A good shepherd lays down his life for the sheep" (John 10:11). This is stressed during the rite of episcopal ordination, which in the liturgical homily underscores that: "As the one chosen by the Father to govern his family, be mindful always of the Good Shepherd, who knows his sheep and is known by them, and who did not hesitate to lay down his life for them."[21] The model of

19 While the dogmatic constitution does not specify that this framework is about the diocesan bishop, using instead the broader term "bishop," the examples given and the specific tasks identified apply only to the diocesan bishop. For example, *LG* 27 speaks of the bishop "giving laws" for his people. No titular bishop in the Church exercises such governing power over a "people."

20 "All to whom the care of souls has been entrusted are subject to the divine command to know their sheep, to offer sacrifice for them, to nourish them by preaching God's word, by administering the sacraments and by the example of good works of every kind, to have fatherly care for the poor and of all others who are wretched, and to be devoted to other pastoral duties." Council of Trent, *Decree of Reform of the 23rd Session*, 15 July 1563, canon 1. English text: Tanner, vol. II, p. 744.

21 Homily at the Ordination of a Bishop; *The Roman Pontifical: Ordination of a Bishop, of Priests, and of Deacons* (USCCB, 2021), 39.

Christ the Good Shepherd "suggests to the Bishop daily fidelity to his mission, total and serene dedication to the Church, joy in leading to the Lord the People of God entrusted to his care, and gladness in gathering into the unity of ecclesial communion the scattered children of God" (*AS* 2).

In what remains one of the most striking points made by *Lumen gentium*, the council teaches that the diocesan bishops "govern the churches entrusted to them as vicars and legates of Christ" (*LG* 27). The same section would go on in detail about the jurisdiction of the diocesan bishop, which is synonymous with his governing power. The Code of Canon Law affirms that "the power of governance, which in fact exists in the Church and is also called the power of jurisdiction" (*CIC* can. 129 §1). As for the diocesan bishop, canon 381 §1 states that the diocesan bishop "in the diocese entrusted to him has all the ordinary, proper, and immediate power which is required for the exercise of his pastoral function except for cases which the law or a decree of the Supreme Pontiff reserves to the supreme authority or to some other ecclesiastical authority" (*CIC* can. 381 §1).[22]

The scope of the pastoral and canonical governance of the diocesan bishop establishes what must be acknowledged as "a proper sphere for the

22 As I have summarized elsewhere:

> Vatican II, the 1983 code, and subsequent papal/curial documents categorize the power of governance of diocesan bishops as being ordinary, proper, and immediate. *Lumen gentium* states that the bishops' power, "which they exercise personally in the name of Christ, is proper, ordinary and immediate..." (*LG* 27). The code reaffirms the idea in canon 381 §1, and Pope John Paul II further noted that the bishops' ordinary, proper, and immediate power is "invested with an objective juridical power meant to be expressed in authoritative acts whereby he carries out the ministry of governance (*munus pastorale*) received in the sacrament" (*PG* 43).

Fredrik Hansen, "Papal Legates and the Jurisdiction of Diocesan Bishops," *The Jurist* 78 (2022): 481, https://dx.doi.org/10.1353/jur.2022.0021

In terms of the specific canonical terms used, they are to be understood as follows: 'Ordinary' power is the jurisdictional power "which by virtue of the law itself is attached to a given office" (c. 131 §1). 'Proper' ordinary power of governance is that which is exercised in one's own name. However, 'proper' in the case of the diocesan bishop is also broader and covers the totality of the governance of diocesan bishops in the particular churches entrusted to them. 'Immediate' power requires no additional or intermediary entity to be exercised, neither approval, consent, nor council.

independent exercise of this authority, a sphere recognized and protected by universal law" (*PG* 56). A crucial part of canon 381 §1 is that it assigns to the diocesan bishop "all . . . power." The *omnis potestas* of the diocesan bishop provides him with all the authority to govern that is required by his ministry as shepherd of the particular Church. It does not, however, signify an absolute power. The supreme authority of the Church—the Roman Pontiff and the College of Bishops *sub et cum Petro*—may restrict his power.[23]

The role and ministry incumbent on bishops—and the expectations for that ministry by the Church and by priests—are clearly very demanding. Even a cursory reading of chapter four of the directory *Apostolorem successores* (on the diocesan bishop's ministry in his particular Church) makes this plain. Added to this are the current complexities of leading a US diocese—among them the legal, financial, and administrative challenges emanating from, on the one hand, the sex abuse crisis and, on the other, parish closures or mergers due to changes in religious practice and demographics. This is an important contextual reality to some of the more critical points raised by the NSCP on the leadership of the bishops, including the widespread perception by the surveyed priests that bishops act more like administrators than shepherds. It may well be that the ministry of diocesan bishops in the United States—including their care for and oversight of priests—would have looked very different if the major and long-running challenges mentioned above had not been present.

The Priests

Priests are at the heart of the NSCP. The numerous replies and the extensive one-on-one interviews conducted provided the most extensive picture of the state of priesthood in the United States. The survey confirms that priests and their ministry must be understood in relation to bishops. This reflects the conciliar decree *Presbyterorum ordinis*, which notes that priests are to "be

23 Any such restriction "would have to be 'for the good of the church or the faithful' (*LG* 27) and does not deny the jurisdiction of the diocesan bishop or release him from his responsibility to govern his particular church." Fredrik Hansen, *The Unity and Threefold Expression of the Potestas Regiminis of the Diocesan Bishops* (PUG Press, 2014), 83. See also Fredrik Hansen, "Sound Decentralization," 383, and Thomas J. Green, "The Pastoral Governance Role of the Diocesan Bishop: Foundations, Scope and Limitations," *The Jurist* 49 (1989): 480, https://heinonline.org/HOL/P?h=hein.journals/juristcu49&i=478

collaborators with the episcopal order in carrying out the apostolic mission entrusted to them by Christ."[24] This foundational point was not only to open the conciliar decree but would serve and still serves as the basis for every postconciliar teaching of the Church on the order of presbyters. This idea is further elaborated by the *Directory on the Life and Ministry of Priests*: "priests participate in the one priesthood of Christ as co-workers of the Bishops: this determination is specifically sacramental in nature and hence cannot be interpreted in merely 'organisational' terms."[25]

Priestly life and ministry cannot be understood without the profound Christological foundation on which stands this clerical order. It is in other words inconceivable without Our Lord: "By virtue of this consecration brought about by the outpouring of the Spirit in the sacrament of holy orders, the spiritual life of the priest is marked, molded and characterized by the way of thinking and acting proper to Jesus Christ, head and shepherd of the Church, and which are summed up in his pastoral charity" (*PDV* 21). The very being of the priests is conformed to Christ, having received a "*deputatio* to act *in persona Christi capitis* in the sacramental life of the Church."[26]

In other words, the priesthood of Jesus Christ (the source of all priesthood as the one high priest) and the bishops (entrusted with the apostolic ministry) provide a framework around priests, by which their holy order is understood and explained.[27] Bishops and presbyters—who both share in the priesthood of

24 *PO* 2. *Presbyterorum ordinis* employs a great number of images to describe the priest and his ministry: "ministers of Jesus Christ" (*PO* 2), "fellow-workers of bishops" (*PO* 4), "patterned to the priesthood of Christ" (*PO* 2), "act in the person of Christ, the head of the body" (*PO* 2), "priests of the new covenant" (*PO* 3), "servants of Christ" (*PO* 3), "good shepherds" (*PO* 3), "sharers in a special way in the priesthood of Christ" (*PO* 5), exercising "the role of Christ the head and the shepherd" (*PO* 6), "educators in the faith" (*PO* 6), "living instruments of Christ the eternal priest" (*PO* 12), "ministers of the word of God" (*PO* 13), and "ministers of sacred rites" (*PO* 13). It must be noted, however, that "co-worker" or similar terms describing the priest in relation to the bishop occupies a unique position.

25 Congregation for the Clergy, *Directory on the Life and Ministry of Priests—New Edition* (February 11, 2013), 6. Hereafter *Directory*, available at vatican.va.

26 David L. Toups, *Reclaiming Our Priestly Character*, Revised Edition (IPF Publications, 2010), 156.

27 Since the post-Apostolic era, the presbyterate has been firmly tied to the episcopacy and these two highest orders of sacred orders have been so united that they cannot fully be understood one without the other. Ignatius of Antioch, recognizing

Christ—are also "constituted as ministers of the apostolic mission. The priests share in the Bishop's solicitude and responsibility in such a way that together they nurture an ecclesial sense at once local and universal" (*AS* 75). The apostolic charge is given to bishops and, through them, entrusted in a partial manner to priests. The Council explains this within the broader apostolic sending of Christ—>apostles—>bishops: "after sending out the apostles as he himself had been sent by the Father, Christ through these same apostles appointed bishops as their successors to share his own consecration and mission; the bishops' office of service was delegated to priests in a subordinate capacity" (*PO* 2).

There are three principal aspects to the priest's participation in the priesthood of the bishop and his aid of the bishop's apostolic ministry. The first gives to the priest a part of the apostolic mission entrusted to the bishop: "by the sacred ordination and mission they receive from bishops, priests are promoted to the service of Christ the teacher, priest and king whose ministry they share, so that the church may be unceasingly built up here on earth into the people of God, the body of Christ and the temple of the holy Spirit" (PO 1).[28] The second communicates to the priest a responsibility to serve with the bishop and in his stead: "In the individual local congregations of the faithful in a certain sense they make the bishop present and they are united with him in a spirit of trust and generosity; and in accordance with their position they undertake his duties and his concern" (*LG* 28). The third brings the priest into

---

in that local Church a true expression of the relationship between bishop and priests, writes to the Ephesians: "Thus it is proper for you to run together in harmony with the mind of the bishop, as you are in fact doing. For your council of presbyters, which is worthy of its name and worthy of God, is attuned to the bishop as strings to a lyre." Ignatius of Antioch, "Letter to the Ephesians," 4, in Michael W. Holmes, *The Apostolic Fathers in English*, 3rd ed. (Baker Academic, 2006).

28 Commenting on *Presbyterorum Ordinis*, Erio Castellucci notes that "Assumendo il modello dei *tria munera*, prima per i vescovi e poi anche per i presbiteri, già in *LG* 28 e poi approfonditamente in *PO* 4–6, il Vaticano II ha inteso ricondurre tutti I compiti presbiterali ad un'unica origine, che è l'ordinazione sacramentale: è Cristo, attraverso il conferimento dell'Ordine, che abilita a predicare, celebrare, guidare." Enrico Castellucci, "La *Presbyterorum Ordinis* cinquant'anni dopo: Genesi, sviluppo, attualità," in Congregazione per il Clero, *Una vocazione, una formazione, una missione: Il cammino discepolare del presbiterio nel 50 anniversario della Optatam Totius e della Presbyterorum Ordinis* (Libreria Editrice Vaticana, 2016), 111.

a particular Church, into a particular presbyterate. A diocesan priest belongs to a presbyterium, "the company of the priests of his own diocese assembled around their bishop, their spiritual father and ruler, the center and the principle of unity in their sacerdotal community."[29] Pope Francis reinforced this idea, noting that a diocesan priest "cannot be separated from the Bishop" and that there "is no spirituality of the diocesan priest without these two relationships: with the Bishop and with the presbytery."[30] The priest's promise of obedience and reverence to his bishop reflects all these three and, thereby, the essential bond between bishop and priest.

The NSCP, which placed an emphasis on the relationship between bishops and priests, amply affirmed that priests see themselves as bound to and ministering under the bishop. This, as the shared understanding of episcopal ministry of both bishops and priests, must be acknowledged as another crucial outcome of the survey—pointing also to the ongoing and already successful reception of the magisterial teaching of Vatican II. On a broader academic note, it must be highlighted, however, that there is limited scholarship on this bond and the rootedness of the priesthood and priestly ministry in the bishop. While significant theological and ecclesiological research on bishops and priests is available, most of it is focused on one or the other of these two holy orders. Scholarship on the episcopal office, on the one hand, is heavily centered on its apostolicity—it being rooted in the ministry and office of the apostles, so central to *Lumen gentium*. Contemporary scholarship on priesthood and priests (including the significant work done on priestly celibacy and spirituality) tends to begin, on the other hand, with the Christological foundation of the presbyter—his configuration to Christ. While this is all rooted in the understanding of the Church, a certain caution here is warranted. Without the profound bond between bishop and priests, too great a distinction between the two holy orders—an apostolic emphasis for bishops and Christological emphasis for presbyters—risks adopting a more theological take on priesthood and a more governmental take on the episcopacy. This would not only lend itself to further verification of the

29 Joseph C. Fenton, *The Diocesan Priest in the Church of Christ* (Cluny Media, 2018), 17.

30 Pope Francis, "Comments During the Meeting with the Priests of the Diocese of Caserta," July 26, 2014; in *Disciples Together on the Road: Words of Pope Francis for Priests* (Libreria Editrice Vaticana, 2016), 50.

impressions garnered by the NSCP, but also move the understanding of the two holy orders back to the medieval sacramental focus on the priest and administrative approach to episcopal ministry.

The Second Vatican Council—in its decree *Christus Dominus*—stresses that the "various relationships between the bishop and his diocesan priests should be held together most of all by the bonds of supernatural charity" (*CD* 28). That the starting point is spiritual affirms that the origin of sacred ministry is Christ, and only in the example of the Good Shepherd will the fullness of priesthood exercised by bishops and priests come to full fruition. This spiritual origin is integral to priestly ministry, not an additional factor. At the same time, the spiritual origin and reality of the priesthood is not opposed to its ministerial expression—to act in the person of Christ for the People of God to aid the common priesthood of all the faithful and in the celebration of the Eucharist and in the sacraments of penance and anointing to assist in bringing forth "a chosen race, a royal priesthood, a holy nation, a people of his own" (1 Pet 2:9). The spiritual origins of the unity between priests and bishop, in other words, serves to "make their pastoral work more fruitful" (*CD* 28).

The data from the NSCP—notably the more detailed interviews conducted with priests—confirmed the practical impact of this point: pastoral efficacy follows from priests being united with and supported by their bishop and a lack of pastoral effectiveness often stems from an absent or fractured relationship between them. The priests serve in their local communities as the expanded ministerial arms, eyes, and ears of bishops, making it important to not only acknowledge this bond, but also include it in the broader pastoral planning of a diocese. Conflict or tension between a bishop and his priests has real, lasting, and detrimental effects on their ministry to and among the People of God.

The Bishop's Governance of Priests

The priests' survey and the individual interviews of the NSCP highlight the negative impact that the sex abuse crisis has had on the relationship between bishops and priests. A central part of this is the concern that many priests have about being falsely accused of sexual abuse, of receiving little or no support from their bishops, of being sacrificed for the good of the institution, and of having their priestly life ended by one of these circumstances. Attention, therefore, to the Church's understanding of the relationship between bishops and priests is key. This relationship is theological-sacramental, ecclesiological, and canonical-pastoral. The theological-sacramental reality is the institution and configuration by Christ of the presbyteral and episcopal grades of the sacrament of holy orders (outlined in the first section above). The ecclesiological-ministerial relationship relates to the bond between the two sacred orders, their ministerial (and joint ministerial) purpose, and the ecclesiological importance of the bishop (outlined in the second and third sections above). And it is canonical-pastoral as it is regulated by ecclesiastical laws and expressed in the life of the Church through the good order provided by legislation aimed at the pastoral end: the salvation of souls.

The governance of the diocesan bishop concerns the totality of the particular Church that has been entrusted to his care. The Council and the directory on the pastoral ministry of bishops define the obligation of the diocesan bishop to govern as nothing less than a "sacred right and duty before the Lord" (*LG* 27, *AS* 64). This governance includes also the presbyterate. Entrusted with power of governments, "distinguished as legislative, executive, and judicial" (*CIC* can. 135 §1),[31] the diocesan bishop governs his priests with true jurisdiction and is as bound to exercise that jurisdiction as any other aspect of his governing power over the diocese. The Church helpfully provides the diocesan bishop with a series of specific governing responsibilities in relation to his priests and to his presbyterate as a whole.

The responsibility of the diocesan bishop for his priests begins by the selection of those who are admitted to priestly formation in seminary and are, therefore, set on the track to God-willing serve as his priests.[32] This

31 It is important to recognize that governing power in the Church is—unlike in the modern constitutional state—not three separate powers. This is not only clear from canonical doctrine, but also from the very text of can. 135. As I have noted elsewhere: "In the first paragraph the power of governance is defined as being 'divided into legislative, executive and judicial power,' using the Latin verb *distinguntur*, which could also be translated into English as is distinguished in. This mirrors the Latin text of principle 7 on the revision of the Code, which uses *distinguatur*. By its very meaning this rules out any separation of powers (in the plural), but implies only a theoretical separation." Fredrik Hansen, *The Unity and Threefold Expression*, 94.

32 The Code of Canon Law calls on the diocesan bishop to accept "only those who are judged qualified to dedicate themselves permanently to the sacred ministries;

is closely followed by the decisions involved in ordaining a candidate to holy orders, first to the order of the diaconate and then to the order of the presbyterate.[33] Following priestly ordination, it falls to the diocesan bishop to order ministerial assignments in the diocese:[34] the appointment and transfer of priests among the various ecclesiastical offices in the particular Church, including those of pastor, associate pastor, chaplain, and various roles in the chancery and other institutions. The Church underscores that such assignments should be guided by objective criteria and not by favoritism or partiality.[35] Seen within the ordering of the particular Church, priestly assignments are both to ensure that the *portio populi Dei* that constitute the diocese receive the sacramental and pastoral care it needs (and to which the Church acknowledges its right), and to be done "giving due consideration to the different aptitudes and legitimate aspirations of each priest, respecting their human and priestly dignity" (*AS* 78). Priests responding to the NCSP noted with frustration where assignments in their diocese seem to be based in bias, "who you know," or perceived loyalty.

---

he is to consider their human, moral, spiritual, and intellectual qualities, their physical and psychic health, and their correct intention" (*CIC* can. 241 §1).

33 The diocesan bishop's decision is not only about determining if one specific candidate is to be ordained. It serves also as a safeguard for the entire presbyterate of the Church, by ensuring that "[o]nly those are to be promoted to orders who, in the prudent judgment of their own bishop . . . have integral faith, are moved by the right intention, have the requisite knowledge, possess a good reputation, and are endowed with integral morals and proven virtues and the other physical and psychic qualities in keeping with the order to be received" (*CIC* can. 1029).

34 "Unless the law explicitly establishes otherwise, it is for the diocesan bishop to provide for ecclesiastical offices in his own particular church by free conferral" (can. 157). This mode of providing for a vacant ecclesiastical office—"free conferral"—is the one that allows the ecclesiastical superior the greatest liberty in making an appointment, as it does not require the approval, intervention, or consent by another entity or office. This is not only a canonical reality, but one closely associated with the required freedom the diocesan bishop needs in shepherding the particular Church in the direction he judges necessary: "In order to distribute more equitably and properly the sacred ministries among his priests, the bishop should possess a necessary freedom in bestowing offices and benefices" (*CD* 28).

35 The directory on the ministry of bishops stresses that the diocesan bishop should "act with the greatest discretion, so as to avoid even the slightest suspicion of arbitrariness, favouritism or undue pressure" (*AS* 78).

The diocesan bishop is also charged with governing "the spiritual, intellectual and material welfare of the priests so that the latter can live holy and pious lives and fulfill their ministry faithfully and fruitfully" (*CD* 16). This includes ensuring a worthy remuneration,[36] the "necessities of their life," including health care and provisions for their retirement. Finally, the diocesan bishop has a responsibility to guide and direct the priests' observance of their obligations to an interior life in accordance with their presbyteral order.[37]

The Church draws specific attention to the diocesan bishop's particular responsibilities when priests find themselves in difficulties. Noteworthy, the directory *Apostolores successores* assumes that the bishop engages in a proactive way in these matters: "Assisted by his regional vicars, the Bishop should seek to anticipate and to resolve any human or spiritual difficulties that priests might experience. He should come lovingly to the help of any priest who finds

36 See can. 281, which reads "§1. Since clerics dedicate themselves to ecclesiastical ministry, they deserve remuneration which is consistent with their condition, taking into account the nature of their function and the conditions of places and times, and by which they can provide for the necessities of their life as well as for the equitable payment of those whose services they need. §2. Provision must also be made so that they possess that social assistance which provides for their needs suitably if they suffer from illness, incapacity, or old age."

37 Canonical legislation exhorts priest to "nourish their spiritual life from the two-fold table of sacred scripture and the Eucharist ... to offer the eucharistic sacrifice daily ... to carry out the liturgy of the hours daily according to the proper and approved liturgical books ... to make time for spiritual retreats according to the prescripts of particular law ... to engage in mental prayer regularly, to approach the sacrament of penance frequently, to honor the Virgin Mother of God with particular veneration, and to use other common and particular means of sanctification" (c. 276 §2). A very similar list is given in *Directory on the Ministry and Life of Priests* 50:

> It is therefore necessary that never lacking in the priest's life of prayer are to be the daily celebration of the Eucharist, with suitable preparation and ensuing thanksgiving; frequent confession and spiritual direction already practiced in the seminary, and often even before that; the complete and fervent celebration of the liturgy of the hours, which is a daily obligation for him; examination of conscience; the regular practice of mental prayer; the *lectio divina*, prolonged moments of silence and colloquium, especially in periodical spiritual retreats and days of recollection; the precious expressions of Marian devotion, such as the Rosary; the *Via Crucis* and other pious exercises; the fruitful reading of the lives of the saints; etc.

himself in a difficult situation" (*AS* 81). In terms of specific situations, the Church urges diocesan bishops to come to the aid of priests who struggle with "loneliness and isolation" (*AS* 81a), "weariness or fatigue" (*AS* 81b), "moral weakness or exhaustion" (*AS* 81c), and priests who "leave the active ministry" (*AS* 81d) or fall into "scandalous conduct" (AS 81e). Inappropriate behavior or sexual abuse committed by priests would be an obvious example of the latter. These specific examples have clearly been listed due to the experience of the Apostolic See in assisting diocesan bishops in difficult cases. In situations when adverse situations or grave difficulties impact priests, the bishop should respect them "and require others to respect their rights and should defend them against unjust criticism. He should act swiftly to resolve controversies, so as to avoid the prolonged disquiet which can overshadow fraternal charity and do damage to the pastoral ministry" (*AS* 77).

Due to the very broad nature of this paternal concern, the diocesan bishop must have a significant understanding of his presbyterate. He "should consider it his sacred duty to know his diocesan priests well, their character, their aptitudes, their aspirations, the depth of their spiritual life, their zeal, their ideals, their state of health, their financial situation, their families and everything which concerns them" (*AS* 77). An important aspect here is the diocesan bishop's efforts to advance the bonds among priests and the unity of the presbyterium. In all this, the Church expects that the diocesan bishop "must have the disposition of a father towards his priests . . . avoiding any distance or a personal style proper to a mere employer. By virtue of his function he must be close to his priests and easily accessible. His first concern must be his priests, his collaborators in his Episcopal ministry" (*Directory* 107). This echoes the call of the Second Vatican Council for the bishop to "hold priests in special regard . . . treat them like sons and friends and so strive to further all the pastoral activities of the whole diocese by being ready to listen to them in an atmosphere of mutual trust" (*CD* 16).

Among the most frequently raised negative observations in the feedback to the NSCP by priests was the lack of care and concern expressed by bishops towards priests accused of abuse. Questions relating to due canonical process, lack of a paternal or fraternal spirit, a sharp distinction between the approach taken in the case of an accused priest compared to an accused bishop should be carefully considered (and are—including among canonists—already under consideration). The responses to the survey pointed also to another perceived deficiency in the relationship between priests and bishops. Not all priests feel that their bishop has an interest in them, desires to spend time with and get to know them, or wishes to hear from priests or engage with their views or input. Some data suggest that these perceptions are either "general" (about most bishops) or aggravated by particular circumstances (such as diverging theological or ecclesial views or opinions between priests and their bishop, or a specific situation or past situations in a diocese). That being said, an indication that priests fail to see in their bishop—or in the hierarchy as a body—this paternal, amicable, and fraternal relationship is concerning. This is true not only because of the emphasis given by Church teaching and theology to this episcopal role vis-à-vis his priest, but also the detrimental impact this breakdown in bonds or failures in the relationship has on the apostolic mission that priests share with and have received from their bishops.

A specific reality that binds diocesan priests further to their bishop is their own incardination in their particular Church—their ecclesiological and canonical belonging to their diocese (*CIC* can. 265ff). From this stems a deeply-rooted charge for the people of that particular Church: "The primary role in the care of souls lies with the diocesan clergy who, being incardinated or appointed to a particular Church, are wholly dedicated in its service to the care of that portion of the Lord's flock" (*AS* 75).[38] Similarly, the same is demanded of priests. Pope Francis, speaking to this from the side of the priest, noted that a "priest who does not have an assiduous relation with his Bishop isolates himself slowly from the diocesan body and his fruitfulness diminishes, precisely because he does not engage in dialogue with the Father of the Diocese."[39] To ensure this, the bishop should "always strive to relate to his priests as a father and brother who loves them, listens to them, welcomes them, corrects them, supports them, seeks their cooperation" (*PG* 47).

The governance of a diocesan bishop of his priests, in other words, not only concerns technical acts of governance but also a much more expansive

38 Dominique Le Tourneau, "Chapter II. The Enrollment and Incardination of Clerics," in *Exegetical Commentary on the Code of Canon Law*, ed. Ernest Caparros (Wilson & Lafleur/ Midwest Theological Forum, 2004), 2/1: 299–304.

39 Pope Francis, "Address to the Community of the Pontifical Lombard Seminary," January 25, 2016; in *Disciples Together on the Road: Words of Pope Francis for Priests* (Libreria Editrice Vaticana, 2016), 140.

set of direction by the diocesan bishop, and one that is ultimately spiritual in nature. The teaching of *Lumen gentium* on the broad governance of the bishop makes the point that the diocesan bishop governs the local Church entrusted to him "by counsel, persuasion and example and indeed also by authority and sacred power" (*LG* 27). An example may provide instructive to this point. The diocesan bishop is to ensure that his priests "fulfil their duty of ongoing formation … so that their enthusiasm for the ministry does not wane, but grows and matures with the passage of time, making the sublime gift they have received more dynamic and more effective" (*AS* 83).[40] In keeping with this, a diocesan bishop wishes to facilitate among his clergy greater theological learning. He may advance this through the exercise of his power of governance by i) expanding the jurisdiction of the episcopal vicar for clergy to include continuing formation, ii) establishing a dedicated fund to support academic-theological gatherings for his priests, iii) enacting guidelines to structure yearly days for formation and support for study days at ecclesiastical universities and faculties. Further, the diocesan bishop may promote such learning "by counsel" by exhorting his priests through *ad clerum* letters and by preaching on theological study at clergy convocations and advancing the matter in the Presbyteral Council, in Deans' meetings, and so on. Finally, by means of his example, the diocesan bishop leads the

40 The United States Conference of Catholic Bishops made an important clarification between initial (seminary) and continuous (post-ordination) formation of priests in their recent guide:

> Ongoing formation is needed to address not only the normal life changes that affect every priest but also the limitations of seminary formation. In some surveys, recently ordained priests have identified gaps in their formation. Some of those concerns are well-founded critiques of seminary programs that rightly point out areas for improvement. Others, however, reveal not so much gaps in seminary formation as the need for further formation. After all, many aspects of priestly life—administrative abilities, financial expertise, leadership, and certain pastoral skills, to take some clear examples—are only fully learned in the field. Rather than shoehorning these important skills into an already burdened seminary curriculum—likely with dubious results—it seems wiser for the Church to provide some basics about these topics during the seminary years while actively fostering their development after ordination.

Guide to Ongoing Formation of Priests (USCCB, 2023), no. 68.

way for his priests by himself taking time each year to engage in continuing formation, keeping updated on the progress of the sacred sciences and other learning. This broad reality of a diocesan bishop's governance of his priests—indeed his relationship with them—is based on the deeper spiritual bond that is the relationship between a bishop and his presbyterate. That is to say that canonical governance without a foundation based on charity among bishop and priests will be partial and less effective.[41]

Following this, ecclesiastical governance begins with the personal example of holiness given by the diocesan bishop,[42] consists of the totality of his words and actions that in one way or another offer direction to the particular Church under his authority, and must continuously be advanced, strengthened, and deepened by engagement, collaboration, and conversations. Further, the bishop must engage with his priests, he must know them, they must know him, and there must be a coherence between all aspects of governance. "In exercising his ministry, the bishop relates to his priests not merely as a ruler towards his subjects, but rather as a father and a friend. He should devote himself wholeheartedly to creating a climate of affection and trust such that his priests may respond with a convinced, pleasing and firm obedience" (*AS* 76). Very concrete expressions of this engagement with priests are found in the two obligatory diocesan bodies prescribed by canon law: the Presbyteral Council and the College of Consultors—both intended to structure the presbyterates support and counsel for the bishop's governance.

41 "The rapport between a Bishop and his presbyterate needs to be inspired and nourished by charity and by a vision of faith, such that their *juridical bonds*, deriving from the divine constitution of the Church, appear as a natural consequence of the spiritual communion each one has with God" (*AS* 76).

42 Cardinal Velasio de Paolis summarizes the importance of the image of the Good Shepherd for the bishop as follows: "L'immagine del buon *Pastore*, come pure quella del *Servo*, è totalizzante. Essa vuole esprimere in modo unitario la figura del Vescovo in quanto vicario e rappresentante di Cristo, buon pastore (Gv 10,11), fattosi agnello sgozzato (Ap 5,5–8) per il gregge; venuto non per essere servitor, ma per servire (Mc 10,45) e per dare la sua vita per la salvezza del mondo, così che gli uomini abbiano la vita e l'abbiano in abbondanza (Gv. 10,10)." Velasio de Paolis, "Stile pastorale di governo e comunione diocesana," in *L'esercizio dell'autorità nella Chiesa: Riflessioni a partire dell'Esortazione apostolica "Pastores gregis,"* ed. Arturo Cattaneo (Marcianum Press, 2005), 25.

Conclusion

Drawing very specific and national conclusions on the bishop-priest relationship based on the NSCP is indeed complicated. Many factors—a belligerent or less-than-enthusiastic priest, an authoritarian or aloof bishop, a diocese inundated by lawsuits due to historic sex abuse cases, a recent and well-known case of an innocent priest who suffered for years due to a false allegation—may all have contributed to some of the more adverse results from the survey. It must also be noted—from the perspective of this chapter—that comparing the theological teaching of the Church (being scholarly and theoretical) to lived reality will often lend itself to the emergence of divergences. This very dynamic has come to the fore in recent years also when comparing the teaching of the Church on Mass attendance and actual numbers in the pews or between the Church's teaching on the sacrament of the Eucharist and what is understood and held by the Christian faithful. At the same time, the adverse indicators of the survey—even with all statistical and analytical realities duly considered—should not be set aside easily.

In that perspective, taking the theological and canonical underpinnings of priesthood, of bishops and of priests, and of the bishop-priest relationship as the starting point, this author believes four succinct conclusions may be drawn at this time: 1) there is a solid understanding among bishops and priests about what the Church teaches as concerns holy orders; 2) both bishops and priests wish for and strive to live according to the Church's magisterium on priestly ministry, and are, even in the face of challenges, reaping great rewards and joy from having assumed the yoke of the Lord; 3) advancing greater unity among the diocesan bishop and his priests, and the diocesan bishop exemplifying that he "manifestly hold his priests in esteem, showing them trust and praising them as they deserve" (*AS* 77) will be crucial to pastoral ministry and the life and well-being of priests; and 4) promoting among the diocesan bishop and his priests a bond that is paternal, fraternal, and amicable from the side of the bishop and filial, fraternal, and amicable from the side of the priest will be key to both improve and fortify the relationship between the diocesan bishop and priests.

A HOUSE DIVIDED: THE DALLAS CHARTER'S ROLE IN FRACTURING PRIEST-BISHOP RELATIONS

Rev. Msgr. Thomas G. Guarino

> *Let the bishop regard his priests as his co-workers and as sons and friends, just as Christ called His disciples now not servants but friends* (Vatican II, *Lumen gentium*, no. 28).

> *Therefore, on account of this communion in the same priesthood and ministry, bishops should regard priests as their brothers and friends* (Vatican II, *Presbyterorum ordinis*, no. 7).

The National Study of Catholic Priests (NSCP) has revealed a far-reaching chasm existing between the American episcopacy and the presbyterate. The primary cause for this cleavage, as the NSCP also makes clear, is attributable to the draconian implementation of the *Charter for the Protection of Children and Young People,* colloquially known as the Dallas Charter. This grave and disturbing "disconnect" between priests and bishops is unhealthy for the life of the Catholic Church since bishops and priests must be co-workers for the Gospel of Jesus Christ, enjoying a relationship marked by mutual trust and respect. The Second Vatican Council taught that bishops and priests should regard each other as "brothers and friends." But, today, as the NSCP indicates, that relationship is not generally marked by fraternal unity. In this chapter, I will reflect on the damage that the implementation of the Charter has done to the relationship between priests and bishops—and why the results of the NSCP are alarming (and at the same time immensely useful)—for the Church in the United States.[1]

First: Why the Dallas Charter? The priestly abuse scandal in the Catholic Church broke in Boston in 2002 in a conflagration that spread from "ecclesiastical Chernobyl" to the rest of the United States. Touted as a treacherous and deceitful cover-up by the Catholic hierarchy, the crisis led to bishops being intensely attacked by the media, by advocacy groups, by lawyers, and by politicians. There was even talk of invoking the federal RICO statute against Catholic bishops, an instrument designed to prosecute mobsters and racketeers. In the face of this ferocious criticism, the US bishops were initially caught off-guard, offering little by way of a coherent response. When they recovered from the torrent of opprobrium, the bishops sought to piece together a program that would be effective in removing abusers from priestly ministry. However, traumatized by attacks on their earlier misprision, their decisions—while rightly acknowledging the profound suffering of victims—were excessive, little informed by Catholic theology or natural justice.

In 2002, the bishops and their house lawyers produced the *Charter for the Protection of Children and Young People*. Appended to this document, although not formally part of the Charter itself, were the "Essential Norms"—practical measures for implementing the bishops' document.

Soon after the Charter's approval, Cardinal Avery Dulles, at that time the premier Catholic theologian in the United States, warned that, because the procedures connected with the Charter were so harsh and unyielding, an "adversarial relationship" would come to prevail between bishops and priests. The NSCP has shown, with pristine clarity, the truth of Dulles's prophetic remark.

In 2004, in an article in *America* magazine, Dulles voiced his concerns about the episcopal Charter.[2] He pointed out that just a few years earlier,

1 As examined in chapter 5, there were high levels of trust between priests and bishops during the years of John Paul II's papacy. Under the influence of the Charter, however, this trust has largely evaporated, as this chapter will explore.

2 Avery Dulles, "Rights of Accused Priests: Toward a Revision of the Dallas Charter and the 'Essential Norms,'" *America* 190 (June 21–28, 2004): 19–23, https://www.americamagazine.org/faith/2004/06/21/rights-accused-priests. See also

in 2000, the US bishops had published *Responsibility and Rehabilitation*, a critique of the American criminal-justice system. In that statement, the bishops rejected easy slogans and "one-size-fits-all" solutions. The cardinal noted that with their Charter, the bishops "have taken positions at odds with these high principles," adopting the very viewpoint they had earlier condemned. In fact, Dulles accused the bishops of having "opted for an extreme response." With the Charter's draconian norms, the bishops undermined priestly morale and struck a blow against the Church itself as an institution in which justice reigns.

Cardinal Dulles remained skeptical that the Charter, and the procedures emanating from it, allowed Catholic priests to be treated justly. He cited a litany of issues: credibility was a term without a clear definition—often meaning nothing more than that some event could have conceivably occurred; there was no room in the Charter for the proper proportionality between offenses and their punishment; statutes of limitation—legal criteria dating back to classical Rome—were routinely ignored; financial settlements with accusers were often regarded as admissions of guilt; accused priests were excluded from ministry for prolonged periods of time, amounting to "forced laicizations"; and there existed no clear guidelines as to when falsely accused priests could be returned to public ministry. As Dulles wisely noted, "Permanent exclusion from priestly ministry is the spiritual equivalent of the death penalty."[3] Again and again, Cardinal Dulles maintained that the Charter would separate the presbyterate from the episcopate. A man of his finely honed theological intelligence saw immediately that the bishops' Charter strained both natural justice and Catholic theology. The NSCP has confirmed Dulles's fears, showing that, as implemented, the well-meaning Charter—while undoubtedly achieving important and critical accomplishments—has also done unfortunate damage to the Catholic Church in the United States.

If the image offered by St. Ignatius of Antioch in the early second century is to hold, with presbyters joined to their bishops as strings to a harp,[4] then

---

Avery Dulles and Germain Grisez, "Sin, Grace, and Zero Tolerance: An Exchange," *First Things* 151 (March 2005): 27–36, https://research.ebsco.com/linkprocessor/plink?id=835c5ea4-436b-3323-b62f-6401843c6957

3 Dulles and Grisez, "Sin, Grace, and Zero Tolerance," 35.

4 "Thus it is proper for you to run together in harmony with the mind of the bishop, as you are in fact doing. For your council of presbyters, which is worthy of its name and worthy of God, is attuned to the bishop as strings to a lyre." Ignatius of

bishops cannot be regarded by priests as men whose central concern is defending their own legal and media flanks from negative publicity, even in the name of protecting minors from abuse.

Causes of the Chasm Between Bishops and Priests

Why did Cardinal Dulles label the bishops' Charter "an extreme response" which undermined priestly morale? After all, one can argue that the Charter and its procedures have effectively cleaned up the abuse problem in the Catholic Church. As Bill Donohue, president of the Catholic League, shows in his excellent book, *The Truth About Clergy Sexual Abuse*, the Catholic Church is the American institution that has most clearly and energetically rooted out child abusers.[5] This is certainly true—and the forceful action of the US bishops must be acknowledged as one of the decisive accomplishments of the Dallas Charter. But having accomplished an important task with a blunt instrument does not prove that a more finely-tuned instrument could not have done the same, but with less collateral damage.

Donohue not only applauds the victories; he is also a keen analyst of the dangerous processes unleashed by the Charter, writing that, because of it, "the average detainee in Guantanamo Bay has more rights than the average accused priest in America does today."[6] A similar comment may be found from the veteran commentator on Catholic issues, Philip Lawler, who writes, ". . . American Church leaders, who once ignored the rights of innocent children, now ignore the rights of accused priests."[7] The bishops and their chancery advisers ought to be deeply troubled by these comments from committed and knowledgeable Catholic laymen—because it is precisely the lack of "rights," the perceived lack of due process for accused priests—that is at the heart of the widespread mistrust of the American episcopacy harbored by many priests today.

Antioch, "Letter to the Ephesians," 4, in Michael W. Holmes, *The Apostolic Fathers in English*, 3rd ed. (Baker Academic, 2006).

5 Bill Donohue, *The Truth About Clergy Sexual Abuse* (Ignatius Press, 2021).

6 Bill Donohue, "Standing Fast for Priests' Rights," Catholic League (January 31, 2019), https://www.catholicleague.org/standing-fast-for-priests-rights

7 Philip Lawler, "Quick Hits" (October 14, 2020), https://www.catholicculture.org/commentary/quick-hits-cardinal-farrells-new-post-priests-belated-vindication

The NSCP has shown that the trust priests place in their bishops has declined significantly over the last two decades, with fewer than half of US priests trusting their local bishops. Moreover, in a truly astounding statistic, *only 24% of priests trust the US episcopacy as a whole.* This is nothing less than a vote of no confidence in current episcopal leadership.

Fundamental Issues

Why does the NSCP reveal such distrust of the episcopacy by Catholic priests? Here are some of the reasons:

1. Civil Suits

In many dioceses, the practice has developed to suspend from ministry any priest who is named in a civil complaint, no matter how bizarre, aged, or flimsy that complaint might be. This is a particularly noxious practice because—without necessarily any evidence to prove a priest's guilt—the priest is called to the chancery office, stripped of his ministerial faculties, made to surrender his "suitability for ministry" card, told he cannot dress or present himself as a Catholic priest, instructed to vacate his parish residence, and made to resign any offices he holds. The accused man is often facing a battery of chancery personnel, including not only the Vicar-General, but attorneys, safe environment coordinators, and financial officers as well.

I have seen this scenario take place time and again—and to men who have rendered decade upon decade of untarnished service to the Church. In these cases, it should be noted, there is no preliminary investigation (even though such investigation is specifically called for by Essential Norm no. 6 appended to the Charter), nor is the case remanded to the diocesan Independent Review Board. Rather, the priest is immediately suspended without even the slightest chance of having the facts carefully examined or with an opportunity to defend himself. The excuse offered for this action is that diocesan attorneys think civil suits need to be resolved before any investigation can take place. Needless to add, this is a violation of the Essential Norms, which insist on a preliminary investigation in every case.[8]

8 As Nicholas Cafardi, a civil and canon lawyer who served as chairman of the Catholic bishops' National Review Board in 2004–2005, commented: "The

This situation—with its lack of due process—has led, just as Cardinal Dulles predicted, to a deep diminution of priests' morale and, as the NSCP shows, to a widespread distrust of the US episcopacy.[9] It seems the main concerns are two: 1) to relieve the bishops from making any judgments at all. Priests are summarily suspended on the grounds of "protecting the faithful" so bishops can never be criticized for being "soft on abuse"; and 2) more dangerously, the concern for "optics"—how will our action (or inaction) appear to the public and the press. More on that below.[10]

Allied to this issue is the Charter's claim that "A priest or deacon who is accused of sexual abuse of a minor is to be accorded the presumption of innocence during the investigation of the allegation" (art. 5). But many priests are removed from ministry upon accusation alone—and for years at a time—often apart from any investigation. How can bishops claim that the presumption of innocence is being respected? As is plain to see, the presumption is of guilt—with the priest treated, de facto, as if he were an abuser, with his reputation now deeply stained. In the third century, the

---

problem is priests are being called into the chancery as soon as [an allegation] comes in and before there's been any kind of preliminary investigation. Technically, that's not supposed to happen. The investigation should be made before you take action against the priest." Cafardi suggested that the American Catholic bishops today "are running extremely scared." See "Effort to Educate Catholic Priests," *National Catholic Reporter* (June 27, 2022), https://www.ncronline.org/news/effort-educate-catholic-priests-what-do-when-accused-abuse-draws-criticism

9 As seen in chapters 3 and 4, the lack of supportive systems for priests—now exacerbated by the policies of the Charter—has contributed significantly to the decline in priestly morale, and to the increased risk of burnout.

10 Michael J. Mazza has noted that dioceses often refuse to take any canonical action on an allegation for fear of being accused [by local prosecutors] of interfering with secular litigation. However, refusing to take canonical action on an accusation against a priest, "betrays either vincible ignorance … or a lack of commitment to carrying it [canonical action] out." Mazza points out that no. 66 of the Dicastery for the Doctrine of the Faith's *Vademecum* (revised 2022) states that "an unjustified delay in the preliminary investigation may constitute an act of negligence on the part of the ecclesiastical authority." See Mazza, "Moral Certainty in Uncertain Times: The Importance of Standards of Proof When Responding to Accusations of Clerical Misconduct," *The Jurist: Studies in Church Law and Ministry* 79 (2023): 321, https://doi.org/10.1353/jur.2023.a915491

theologian Tertullian warned against arguing about Scripture with heretics. He noted that such discussions always end with listeners having a doubt planted deep in their hearts.[11] Similarly, when a man is removed from priestly ministry based on an accusation alone—apart from any significant evidence—are not the bishops planting a doubt about a man's character deep in the hearts of his parishioners, and of the laity in general?

2. Transparency and Terminology

Outside of civil suits, there are those priests who are accused in other ways, e.g., by a simple report, phone call, or letter to the chancery office. Unlike the way civil suits are treated (in many dioceses), these accusations at least go before an Independent Review Board (IRB) sponsored by a diocese or religious order. The IRB is a consultative body intended to assist bishops in determining the veracity of allegations of sexual abuse by clerics. As such, the IRB is crucial in the decision as to whether an accused priest remains in public ministry.

Recently, the Men of Melchizedek (MoM), an extraordinarily thoughtful advocacy group that seeks justice for both victims and accused priests, published a handbook intended to advise and assist Independent Review Boards. The volume makes several crucial points, among which that the canonical investigation of an allegation (the results of which must be considered by the IRB) "is distinct from any civil or criminal investigation performed by a government employee or official and must be performed promptly."[12] It is the issue of promptness that is crucial since many priests are summarily suspended and then wait years before their cases are adjudicated. As the MoM volume points out, both Essential Norm no. 6 and the *Vademecum* no. 66 call for the canonical investigation to be conducted promptly. The *Vademecum* is a Vatican-sanctioned guide for handling cases of sex abuse, published in 2020 and revised in 2022. Indeed, the *Vademecum* specifies that delay in the preliminary investigation "may constitute an act of negligence on the part of the ecclesiastical authority."[13]

11 Tertullian, *The Prescription Against Heretics*, chapters 17–19.

12 See Men of Melchizedek, *Independent Review Board Member Orientation Handbook* (MoM, 2023), 9.

13 Dicastery for the Doctrine of the Faith, "*Vademecum* on Certain Points of Procedure" (June 5, 2022). Available at vatican.va.

The MoM *Handbook* also warns IRB members against the temptation to shade information in order to protect the reputation of a diocese from negative publicity—and against the desire to be seen as "doing something" in response to an accusation. Importantly, it should be noted that at this point—with an accusation in the hands of the IRB—the priest who is under investigation has had no opportunity to defend himself. The task of the IRB is merely to help the bishop decide if an allegation has at least a "semblance of truth" (*saltem veri similem*). As the handbook points out, this is a very low standard, "even lower than the 'preponderance of evidence' used in civil trials."[14] It warns, therefore, that "some IRB members might be inclined to 'err on the side of caution' by routinely ruling against clerics, almost as a matter of practice."[15] Indeed, the handbook worries that IRB members might be tempted to think almost all allegations satisfy the low bar of "semblance of truth." But this would be "a gross dereliction of duty and could inflict serious damage on individual priests and the ecclesial community in general."[16]

As all priests know, an IRB decision that an individual has been "credibly accused" has colossal consequences. In truth, this is an understatement. One bishop has even spoken about possibly laicizing all priests who have been credibly accused. Simply considering such an action—against men who may be guilty of no crime whatsoever—indicates a shocking lack of understanding of Catholic theology and of the priesthood itself. And it goes a long way toward explaining the fissure between bishops and priests in the United States which the NSCP has exposed.

The Men of Melchizedek's *Handbook* also makes important suggestions about the terminology currently in use. It notes that "terms such as 'credibly accused' should be avoided," especially since there is no clear definition of the term "credible," with the word's meaning fluctuating from diocese to diocese.[17] The word "substantiated" is also problematic not only because an IRB decision is merely advisory but because the decision "has been reached

14 MoM Handbook, 11.

15 MoM Handbook, 14.

16 MoM Handbook, 14.

17 MoM Handbook, 15. As Mazza has noted, "The lack of a generally accepted definition [of credibility] raises significant concerns. In the USCCB's 2016 Annual Report on Child and Youth Protection, for instance, the words 'credible' and 'credibility' are not defined, despite being used over four dozen times." See Mazza, "Moral Certainty," 306.

without the accused having had an opportunity to defend himself."[18] Can an accusation be "substantiated" before the accused has had the chance to explain his side of the story?

The civil and canon lawyer Michael J. Mazza notes that there exist other problems with the term "substantiated." In 2022, the USCCB's annual report spoke of an allegation as "substantiated" when "the diocese/eparchy has completed an investigation and the allegation has been deemed credible/true based upon the evidence gathered through the investigation."[19] But, as Mazza notes, this language raises more questions than it answers. One must wonder, for example, "whether the words 'credible' and 'true' now mean the same thing, whether they instead represent different positions on a sliding scale, or whether the word 'credible' has morphed from its etymological meaning—tied to being capable of belief—to being employed now as a synonym for reality itself."[20] As Mazza points out—and as the NSCP confirms—a troubling issue is the effect that this uncertainty about standards has on the morale of the thousands of priests working in the United States. Further, a judgment by the IRB that a cleric has been "credibly accused" means, in most cases, that the priest's name will now be published on the internet. Just here, the MoM *Handbook* issues a stern warning, noting that "*this practice has been repeatedly criticized by the Holy See* and can inflict a lasting wound upon the cleric's reputation, *given the fact that the allegation has yet to be proven.*"[21]

In their rush to respond to unfavorable publicity and to a headline-hungry press, the US bishops constantly invoked the terms "transparency" and "accountability." But there normally exists no civil mandate to publish the names of accused priests. Under the rubric of "transparency," the bishops have adopted practices that have called into question natural justice and tarred the reputations of many priests. And this despite the eighth commandment, which prohibits rash judgment, calumny, and detraction. In significant statements about the eighth commandment, pertinent to the issue at hand, the Catechism of the Catholic Church teaches:

18 MoM Handbook, 16.

19 USCCB, 2017 Annual Report: Findings and Recommendations (April 2012), 23, available at https://www.usccb.org/issues-and-action/child-and-youth-protection/ upload/2017-Report.pdf. Cited in Mazza, "Moral Certainty," 307n79.

20 Mazza, "Moral Certainty," 307.

21 MoM Handbook, 16, emphasis in original.

> *Respect for the reputation* of persons forbids every attitude and word likely to cause them unjust injury. One becomes guilty:
>
> - of *rash judgment* who, even tacitly, assumes as true, without sufficient foundation, the moral fault of a neighbor;
> - of *detraction* who, without objectively valid reason, discloses another's faults and failings to persons who did not know them;
> - of *calumny* who, by remarks contrary to the truth, harms the reputation of others and gives occasion for false judgments concerning them. (*CCC* no. 2477, emphasis original).

Do the present practices skate too closely to the very actions condemned by the Church? As noted, the practice of listing names of accused employees "is entirely unheard of in the American employment experience."[22] No employer or government entity publishes the names of individuals against whom "credible" (once again, a variable term) accusations have been made. As Mazza has pointed out,

> A man who has been unjustly labeled as having a "credible," "substantiated," or "established" accusation of sexual abuse against him can suffer serious and long-standing damage, not to mention his family, friends, and the people he has served as a priest of Jesus Christ. Having one's name published on the internet in this way can only be seen as a form of punishment, and an especially severe one at that.[23]

Given the quasi-permanent nature of lists on the worldwide web, does it make sense to publish the names of accused priests—even those who fall under the widely variable term "credible"—thereby damaging their lives and reputations? As has been rightly noted, "What priest will not wonder whether

22 Joseph R. Maher and David A. Shaneyfelt, "When the Church Defames Her Priests," *Homiletic and Pastoral Review* (July 21, 2017), https://www.hprweb.com/2017/07/when-the-church-defames-her-priests. See also Michael J. Mazza, "*Bona Fama* in an Age of 'Transparency': Publishing Lists of 'Credibly Accused' Clerics," *The Jurist: Studies in Church Law and Ministry* 78 (December 2022): 445–76, https://dx.doi.org/10.1353/jur.2022.0020

23 Mazza, "Moral Certainty," 312.

his name will be publicized, and forever connected to heinous misdeeds, if some allegation is made against him ... and if his bishop (or his delegate) finds the claim 'credible'?"[24]

3. Optics and Fear

Why, one might ask, would bishops allow all of this? Why would church leaders expose their own men to opprobrium and severe penalties, including complete exclusion from public ministry, when many accusations are supported by no evidence at all or very weak evidence at most?

One issue, certainly, is that US bishops were under extraordinary pressure from many groups, including politicians and the media. As one priest states, in the interviews conducted by the NSCP, "I think this kind of crisis is really much more focused on the bishops, and they were the ones really taking the hit." Indeed, the bishops as a whole were accused of widespread and willful misprision—and the intense societal pressure brought to bear on them caused panic—followed by an excessive reaction.

But another problem revealed by the NSCP is that some bishops appear to be so isolated and detached from their priests as to not even recognize that there exists a serious problem in their relationship. According to the NSCP, over 90% of US bishops claim that they would be helpful to priests who are dealing with personal struggles. Compare this with the fact that only 36% of diocesan priests think their ecclesiastical superiors care about their difficulties. Bishops clearly think of themselves in a much more favorable light—and with much greater self-regard—than do their own priests. What is the cause of this presbyteral alienation?

Peggy Noonan has written in the *Wall Street Journal* that the established political class in the United States is no longer trusted by ordinary citizens because this "protected class" lives in a bubble. It makes public policy but does not have to live with it, while the "unprotected class" does.[25] *Mutatis mutandis*, these words apply to many priests' perception of bishops—who do not fall

24 Maher and Shaneyfelt, "When the Church Defames Her Priests."

25 See Peggy Noonan, "Trump and the Rise of the Unprotected: Why Political Professionals Are Struggling to make Sense of the World They Created," *Wall Street Journal*, Feb. 26, 2016, https://www.proquest.com/blogs-podcasts-websites/trump-rise-unprotected-why-political/docview/1768059361/se-2

under the precise strictures of their own Charter. Bishops are subject to a different set of rules, one that handles cases much more expeditiously than those applied to priests. This is another reason for the current chasm between priests and bishops.

In 2023, the Men of Melchizedek sponsored an online webinar with several attorneys discussing the role of Independent Review Boards in ensuring the rights of accused priests.[26] One speaker, Mr. Joseph Richotte, a Michigan attorney, noted the high stakes involved in IRB decisions—nothing less than the continued ministerial work of a priest. In other words, a man's entire vocation is on the line in their decisions. Mr. Richotte told the sad tale of a religious order priest who had been accused of abuse. The diocese in which the priest worked conducted an investigation—a rather hasty and slipshod affair. Mr. Richotte conducted his own thorough inquiry—and then challenged the quality of the diocese's work—as well as the decision to suspend the priest on the basis of an uncorroborated accusation. The attorney said he was stunned with the response. He was told, "Do you have any idea what the reaction would be in the press if we had left this priest in ministry?" As Mr. Richotte points out, this is not how Catholics should think; concern with optics is how the world thinks. Are we concerned primarily with the media? Or with how God judges our search for justice?

Catholic priests in the United States are well-aware that some bishops are deeply concerned with the bad press they might receive by leaving an accused priest in ministry—even though the accusation may be flimsy and aged.[27] As the NSCP has shown, an extraordinary 82% of priests live in fear of a false accusation. They know that almost any accusation, even if weakly supported, can easily end their priestly ministry. Is it healthy for men in any profession to live with such overweening and inordinate anxiety?

At the same time, let it be stated clearly that the NSCP also shows that two-thirds of priests acknowledge that the bishops needed to act vigorously to create safe environments for children. Priests certainly do not harbor a

26 See Men of Melchizedek, Independent Review Board Webinar (September 21, 2023), https://menofmelchizedek.org/independent-review-board-webinar

27 As Cardinal Dulles has written about decades-old accusations: "It is very hard for a priest to defend himself against accusations from the remote past, since memories fade, witnesses die or leave the area, and physical evidence is difficult to obtain. The 'recovered memories' stimulated by psychotherapy are notoriously unreliable." See Dulles and Grisez, "Sin, Grace, and Zero Tolerance," 34.

lackadaisical view of child abuse. Indeed, the vast majority of priests strongly sympathize with victims of abuse and support forceful zero-tolerance measures *for those who are truly abusers*. The quarrel is not—and never has been—with the need for compelling episcopal action; the controversy revolves around the harsh manner in which the US bishops have, in fact, acted toward priests who are merely accused. As Cardinal Dulles insisted, the "good of the totality must not override the rights of individual persons."[28]

Priests' Voices

The in-depth interviews conducted by the National Study of Catholic Priests are revelatory—and often bittersweet—in that they display a great love for the Church, the priesthood, and frequently for the local bishop. Indeed, the NSCP shows that there often exists a significant level of trust toward individual bishops, even when this is combined with deep-seated disappointment with episcopal leadership in general. As one priest says,

> How many times has Pope Francis said that the bishop has to be a father and a shepherd? And very often, bishops can be tempted to just be bureaucrats and the overseers. And . . . the priests have to feel like he is an advocate for them, and will be fair to them. And not just someone who will throw them under the table. *Because of the clerical sex abuse crisis, every priest feels like he's got a knife to his throat.* Because anyone can say anything at any time. And it's credible. And the priests have to know that the bishop will at least be fair with them. And that isn't always the case (emphasis added).

"Every priest feels like he's got a knife to his throat." That's a powerful image, and a true one. Among themselves, priests engage in gallows humor: "One phone call and my life is over." And, "I have a gun to my head and I'm not even in the mob." These images make the same point: Every priest has a knife to his throat, and a Damoclean sword hanging over his head.

Given this perilous situation, can any American priest today encourage vocations with a clear conscience? Can intelligent young men be invited to

28 Dulles, "Rights of Accused Priests," 20.

consider a vocation when the chances for injustice are so great? Another of the interviewed priests encapsulates the problem:

> There is no trust, fundamentally, between the priests and the bishop, or between the bishop and the priests. . . Every priest knows that at the drop of the hat, the bishop will pull the rug out from under you, because that's how life is. And priests kind of expect the bishop to sacrifice them. So I think that there is a fundamental lack of trust all the way around, and I'm not quite sure that anybody can really be blamed for that. It's just a consequence of everything we've been through.

A religious priest voices a similar sentiment, noting the very low morale among diocesan priests because of distrust of their bishops:

> So I would say trust, at the level of the archdiocese and the bishop, is about as low to zero as you can get. So there's a real sense, and that's not just here, because I was in a previous diocese . . . and it was the exact same. There's a definite sense and justification from some situations that as a priest, no matter what you do, the bishop's gonna run you over. That it will always be your fault, that everything's your fault, and you'll be thrown under the bus no matter what. And I've never seen morale—any organization I've worked [with] in the church, outside or otherwise—so low. There's a real sense that the bishop will never have your back and to cover himself the priest will always be guilty. So there's very low trust. And that's a real problem.

The sentiments voiced in these few citations could be multiplied endlessly in the interviews conducted by the NSCP.

Theology of the Priesthood

Probably the greatest tragedy to come from the bishops' Charter is the damage it has done to the Church's own faith. After all, the Catholic Church's greatest gift to the world is the *depositum fidei*, that is, God's self-revelation to humanity as mediated through the history of ancient Israel and pre-eminently in Jesus Christ.

The disconnect between priests and bishops revealed by the NSCP is not only because priests believe they have been treated poorly, but because of their sense that the Charter has damaged the theology of the priesthood itself. As Cardinal Newman wisely stated in his preface to *The Via Media of the Anglican Church*, "Theology is the fundamental and regulating principle of the whole Church system."[29] But if theology is the regulating principle of the entire Church, then, inexorably, when the theology of the priesthood is damaged, the entire intellectual architecture of Catholicism begins to wobble.

What theological understanding of the priesthood is purveyed when, in a split-second, this sacred vocation becomes nothing more than an employer-employee contract? When priests are reduced to members of the gig economy? At priestly ordinations and anniversaries, choirs often sing, "*Tu es sacerdos in aeternum,*" echoing Psalm 110, "You are a priest forever, according to the order of Melchizedek." But does the Church still believe it? Or should the choir more accurately sing, *Tu es sacerdos usque ad revocationem*? You are now a priest only until a bishop, his house lawyers, and PR flacks decide otherwise. As noted, one American bishop was recently considering laicizing all of his credibly accused priests. But "credibly accused" men are not necessarily guilty of any crime whatsoever. And as Cardinal Dulles rightly stated, laicization should be "exceedingly rare, since it obfuscates the very meaning of ordination, which confers an indelible consecration. It reinforces the false impression that priesthood is a job dependent on contract rather than a sacrament conferred by Christ."[30]

Have some US bishops, perhaps living in a "protected bubble," forgotten the significant sacrifices that the priesthood entails? Those sacrifices are more easily borne with the knowledge that one is living a sacred vocation. Unfortunately, many priests have concluded that certain bishops now regard their priestly "vocation" as little more than a job like any other, except with longer hours and lower pay. The procedures emanating from the Charter eat away at the theological and ontological density of the sacrament of holy orders, reducing the

29 John Henry Newman, *The Via Media of the Anglican Church*, 3rd ed. (Longmans, Green, 1877), xlvii.

30 Dulles, "Rights of Accused Priests," 22.

priesthood to a transitory, contractual position. Is the priesthood truly a sacred vocation, rooted in a unique divine call, marking one—like baptism itself—with an indelible character? Or does the Charter now whisper—and more than whisper—that such theology belongs to the discarded baggage of the past, as critics of the Catholic Church have long desired?

Is it any wonder that some priests have stopped encouraging vocations? Several fine priests have told me that they cannot, in good conscience, encourage a man to enter the seminary today. His reputation could be smeared, and his life thrown into turmoil by one weakly supported accusation. Even without conclusive evidence, he might be forced to wear the scarlet letter of abuse for the rest of his life. His name and reputation would be permanently stained on the worldwide web. Another priest advises men to obtain secular credentials—an MBA or a law degree—before beginning theological studies. Then at least they will be able to make a living if they are suspended from ministerial activity because of some flimsy or spurious allegation.

One diocesan priest sums up the problem:

> Well, I mean, living in constant fear of a life-ending accusation definitely puts a cloud over the priesthood. And honestly, I think most priests have that. Because the life-ending accusation doesn't have to be based in any reality. You know, it can just come out of somebody's three years of recovered memory, therapy, and have no ground in anything that ever really happened, but you're still doomed when it happens. And everybody knows that.

A religious priest is even more pointed in his remarks about future seminarians:

> But you know, to have zero tolerance, and to be guilty until proven innocent, is just who in God's name, would want to be a priest? You have to be out of your goddamn mind to say, oh, yeah, I'll be joining that group. And then, you know, somebody calls up next thing you know, you're out of ministry for the rest of your life. Due process, completely nonexistent. So if you're a priest, today, I can say you're a walking target for anybody . . . I don't know any priests, to be honest with you, that think that we're being treated with any kind of fairness or justice.

The NSCP, using the Harvard Flourishing Index for quantitative measurement, reports that the vast majority—a full 77% of priests—are flourishing in their ministry. So, clearly, the distrust of the US hierarchy is not related to priests' dissatisfaction with their lives and work. The reasons, as the interviews make clear, are almost entirely related to the draconian implementation of the Charter—and the severe anxiety this has caused among priests.

Scores of priests have been removed from ministry upon accusation alone, absent any significant evidence and, at times, even without even a brief investigation. In their legitimate desire to address the abuse crisis forcefully, the US bishops have instantiated norms that encumber both natural justice and Catholic theology. It is no surprise, then, that the NSCP has revealed that a priest would turn to his bishop for support only after all other avenues have been exhausted. In a ranking of social support for the clergy, the categories priests listed (in descending order) are: lay friends; family; parishioners; fellow priests; and, finally, the local, diocesan bishop. Unfortunately, many priests believe that bishops no longer have their best interests at heart.

Every year at Mass, there is a reading from the prophet Daniel—the well-known story of Susanna, who was herself falsely accused of sexual impropriety. Daniel's words leap off the pages of the lectionary: "Are you such fools, O children of Israel, to condemn a daughter of Israel without clear evidence?" (Daniel 13:48). That scriptural passage should force an examination of conscience by every American bishop: Should one condemn a priest of Jesus Christ without clear evidence? Should one allow a flimsy allegation to ruin a man's reputation and life?

Conclusion: Rectifying the Current Failures

Let it be stated clearly and without hesitation: the US bishops have been exemplary in their concern for the victims of abuse. They have rightly pledged that never again must such horrible crimes and reprehensible betrayals occur in the Catholic Church. The bishops have taken extraordinary measures to ensure that church-related institutions are, in name and in fact, safe environments. They have created a powerful culture of assessment to ensure compliance with their good proposals. And they have made appropriate restitution to those victims who have suffered the horror of abuse. All of these are praiseworthy and necessary actions. We applaud the bishops for them. Let it also be said, to their great credit, that the US Catholic bishops, exercising their apostolic ministry, often boldly defend unpopular truths—about religious freedom, about the sanctity of life, and about the nature of marriage.

However, with the country in the grip of a moral panic—overwhelmed by the perception that clergy abuse was rampant and unrestrained—the bishops themselves succumbed to excess and were sold an a-theological bill of goods. The US bishops adopted a false either/or proposition: Protect possible victims *or* protect the rights of priests. True leadership means caring for both the victims of abuse and the victims of false accusations. But for many bishops, showing serious interest in the plight of abuse victims—an interest that was and is abundantly warranted—meant treating accused priests without the necessary juridical safeguards. By accepting this fateful dichotomy, the US bishops—as the NSCP reveals with sterling clarity—have become estranged from their own priests. There has been a rush to judgment of many priests, who have been suspended from their ministry based on flimsy charges.

As Michael Mazza has insightfully noted,

> Some Catholic dioceses and religious orders all too often appear to be rushing to judgment, condemning men without sufficient due process and taking punitive actions (like publishing names on the internet) without having first reached the requisite level of moral certainty demanded by canon law and fundamental principles of justice. Such practices, it must be said, express not only a worrying disregard for the rule of law, but threaten the integrity of the Church's entire juridical system and, by extension, the Church's mission to the world.[31]

Even worse, the bishops do not appear eager to emend a process they must now realize is damaging to the Church. Fearful of the media, fearful of politicians, fearful of advocacy groups, fearful of incessant criticism, fearful of being sued, fearful of being labeled insufficiently punitive, the bishops are paralyzed. Paralysis, however, in this crucial matter, is a disastrous recipe—disastrous for justice, for priestly morale, for vocations, and for the future of the Catholic Church in the United States. Only strong episcopal action, based on natural justice and Catholic theology, will convince priests that the

31 Mazza, "Moral Certainty," 322.

leadership of the Catholic Church in the United States is deeply concerned about *both* victims *and* accused priests.

The bishops should learn from other recent events. For example, there remains seared in American memory the 2006 tragedy of the Duke University lacrosse team, with three members of that squad having been accused of rape. Their story quickly became a national parable about race, class, and gender, with the athletes widely condemned in the court of public opinion prior to their exoneration. So hasty was their denunciation—on campus and off—that the attorney general of North Carolina subsequently condemned the "tragic rush" to accuse the students.

Or one can point to the case of Alan Dershowitz, the well-known Harvard Law professor who tells his own frightening story of a false accusation. Dershowitz's reputation for integrity, built over the course of a lifetime, was threatened by an uncorroborated allegation of sex with an underage woman. While that accusation has now been stricken from the record, Dershowitz notes that "You can't un-ring a bell," his sterling career and good name having been called into question.[32]

These high-profile episodes should make us think, once again, about Catholic priests who have been falsely accused of sexual abuse, and about the need for a just process in dealing with their cases. Priests today are trapped in a vise between the Church's proper desire to remedy past injustices and her equally proper desire to avoid the slightest appearance of tolerating abuse. As such, the Dallas Charter is an open wound that festers still, deeply scarring the priesthood and the Church in the United States.

This essay opened with two citations from the Second Vatican Council, both insisting that bishops, since they share in the same priesthood of Jesus Christ, should regard priests as their brothers and friends. But, as the NSCP has revealed, episcopal fear has harmed any semblance of fraternity.

The National Study of Catholic Priests has done the Catholic Church in the United States a great service. By its extensive survey of priests (from 191 dioceses and eparchies) and through its wide-ranging in-depth interviews, it has shone a bright light on the current chasm that exists between US bishops and priests—and has amply explained the primary reason for this cleavage. *Now is the time for healing the wound.*

32 Alan M. Dershowitz, "How It Feels to Be Falsely Accused," *Observer* (April 10, 2015). https://observer.com/2015/04/how-it-feels-to-be-falsely-accused

A significant step toward healing would be to constitute a national commission of bishops, theologians, and canonists to examine the Charter's norms and implementation with theological intelligence and Christian fortitude.[33] Yes, the bishops will be roundly criticized for this—by politicians, lawyers, media, advocacy groups, and so on. It will be claimed that bishops are "sweeping sexual assaults under the rug," "protecting rapists," and "attacking survivors." Not only will bishops be subject to recriminatory language, their PR flacks, house lawyers, and risk managers will do everything possible to dissuade them from re-thinking the issue.

But precisely now is when Spirit-guided courage is so desperately needed in the Catholic Church.

Bishops often remark that they "promised the Catholic people" they would be tough on abuse. But no promise, however well-intentioned, can stand on a foundation of shabby theology. In convening this commission, the bishops will begin a process that will, in time, ensure due process for accused priests, restore the confidence and trust of the clergy, and establish procedures for the accused on the solid bedrock of Catholic theology and natural justice. And all of this can be accomplished while fully respecting the plight of victims and maintaining adamantine measures against abuse in any form. As Cardinal Dulles concluded, "After doing everything necessary to create a safe environment for children, the bishops should strive to do what they can to see that innocent priests are not treated as if they were guilty and that all priests are treated with justice and Christian charity."[34]

May the Lord bestow fortitude and wisdom on the American episcopacy.

33 Editor's note: For a sterling canonical analysis of the sexual abuse scandal and the prospect of further reforms to canon law pertaining to abuse, see Susan Mulheron, "Canonical Considerations in Response to the Scandals in the Church," *Proceedings of the 80th Annual Convention: Phoenix, Arizona, October 8–11, 2018* (Canon Law Society of America, 2019), 297–317.

34 Dulles, "Rights of Accused Priests," 23. While re-thinking the Charter's implementation must be the cornerstone for rebuilding trust and communion between bishops and priests, other practical strategies will be examined in Chapter 10.

CHAPTER EIGHT

SPIRITUAL FATHERHOOD: A PATH TO GREATER COMMUNION AMONG CLERGY

David Songy, OFMCap.

The 2022 National Study of Catholic Priests (NSCP)[1] conducted during the twenty-year anniversary of the approval of the USCCB Dallas Charter,[2] produced significant observations on the experiences of clergy since 2002. The survey results point to a need for a restoration of trust between Catholic priests and bishops, who apparently possess quite divergent views of each other. Bishops view their relationship with priests as spiritual fathers and sons—or brothers in the vineyard. Compare this to priests who see their bishops as mere administrators and themselves as powerless subjects. While the summary of the results is sobering, a closer look at the data is important in order to address this underlying question

1 Brandon Vaidyanathan et al., "Well-Being, Trust, and Policy in a Time of Crisis: Highlights from the National Study of Catholic Priests." The Catholic Project. The Catholic University of America, 2022, https://catholicproject.catholic.edu/national-study-of-catholic-priests/well-being-trust-and-policy

2 United States Conference of Catholic Bishops, *Charter for the Protection of Children and Young People*, revised 2018, https://www.usccb.org/resources/cyp-charter-2018

in the wake of the Church's response to the clergy sex abuse scandal: If today there truly exists a crisis of communion among diocesan clergy and bishops, how does the Church respond?[3]

The necessity of a safe environment culture within the Church is clear, but it must be founded upon ecclesial communion. In the priest interviews, several recommendations were made for moving forward, the first involving their relationship with bishops, desiring that they act more as spiritual fathers and brothers. This offers an excellent starting point for this process. Given the apparent desire of bishops to be spiritual fathers to priests and the NSCP data indicating a significant disparity in the experience of such fatherhood by priests, this chapter will outline the tension that exists, explore the nature of fatherhood from both psychological and spiritual perspectives, emphasize its importance at this moment in the Church, and offer recommendations for addressing the gap between the principle of spiritual fatherhood professed by bishops and priests and its concrete expression today.

A Look at the Data Suggesting a Crisis of Communion

Despite the tensions of the current crisis, the survey found that an overwhelming number of priests and bishops are "flourishing."[4] In fact, while 87% of clergy who report a great deal of trust in their bishop seem to be flourishing, 77% are flourishing who report very little trust in their bishop.[5] Catholic clergy continue to find meaning and purpose in their vocation. How is it possible that this same group is experiencing significant burnout and suffering from a crisis of mistrust?

A closer look at the data indicates that almost half of the priests completing the survey reported one or more symptoms of ministry burnout. Yet of those three factors measuring burnout, the one most indicative of priest burnout was low. Rossetti and Rhoades studied the unique factors of burnout

3 While the study also references religious priests and their relationships with superiors (for whom the element of mistrust seemed lower), the focus of this chapter will be on diocesan clergy.

4 Using the measure developed by the Harvard Flourishing Program. See Tyler J. VanderWeele, "On the Promotion of Human Flourishing," *Proceedings of the National Academy of Sciences* 114, no. 31 (2017): 8148–56, https://doi.org/10.1073/pnas.1702996114

5 Vaidyanathan et al., "Well-Being, Trust, and Policy in a Time of Crisis."

among Catholic clergy and discovered that being tired and overworked had less of an impact on this population of clergy than whether they were enjoying ministry and having a strong sense of inner peace.[6] In the NSCP, while a third of respondents admitted feeling worn out and tired in their ministry and another third reported being emotionally drained, only a small percentage indicated that they speak about their ministry negatively. Consistent with Rossetti and Rhoades,[7] the nuance in the data suggests that burnout may be less of a problem than it initially appears, since few respondents were wrestling with negative thoughts about their ministry and priestly identity. Like many priests in ministry throughout history, they do not cling to cynicism, even though many feel overworked, emotionally drained, and frustrated with Church leadership.

The survey clearly indicated divergent perceptions of the relationships between priests and their bishops, such as the willingness expressed by bishops to help a priest with personal struggles versus the unwillingness expressed by priests to entrust a bishop with such struggles. A review of the follow-up interviews with over 100 priests confirmed extreme frustration and fear by many (though not all) in relation to their bishop. These interviews confirm a sense of discommunion, rooted in not being treated with the dignity of a mature, adult son. These results are similar to the results of the qualitative survey of priests conducted by Kane's 2008 research[8] on the attitudes of priests towards bishops after the 2002 Dallas Charter.

One of the most disconcerting survey responses, which is difficult to argue away—though possibly the one that offers the best opportunity for addressing a key issue—is that 82% of priests "strongly agree" or "agree" that they regularly fear being falsely accused of sexual abuse. Given the percentage of clergy who have been found to abuse (e.g. 4.4% according to the John Jay College of Criminal Justice),[9] it would seem logical that most priests responding to this

6 Stephen J. Rossetti and Colin J. Rhoades, "Burnout in Catholic Clergy: A Predictive Model Using Psychological and Spiritual Variables," *Psychology of Religion and Spirituality* 5, no. 4 (2013): 335–41, https://doi.org/10.1037/a0033639

7 See also Mary L. Gautier et al., *Same Call, Different Men: The Evolution of the Priesthood Since Vatican II* (Liturgical Press, 2012).

8 Michael N. Kane, "A Qualitative Survey of the Attitudes of Catholic Priests Toward Bishops and Ministry Following the Sexual Abuse Revelations of 2002," *Pastoral Psychology* 57 (2008): 183–98, https://doi.org/10.1007/s11089-008-0171-9

9 John Jay College of Criminal Justice, *The Causes and Context of Sexual Abuse*

question would experience such fear not because they are hiding some dark secret, but because they are afraid of events spinning out of their control. Just as disconcerting is the low percentage of diocesan priests who believe they would receive sufficient resources in the case of a false accusation. It would be difficult for bishops to argue that clergy have been given the necessary resources, when this is reportedly not the case at even higher levels in the Church.[10] In addition, the application of principles underlying the Dallas Charter to the cases of bishops who are accused of abuse only came into play in the 2019 Motu Proprio of Pope Francis, *Vos estis lux mundi*.[11]

In sum, the NSCP survey results point to the need for greater communion between bishops and clergy—and within the Church.

A Theological Reflection

A theological reflection on the relationship of the bishop and his presbyterate and their communion with the People of God could be a great step toward addressing this crisis of trust. The positive evidence of flourishing clergy—despite various challenges of the past twenty years—points to the crucial importance of priestly identity as essential to clergy resilience. The data from the NSCP suggests that priests are frustrated when bishops do not act as spiritual fathers and shepherds. Despite an emergent agreement among several theologians on the importance of spiritual paternity as key to priestly identity,[12] the obvious dissonance between the episcopate and presbyterate on the nature of spiritual fatherhood and its expression in the contemporary Church demands further reflection in order to bridge this deepening gap of trust between bishops and clergy, which affects communion within the entire Body of Christ.

---

of Minors by Catholic Priests in the United States, 1950–2010 (The City University of New York, 2002), https://www.usccb.org/offices/child-and-youth-protection/research

10 See, e.g., Elise A. Allen, "Top Anti-Abuse Expert Sets Record Straight on Resignation from Vatican Body," *Crux*, April 18, 2023, https://cruxnow.com/vatican/2023/04/top-anti-abuse-expert-sets-record-straight-on-resignation-from-vatican-body

11 Pope Francis, Apostolic Letter issued Motu Proprio *Vos estis lux mundi* (May 7, 2019). Available at vatican.va

12 See Anthony Isacco and David G. Songy, "Spiritual Fatherhood of Catholic Priests: Conceptualization and Practical Applications," *Spirituality in Clinical Practice* 9 (2022): 115, https://doi.org/10.1037/scp0000293

Essential Qualities for the Development of Spiritual Fatherhood

St. Paul had written about his own experience of spiritual fatherhood in the First Letter to the Corinthians: "It was I who begot you in Christ" (1 Cor 4:16). In the Second Letter to the Corinthians, he writes about his willingness to give his life for the souls of the people: "I will most gladly spend and be spent for your souls" (2 Cor 12:15). Every priest participates in this tradition, embracing the Church as spouse and the people of God entrusted to him as a spiritual father.

Numerous Catholic theologians have described spiritual fatherhood, a tradition dating back to pre-Christian times. Essentially, spiritual fatherhood is an aspect of priestly *character*, in which the sacrament of holy orders "configures the recipient to Christ by a special grace of the Holy Spirit, so that he may serve as Christ's instrument for his Church."[13] The Catechism of the Catholic Church places the sacrament of holy Orders under the heading "Sacraments at the Service of Communion" (*CCC* no. 1533–35). Matrimony and holy orders are "directed toward the salvation of others" (*CCC* no. 1534). Both matrimony and holy orders have spousal and generative elements, calling all who have received such sacraments to experience holiness by donating themselves for the salvation of another.[14]

According to Christopher Lockwood,[15] a priest generates new life in the order of grace and represents Christ and the Father as an *agent*, *icon*, *instrument*, and *merciful face*. The priest teaches, sanctifies, and shepherds in collaboration with God—as Christ did. Spiritual fatherhood "cannot be reduced to spiritually generative sacramental actions but is meant to flow into fatherly identity and behavior: to *protect, provide for, rear and mentor, teach, sanctify, and shepherd—to love with the love of God*."[16]

13 *Catechism of the Catholic Church* (Libreria Editrice Vaticana, Catholic Book Publishing Co., 1994), no. 1581.

14 Cf. David G. Songy, *Spiritual Direction for Priestly Celibacy* (Capuchin Province of Mid-America, 2012), 101.

15 Christopher Lockwood, "Spiritual Fatherhood After the Model of Christ in the Gospel According to John," *Greek Orthodox Theological Review* 59 (2010): 81–127.

16 Roger J. Landry, "Renewing Spiritual Fatherhood," *National Catholic Register*, February 23, 2019, emphasis mine, https://www.ncregister.com/commentaries/renewing-spiritual-fatherhood

A review of magisterial documents and theological works on the process of seminary formation can contribute to an understanding of how the Church views spiritual fatherhood. The Congregation for the Clergy in *The Gift of the Priestly Vocation: Ratio Fundamentalis* (*Ratio*) outlined several elements of the priestly formation process requiring significant renovation and pointed to the importance of forming spiritual fathers. "As a member of the holy People of God, the priest is called to cultivate his missionary zeal, exercising his pastoral responsibility with humility as an authoritative leader, teacher of the Word and minister of the sacraments, practicing his spiritual fatherhood fruitfully."[17]

In describing the formation of a spiritual father, seminary professor Father Lucio Casto suggested several essential areas to be developed: affective maturity, pastoral charity, prayerfulness, awareness of the other as a child of God, and being in communion with the Church.[18] In my previous work, I have described six important human qualities of the priestly celibate: human freedom, affective maturity, the capacity to relate to others, an integrated human sexuality, a well-formed conscience, and virtue.[19] Diocesan seminary rector Father Carter Griffin recommended human formation in masculine identity, sacrificial self-giving, responsibility, making and keeping commitments, sincerity and humility, warmth, tenderness, fortitude, and seriousness.[20] Father Jacques Philippe of the Community of the Beatitudes has recently described the importance of unconditional love and words of authority for priests as spiritual fathers and describes several behaviors that hinder spiritual fatherhood: absence, severity, chumminess, the Superman, the Businessman, and power.[21] Interestingly, Philippe's description of behaviors that hinder spiritual fatherhood in priests echoes many priests' descriptions of bishops in the NSCP.

In April of 2022, the United States Conference of Catholic Bishops (USCCB) promulgated the sixth edition of the *Program of Priestly Formation*

17 Congregation for the Clergy, *The Gift of the Priestly Vocation: Ratio Fundamentalis Institutionis Sacerdotalis* (L'Osservatore Romano, 2016).

18 Lucio Casto, *La direzione spirituale come paternità* (Effatà Editrice, 2003).

19 Songy, *Spiritual Direction for Priestly Celibacy.*

20 Carter Griffin, *Why Celibacy? Reclaiming the Fatherhood of the Priest* (Emmaus Road Publishing, 2019).

21 Jacques Philippe, *Priestly Fatherhood: Treasure in Earthen Vessels* (Scepter Publishers, 2021).

(*PPF*), outlining the revised program of training for seminarians in the United States and promoted the importance of spiritual fatherhood:

> The diocesan priest entrusted with the care of souls in many ways normally serves in parochial ministry. In the parish he will encounter the day-to-day joys and sorrows of the faithful as he accompanies them throughout life, continually leading them to encounter Christ. This art of accompaniment, which develops in the heart of the seminarian and continues to deepen in the heart of the priest, allows him lovingly to accompany the flock entrusted to him; he thus becomes a **spiritual father** to his people.[22]

The *PPF*, quoting extensively from the *Ratio,* noted that a key element in formative accompaniment is **mutual trust**.

> It is essential that "the seminarian should know himself and let himself be known" (*Ratio Fundamentalis*, 45). This openness is required for real formation to happen. If a man hides his struggles in formation, growth cannot happen. The seminary community should seek to create the conditions that foster this peaceful climate of trust and mutual confidence through relationships marked by "fraternity, empathy, understanding, the ability to listen and to share, and especially a coherent witness of life" (*Ratio Fundamentalis*, 47). This climate of mutual confidence will be helped by the formators accompanying the seminarians outside of formal meetings in meals, recreation, and other potentially formative experiences. These times can provide excellent opportunities to know the seminarians and provide the formation that comes from witness of life and ordinary encounters. *When the seminarian experiences that the priest formators live true fatherhood seeking his good, and that the life of the seminary is marked by a spirit of true fraternity, this trust will not be difficult to establish.*[23]

22 United States Conference of Catholic Bishops, *The Program of Priestly Formation in the United States of America*, 6th ed. (USCCB, 2022), no. 44, emphasis mine. Hereafter *PPF.*

23 *PPF,* 6th ed., no. 101, emphasis mine.

These words on the connection between spiritual fatherhood and the importance of mutual trust could suggest that the current crisis in communion between clergy and superiors points to a need to strengthen the relationship in a manner consistent with the very principles clergy and superiors profess.

The *PPF* described several "benchmarks" to determine whether a seminarian has responded freely to the graces that would engender a mature priesthood.[24] Benchmarks are evaluative principles to help formators and seminarians discern sufficient growth in formation. The human formation benchmarks touch on self-knowledge and awareness, relational skills, self-discipline, a trusting relationship with formators, and healthy habits of self-care.

- Self-knowledge and awareness refer to a seminarian's growth in human virtues, i.e., the ability to internalize values and overcome individualism. They need to possess interior freedom, self-possession, self-motivation, and direction. Such self-knowledge permits ongoing growth.
- Relational skills include the capacity for healthy, deep friendships; the ability to maintain appropriate boundaries; the development of social skills and good manners, flexibility, and adaptability; empathy and the capacity for appropriate emotional sharing; solidarity, compassion, and attentive listening; the ability to relate to peoples from various states of life and different cultures; wholesome friendships with priests and others; and demonstrating the ability to live the communal nature of the priesthood.
- Self-discipline refers to hard work, the appropriate use of time, basic self-control, and academic responsibility.
- A trusting relationship with formators involves openness to correction, transparency, and accountability, leading to an ability to exercise authority and leadership well among peers and a commitment to mentoring relationships with men and women who assist in his pastoral placement.

24 *PPF*, 6th ed., no. 163.

- Healthy habits of self-care include maintaining good health, managing stress, developing a workable strategy for handling psychological issues in one's life, and having well-established habits regarding the proper use of technology.

Interestingly, the *PPF,* in discussing every dimension of formation—i.e., human, spiritual, pastoral, and intellectual—never mentions "fatherhood" as a benchmark to be reached. It does, however, tie fatherhood to the role of formator: "The rector ... is seen as the father of the entire seminary community,"[25] and "the formator helps to discern whether a call is present and to foster it to its fullness by relating to the man as a shepherd and a father."[26]

If shepherding and fathering are inherent to the initial formation of seminarians, it would seem incumbent on bishops and clergy to embrace these qualities. Every bishop or priest has been formed in a seminary or house of religious formation, having been taught essential characteristics of priests as spiritual fathers. In addition, the *Directory for the Pastoral Ministry of Bishops: Apostolorum successores* (Congregation for Bishops, 2004) makes clear the essential role of bishops as fathers and shepherds:

> Some dynamic images of the Bishop, drawn from Scripture and from the Tradition of the Church, such as the image of the shepherd, the fisherman, the father, the brother, the friend, the comforter, the servant, the teacher, the leader, the *sacramentum bonitatis,* point to Jesus Christ and characterize the Bishop as a man of faith and discernment, a man of hope and serious commitment, a man of gentleness and compassion, a man of communion. These images indicate that to enter into the Apostolic succession is to enter into combat for the Gospel. Among the different images, that of the *shepherd* illustrates with particular eloquence the breadth of the episcopal ministry, in that it expresses its meaning, purpose, style and evangelical missionary dynamism.[27]

25 *PPF,* 6th ed., no. 98.

26 *PPF,* 6th ed., no. 99.

27 Congregation for Bishops, *Directory for the Pastoral Ministry of Bishops: Apostolorum successores* (L'Osservatore Romano, 2004), no. 2, emphasis mine.

The document is replete with references to the bishop as a father: "He should behave like a father towards everyone."[28] "This human and affective maturity is required of the Bishop if, like a good father, he is to exercise his episcopal authority as an authentic service to the unity and right ordering of the family of God's children."[29] "The Bishop, realizing that he is not only father and head of the particular Church, but also a brother in Christ and a member of the Christian faithful, does not act as if he were above the law, but observes the same rule of justice which he applies to others."[30] "The Bishop is father of the priestly family and through him the Lord Jesus Christ is present among believers."[31] Indeed, one section of the document is entitled: "76. *The Bishop: Father, Brother and Friend of Diocesan Priests.*" The document insists that a bishop should have a personal acquaintance with his priests and be attentive to their needs, especially "priests in difficulties."[32] However, there are times when the bishop is to intervene charitably but with justice in mind:

> In the event of *scandalous conduct*, the Bishop should intervene with charity, yet firmly and decisively: whether through admonition or correction, or by taking steps towards removal or transfer to an office in which the occasion for such misconduct does not arise. If these measures are unsuccessful or insufficient, in view of the gravity of the misconduct or the obstinacy of the cleric, the Bishop should impose the penalty of suspension according to the law or, in extreme cases provided for in canonical norms, he should initiate a penal process aimed at dismissal from the clerical state.[33]

The apparent crisis in communion among clergy and Bishops points to the need for ongoing formation for all parties, i.e., religious and diocesan priests, religious Superiors, and Bishops.

The USCCB recently published a *Guide to Ongoing Formation of Priests* (2023), which addresses ongoing formation for spiritual fatherhood.

28 *Apostolorum successores*, 45. Hereafter *AS*.
29 *AS*, 50.
30 *AS*, 66.
31 *AS*, 75.
32 *AS*, 81.
33 *AS*, 81, emphasis mine.

> The priest's spiritual fatherhood is more than a mere metaphor for his ministry. Like a natural father, he shares in the Fatherhood of God by generating life and loving in a distinctly paternal way. For example, the priest provides for his people in the order of grace, particularly by administering the sacraments. He guides them along the way of truth and salvation, especially in his preaching and teaching. He protects them from harmful spiritual and moral influences through his courageous and loving counsel and personal sacrifice. These and other paternal responsibilities depend upon a constellation of human virtues that natural and spiritual fathers have in common.[34]

The document goes on to describe important markers of ongoing formation in spiritual fatherhood: the capacity to sacrifice and be generous; discipline and responsibility, and "humility in the exercise of paternal authority"; sincerity, patience, and kindness; the "courage to protect his family"; and commitment.[35]

Fatherhood in Psychology

Until recently, little psychological scholarship had examined the spiritual fatherhood of Catholic priests.[36] In our article, Isacco and I focused on three major themes in the psychological literature on fatherhood and sonship that can help inform a discussion on spiritual fatherhood for Catholic priests: father involvement, paternal identity, and masculinity.

Lamb and Pleck have both researched father involvement, that is, the importance of fathers being present and engaging in positive activities with their children.[37] Fathers have a positive impact on their families when they are accessible and available, warm and responsive, and at the same time

34 United States Conference of Catholic Bishops, *Guide to Ongoing Formation of Priests* (USCCB, 2023), no. 114.

35 *Guide to Ongoing Formation of Priests*.

36 Cf. Isacco and Songy, "Spiritual Fatherhood of Catholic Priests."

37 Michael E. Lamb, "How Do Fathers Influence Children's Development? Let Me Count the Ways," in *The Role of the Father in Child Development,* 5th ed., ed. Michael Lamb (Wiley, 2010), 1–26. Joseph Pleck, "Paternal Involvement: Revised Conceptualization and Theoretical Linkages with Child Outcomes," in Lamb, *The Role of the Father*, 58–93.

responsible for their children: caring for, providing, and protecting. This leads to positive child development.[38] Isacco conducted a qualitative study, asking priests, "What are the characteristics of a good priest?" Three were identified: "generously available to the people"; "People-oriented"; and "Be and bring Christ to people."[39] It should be noted that the data in the NSCP clearly indicates that many priests find this element of fatherhood lacking in their experience of bishops in the US.

Paternal identity refers to "the set of interior mechanisms that relate to external fulfillment of paternal roles, i.e., the concrete experience of being a father and caring for the needs and development of children."[40] The crisis of communion among clergy seems to be directly tied to this issue: varied understandings of paternal identity. Most men develop this sense from their own experience of having a father or seeing other paternal models. Research has shown, however, that a man's ideal of his paternal identity is not always consistent with his behaviors.[41] In considering the data from the NSCP, one may posit that many priests see the professed spiritual father identity of their bishops as inconsistent with their actions. At the same time, at the root of the clergy child abuse crisis was a failure on the part of many—priests and bishops alike—to act as spiritual fathers. Needless to say, sexual abuse is the polar opposite of a truly fatherly way for priests to relate to young people or those under their authority. In a similar way, confusion regarding paternal identity among bishops has contributed to the crisis of communion.

The study of the psychology of masculinity has undergone numerous developments in recent years.[42] One useful resource that may be acceptable

38 See also Ross D. Parke, *Fatherhood* (Harvard University Press, 1996).

39 Anthony Isacco, "A Developmental Model of Evidence-Based Interventions for Catholic Clergy," Paper presented at the *Catholic Psychotherapy Association Annual Conference,* Scottsdale, AZ, May 2020.

40 Isacco and Songy, "Spiritual Fatherhood of Catholic Priests," 119.

41 See Kari Adamsons and Kay Pasley, "Parents' Fathering Identity Standards and Later Father Involvement," *Journal of Family Issues* 37 (2016): 221–44, https://doi.org/10.1177/0192513X13514407, and Sandra Tremblay and Tamarha Pierce, "Perceptions of Fatherhood: Longitudinal Reciprocal Associations Within the Couple," *Canadian Journal of Behavioural Science* 43, no. 2 (2011): 99–110, https://doi.org/10.1037/a0022635

42 Anthony Isacco and Jay C. Wade, *Religion, Spirituality, and Masculinity: New Insights for Counselors* (Routledge, 2019).

to a Roman Catholic clergy population is the Positive Psychology–Positive Masculinity (PPPM) paradigm, which focuses on the traditional, positive aspects of masculinity.[43] The PPPM suggests that there are "eleven positive characteristics to traditional masculinity that are worth promoting among men and priests."[44] These include relational style, caring, generative fatherhood, self-reliance, worker-provider tradition, respect for women, courage, group and team orientation, service, use of humor, and heroism. Many of these characteristics have been identified in the Church documents on initial and ongoing formation.[45]

The Broader Historical and Social Perspective

A broader crisis in fatherhood in contemporary American culture is attested to by numerous authors.[46] Absent fathers impact not only the children directly affected but society itself. More than 20 million children in the US grow up without fathers in the home. Children without fathers often leave school before graduating and struggle more in developing careers.

Many Church leaders and intellectuals have addressed the crisis of fatherhood and its effects on the contemporary Church, including Pope Francis in *Patris corde: An Apostolic Letter on 150th Anniversary of the Proclamation of St. Joseph as Patron of the Universal Church*:

43 Mark S. Kiselica et al., "Accentuating Positive Masculinity: A New Foundation for the Psychology of Boys, Men, and Masculinity," in *APA Handbooks in Psychology: APA Handbook of Men and Masculinities*, ed. Y. Joel Wong and Stephen R. Wester (American Psychological Association, 2016), 123–43.

44 Isacco and Songy, "Spiritual Fatherhood of Catholic Priests," 120.

45 Cf. *Ratio Fundamentalis*, 2016; *PPF*, 6th ed.; *Guide to Ongoing Formation of Priests*, 2023.

46 Cf., e.g., David Blankenhorn, *Fatherless America: Confronting Our Most Urgent Social Problem* (HarperCollins, 1996); Angelica Yolanda Barrera, "Educational Attainment and Growth Among Individuals with Absent Fathers" (PhD diss., Walden University, 2021); Autumn P. King, "The National Fatherhood League: Increasing Father Involvement in the Black American Community" (DSW diss., California Baptist University, 2022); and Flory L. Perone Seidel, "The Proclivity of Juvenile Crime in Fatherless Homes: An Urban Perspective," (PsyD diss., University of Arizona, 2021).

> Children today often seem orphans, lacking fathers. The Church too needs fathers. Saint Paul's words to the Corinthians remain timely: "Though you have countless guides in Christ, you do not have many fathers" (1 Cor 4:15). Every priest or bishop should be able to add, with the Apostle: "I became your father in Christ Jesus through the Gospel." Paul likewise calls the Galatians: "My little children, with whom I am again in travail until Christ be formed in you!" (4:19).[47]

Pope Francis's predecessors also pointed to a crisis of fatherhood, which affects not only relationships between priests and bishops, but also relationships between clergy and the faithful. St. John Paul II wrote about this crisis as an ongoing consequence of original sin, which "*attempts to abolish fatherhood,* destroying its rays which permeate the created world, placing in doubt the truth about God who is Love and leaving man only with a sense of the master-slave relationship."[48]

Pope Benedict XVI began to address the crisis of fatherhood long before he took on the papal mantle:

> The crisis of fatherhood that we are experiencing today is a basic aspect of the crisis that threatens mankind as a whole. Where fatherhood is perceived only as a biological accident on which no genuinely human claims may be based, or the father is seen as a tyrant whose yoke must be thrown off, something in the basic structure of human existence has been damaged.[49]

As pope, he would describe the importance of divine fatherhood for communion in the Church and world:

> God's fatherhood is more real than human fatherhood, because he is the ultimate source of our being; because he has thought and willed us from all eternity; because he gives us our true paternal home, which

47 Pope Francis, *Patris corde: An Apostolic Letter on the 150th Anniversary of the Proclamation of St. Joseph as Patron of the Universal Church* (December 8, 2020), 7. Available at vatican.va

48 John Paul II, *Crossing the Threshold of Hope* (Knopf, 1994), 228, emphasis mine.

49 Joseph Ratzinger, *The God of Jesus Christ: Meditations on God in the Trinity* (Franciscan Herald Press, 1979), 29.

> is eternal. And if earthly fatherhood divides, heavenly fatherhood unites. Heaven, then, means that other divine summit from which we all come and to which we are all meant to return. The fatherhood that is "in heaven" points us toward the greater "we" that transcends all boundaries, breaks down all walls, and creates peace.[50]

Within the theological literature on the subject, Father José Granados's masterful article, "Priesthood: The Sacrament of the Father," employed the wisdom of various philosophers and theologians. He began with the following account, touching on the crisis of fatherhood in the 19th century Church:

> In his play *Le Père humilié* (The Humiliated Father), Paul Claudel depicts the suffering of Pope Pius IX during the siege of the Vatican in 1870. The pope, about to be made a prisoner, speaks as a father who is wounded by the hatred of his children. In his dialogue with a humble Franciscan who has just heard his confession, he says: "Will they be any happier when they have no Father? If I am no longer with them, through whom will they be brothers? Will there come among them greater amity and love? . . . Does a child ever grow up sufficiently to be able to do without his father? Can a father ever grow so old that he has no need of his children?"[51]

Granados goes on to explain that Claudel juxtaposes the threatened loss of the spiritual fatherhood of the pope with the loss of fatherhood in the world. According to Granados, "we are no longer able to understand who a priest is because we no longer know who a father is. In addition, the lack of understanding of priestly fatherhood . . . has contributed to the current eclipse of fatherhood in our society."[52]

Finally, the *Guide to Ongoing Formation of Priests* addresses the impact of the wider American culture on the communion within the Church. The document acknowledges the increase in social divisions, new prejudices,

50 Benedict XVI, *Jesus of Nazareth: From the Baptism in the Jordan to the Transfiguration* (Doubleday, 2007), 141–42.

51 José Granados, "Priesthood: A Sacrament of the Father," *Communio: International Catholic Review* 36, no. 2 (2009): 186, https://www.communio-icr.com/files/Granados_Paternity_Format.pdf

52 Granados, "Priesthood," 187.

intensifying political ideologies, and polarized worldviews: "This atmosphere of bitter antagonism has seeped into the Church and even into the priesthood. It does not make the pursuit of holiness any easier for our priests, who themselves are sometimes swept into a highly emotivist approach to resolving conflict."[53] A "highly secularized society" is placing pressure on the Church to change doctrine and has "championed a view of the human person and human sexuality that directly opposes the Christian point of view."[54] This section concludes with a stark summary:

> The situation seems bleak, especially if we priests are not finding strength and consolation in our union with God. A priest who lacks deep roots can easily be carried away by any—let alone all—of these obstacles. Building strong foundations of a holy, healthy priesthood is ever more necessary if we are to respond to these obstacles with confidence, peace, and joy. This document proposes a way of life that will make it possible.[55]

Recommendations for Bridging the Gap

The priests interviewed in the NSCP identified three needs for improving trust in their bishops: bishops should strengthen their personal relationships as fathers and brothers with priests, improve transparency and communication, and be accountable themselves. Notably, all of the recommendations involved changes to be made by bishops. In addition, the suggestions cover a wide range of expectations.

The *PPF* offers an excellent format for the formation of seminarians, which is based on the important movement from self-knowledge to self-possession to self-gift.[56] The USCCB's *Guide to Ongoing Formation for Priests* employs this language as well. If the Church in the United States were to take a cue from its own models of priestly formation, it would make sense that the restoring of trust begin with a period of growth in self-knowledge, followed by a process that would bring about greater self-possession rooted in

53 *Guide to Ongoing Formation of Priests*, no. 55.
54 *Guide to Ongoing Formation of Priests*, no. 57.
55 *Guide to Ongoing Formation of Priests*, no. 58.
56 *PPF*, 6th ed., no. 100.

priestly identity, and culminate in an experience of self-gift and a consequent experience of communion.

Psychologists employ a competence model of learning that could aid in this process. It involves three factors: (a) Self-awareness, (b) Knowledge, and (c) Skills. "Self-awareness is the key mechanism to gaining knowledge and developing skills."[57] It is essential to bridge any gaps between priestly identity as fathers and shepherds and behaviors that are inconsistent. Self-awareness can be achieved by asking the simple question, "How am I at being a man/masculine/a father?" Knowledge is found in answering the query: "What does it mean to be a man/masculine/a father?" Finally, "What do I need to learn about being a man/masculine/a father?" can help clergy to identify which skills need to be developed. Such questions need to be asked by all parties, both priests and bishops.

The institution for which I work, Saint Luke Institute Clergy & Religious Health Monitor,[58] is an example of an instrument designed to help a diocese or religious order begin a process of greater self-awareness among clergy or religious, helping leaders to understand organizational strengths and challenges and serving as a starting point for dialogue. Such an instrument could be adapted to help clergy grow in self-awareness regarding any crisis of communion within their local church environment. Greater self-awareness by all parties could lead to proposals to promote knowledge that can contribute to better mutual understanding of people and issues, as well as determining which skills need further development. Knowledge and skills may be accrued through various educational events. In addition, clergy could benefit from forming groups to discuss mutual experiences, increasing the self-awareness of the local Church. A diocese could use this process to develop ongoing formation goals and a process of ongoing evaluation of progress that leads to deeper communion.

Crucial to any process will be a reflection on spiritual fatherhood and priestly identity by priests and bishops. They need to explore whether their behaviors reflect their identity as spiritual fathers and brothers. It would be helpful for them to discuss their operating models of paternity and masculinity and confront the reality of clericalism or indifference. There

57 Isacco and Songy, "Spiritual Fatherhood of Catholic Priests," 124.

58 Saint Luke Institute Clergy & Religious Health Monitor, last accessed July 27, 2024, https://sli.org/health-monitor

should be transparent conversations to address specifically the fear of priests regarding false accusations. Every priest should be familiar with processes for dealing with accusations and should feel free to discuss its impact on being in communion with his bishop.

Some dioceses have created the role of a priest mentor or clergy companion. It could be helpful for various parties to work on developing a position description that provides for the necessary support of individual clergy as well as an atmosphere of communion. This may seem idealistic, but the more the Church embraces her spiritual values and fosters priestly identity, the greater the possibility of success. A priest mentor or clergy companion would not be a civil or canon law advocate, nor would he be someone in the chain of command above the priest. Rather, he would take on the role of a spiritual father or brother to accompany a peer through any challenges. If a priest has hurt another, he should be responsible for the consequences of his actions. This could mean significant loss and humiliation for the offender. However, a priest mentor could be a spiritual father to him in this situation. This may lead to a greater acceptance of consequences and a transformational experience of forgiveness.

St. Francis of Assisi wrote a letter to a Superior in the Order, offering the following advice for dealing with a sinful brother:

> I wish to know in this way if you love the Lord and me, His servant and yours: that there is not any brother in the world who has sinned—however much he could have sinned—who, after he has looked into your eyes, would ever depart without your mercy, if he is looking for mercy. And if he were not looking for mercy, you would ask him if he wants mercy. And if he would sin a thousand times before your eyes, love him more than me so that you may draw him to the Lord; and always be merciful with brothers such as these.[59]

This is the experience priests desire. Consequences must be faced, but facing them with the help of a father or brother could help bridge the gap and heal the crisis of communion in the Church today. By providing such a priest mentor, a bishop could show his fatherhood to his priests when offering such

59 Francis of Assisi, "A Letter to a Minister (1221–1223)," in *Francis of Assisi: Early Documents*, vol. I, ed. Regis J. Armstrong et al. (New City Press, 1999), 97.

accompaniment is difficult to do directly given his own legal responsibilities and position of power. Whether through this means or some other, showing mercy to his priests while still providing justice and restitution for victims is what is required of the bishop as a spiritual father to all in his diocese. It is also consistent with Canon 1752, emphasizing "the salvation of souls, which is always the supreme law of the Church (*salus animarum suprema lex*)."[60]

60 *Code of Canon Law: Latin-English Edition* (Canon Law Society of America, 1999), can. 1752.

FROM CRISIS TO COMMUNION: REBUILDING TRUST WITHIN THE PRIESTHOOD IN THE DIOCESE OF FALL RIVER

Most Rev. Edgar M. da Cunha, SDV, and Matthew Robinson

The universal Church, the Church in the United States, and the local Church here in the Diocese of Fall River, Massachusetts, have been incredibly blessed by the profound work of The Catholic Project at The Catholic University of America.

Specifically, in the coming pages, we hope to share the impact on our diocese of the National Study of Catholic Priests in 2022, which, as the most extensive priesthood study in over fifty years, looked at priestly well-being in the context of the Church's response to the abuse crisis.

One of the things that we appreciate most regarding the work of The Catholic Project and the study at hand is that they have clearly and courageously answered the call of the Second Vatican Council to utilize the secular sciences and place them at the service of Christ and His Church. For example, we read in *Gaudium et spes*: "In pastoral care, sufficient use must be made not only of theological principles, but also of the findings of the secular sciences, especially of psychology and sociology, so that the faithful may be brought to a more adequate and mature life of faith."[1] While we often think

1 Vatican Council II, *Gaudium et spes* (December 7, 1965), no. 62. All Vatican documents are available at vatican.va unless otherwise noted. All Vatican documents available at Vatican.va unless otherwise noted.

of pastoral care in terms of the Church's efforts to bring the truth and love of Christ to the laity in various moments of life, we must never forget that our priests and bishops—as human beings and disciples first and foremost—need their own pastoral care as this study clearly affirmed.

One might ask, what difference does offering pastoral care to our own shepherds make? When we read the National Study of Catholic Priests, which, as we shall explore further in a moment, highlights the pivotal need for supporting our priests and the importance of the bishop-priest relationship toward that end, we were reminded of the famous story of compassion offered by Pope Saint John Paul II to the "beggar priest."

For those unaware of this story, Scott Hahn has often recounted the true story of one of his priest-friends who was visiting Rome. Among other commitments, this priest was scheduled for a private audience with Pope John Paull II. When the day of the private audience arrived, the priest happened across a group of poor beggars outside a church in Rome. To his amazement, he recognized one of the beggars saying, "Do I know you?" "Yes," the beggar replied. "I studied for the priesthood with you here in Rome and was ordained." The "beggar priest" would go on to explain how he encountered a crisis and lost everything.

This encounter weighed heavily upon the priest's heart and mind at the papal audience. In fact, he relayed this experience to Pope John Paul II, who, to his amazement, asked him to bring the "beggar priest" over for dinner.

After dinner, the Pope was left alone with the "beggar priest" for a private visit. After about 15 minutes, the "beggar priest" departed from his private papal visit in tears. He would later recount that the Holy Father heard his confession and asked him to hear his own, saying, "My son, once a priest, always a priest. We are all beggars."

This moment of love, compassion, and mercy offered by the Holy Father to a priest not only completely changed that priest's life, but offers the Church a stunning example of a holy relationship between bishops and priests.

As the Church continues to reflect upon the findings of the NSCP, we hope and pray that the following reflections may provide a practical example of how each of us, in our own capacity as clergy, laity, or religious, can work towards strengthening and supporting our priests for the ultimate benefit of furthering the mission of the Church.

The Foundational Reason to Strengthen, Support, and Renew Our Priests

Before highlighting specific findings and their impact on the Diocese of Fall River, perhaps a prior question must be asked: Why is it essential for bishops, the Church, and various apostolates (such as The Catholic Project) to continually study, pray, and implement practical strategies that focus on the health, holiness, and pastoral effectiveness of our priests?

As a starting point, it is essential to recall the consistent research showing that ***thriving parishes and Church apostolates are generally led by happy and thriving priests***. Let us repeat that truth once more: flourishing priests are key to flourishing parishes. In other words, there is a connection between the priest's personal life (i.e., natural well-being and spiritual holiness) and authentically flourishing ministries. This recognition must take hold within our dioceses and church institutions.

Consequent to this truth (and continuing the theme of using the natural order and placing it in service of the Church), we might say that each presbyterate must be "the center of gravity" for the diocese. The concept of center of gravity within an organization originated from the US military, and it is defined as the source of power that provides moral or physical strength, freedom of action, or will to act. The center of gravity is usually seen as the "source of strength." Therefore, foundational in our work to move the local Church forward in relationship to Christ should always be to bring more stability, hope, holiness, and wellness to the presbyterate.

There is spiritual precedence for this reality as well. For example, the Spiritual Law of Causality states that there is a causal relationship between priests' holiness and the laity's holiness. As the Congregation for Clergy puts it in *The Priest, Pastor, and Leader of the Parish Community*, "a certain osmosis exists between the faith of the priest and that of the other faithful."[2] Or, as Dom Jean-Baptiste Chautard, OCSO, describes it in *The Soul of the Apostolate*: "If the Priest is a saint, the people will be fervent; if the priest is fervent, the people will be pious; if the priest is pious, the people will at least be decent; if the priest is only decent, the people will be godless. The spiritual generation is always one degree less intense in its life than the one who begets it in Christ."[3]

2 Congregation for the Clergy, *The Priest, Pastor, and Leader of the Parish Community* (August 4, 2002), no. 16.

3 Jean-Baptiste Chautard, *The Soul of the Apostolate* (TAN Books, 1946), 39.

To summarize, why should the bishops and the Church continually study, pray, and implement practical strategies that focus on our priests' health, holiness, and pastoral effectiveness? Because the very mission of the Church to preach the Gospel and dispense the mysteries of salvation depends on it.

One of the practical repercussions of such a reality is that perhaps the time has come for each diocese to consider further how to be more single-minded in strengthening and renewing its presbyterate, given the complex and challenging realities established in this study. Perhaps we do not need to try to evangelize the entire diocese at once; each parish only requires one person who is thriving personally and on fire for the Lord, the priest. A diocese with a presbyterate living their best lives will be a diocese that is set aflame for the love of the Lord (and probably in relatively short order). Was this not the model handed down by our Lord Himself, Who started with twelve apostles and changed the world? If it worked for Him, it will work for us.

The Urgent Need to Strengthen, Support, and Renew Our Priests

While the foundational and perennial importance of supporting and renewing our priests has been established due to the very nature of the priesthood and its intrinsic connection to the success of the Church, we now focus on the *urgent* need to do so, given the current secular and ecclesial landscapes.

Why might there be an urgent need to strengthen, support, and renew our priests? Obviously, the NSCP delivered to the Church a number of significant albeit difficult contemporary realities that have ignited in our diocese a heightened sense of urgency. In many ways, the study renewed in our minds the perhaps prophetic words of Servant of God Fr. John Hardon, SJ: "Having taught priests over 30 years, having lived with priests, and having labored for them, loving them and suffering with them—no words I can use would be too strong to state that the Catholic priesthood needs prayer and sacrifice as never before since Calvary. One saint after another has declared that the devil's principal target on earth is the Catholic priest. Priests need, Lord how they need, special graces from God."[4]

4 John A. Hardon, SJ, "The Value of Prayer and Sacrifice for Priests," "Lent: Praying the Sorrowful Mysteries for Priests," *Father John A. Hardon, S.J. Archives* (The Real Presence Association, 1998), http://www.therealpresence.org/archives/Prayer/Prayer_014.htm

If that was true a few decades ago, it seems all the more true today. The first author's experience of over 42 years of priesthood, serving in multiple capacities, including in vocations and seminarian formation with the Vocationist Fathers, as well as 21 years as a bishop, certainly has confirmed that despite the many joys of the priesthood, many presbyterates are in a great need of healing and renewal. Obviously, The Catholic Project's findings and other scientific data provide ample evidence of this reality. It seems priests need our support more than ever in Church history, as Fr. Hardon prophesized.

What evidence can we garner to make such a claim? One of the great benefits of the NSCP is that it provided a glimpse into our priests' inner—or perhaps hidden—lives. Priests are men of mystery to many in the Church. We tend to see them only in their ministerial capacity, but there is much that goes on in their hearts, minds, and lives!

Before considering this, a disclaimer is important. Every vocation has its joys and struggles. We are sure those who are married are fully aware of this reality. So, while we are considering the reality of challenges facing the priesthood, we should not make it seem like the priesthood is any different than other vocations in that sense. Second, we have many devoted, holy, and happy priests. Even the NSCP points out that, despite grave challenges facing our priests due to the continued fallout from the abuse crisis, 77% of priests are categorized as "flourishing." For the first author of this chapter, it has been and continues to be one of the great joys of his life to be able to minister alongside his brothers, both priests and bishops. He speaks for the Church when he says how grateful he is to the priests of the Diocese of Fall River and all priests and bishops worldwide. Ministry is a team sport, which we must never forget.

However, these realities do not mean we shouldn't look clearly and courageously at some of the severe struggles and trials many priests face. It is naïve to view priests as individuals alone without reference to the broader context of priestly morale, well-being, and ministerial effectiveness.

We are brought back down to earth quickly when we see that, according to the NSCP, almost 50% of priests report at least one symptom of ministry burnout. This is very concerning as burnout can lead to many adverse outcomes such as exhaustion, lack of motivation, cynicism, decreased satisfaction, frustration, inability to concentrate, negative outlook, self-doubt, mood changes, social isolation, and depression. We also know that while burnout exists in all vocations, priests are typically less likely to admit experiencing it, making it difficult to treat.[5]

Why is this happening? In general, seeing behaviors as a sort of "language" can be helpful. In other words, what might the behaviors associated with priest burnout be saying to us? In the Diocese of Fall River, we try to approach that question through two lenses: the lens of the individual priest and the lens of the organization and environment surrounding the priest. Both views are essential because we know that a person's behavior is not just the product of their choices but of the powerful way that the environment influences them one way or another. Sometimes, in the Church, there can be an emphasis on the priest's behaviors without taking into account the situation and environment surrounding the priest. This method must be rejected in favor of a holistic understanding of human behavior.

Let us return to the question of why priestly burnout may happen from the individual and organizational perspective. Some influential individual factors may include a lack of sufficient human formation, isolation, loneliness, and poor physical health. Some influential organizational factors may be too many parishes combined with a priest shortage, expectations for the superhuman performance of priests, parish ministry unyielding to priestly mission, untrained support/parish staff, poor clerical culture, lack of direction and accountability, and untenable rectory living situations. All of this leading to an exhaustion pandemic that has become normal. Many priests simply learn to tolerate being "out of gas."

Another very significant and startling statistic from the NSCP—which calls for a sense of urgency in the Church's care for priests—is the number of priests who report living in a state of fear regarding false accusations (82%).[6] This is a secondary trauma in the priesthood relating to the clergy abuse crisis and the lack of confidence some priests feel in due process protection. Among many significant negative repercussions of this finding is that feelings

5 Editor's note: In chapter 3, Maureen Day makes the point that the term "burnout" seems to carry a certain stigma among respondents to the NCSP; even if they admit to the elements of burnout, they do not "own" the term as such. But in chapter 8, Fr. Songy gives a hopeful reading of the data.

6 Editor's note: this fear and the strong reasons on which it is founded comprise chapter 7 of this book by Msgr. Thomas Guarino.

of unsafety can contribute to an "isolationist priesthood" (i.e., a priesthood that is lived "from a distance"—staying in an office/behind a desk, attending meetings, focusing on non-pastoral activity, even "hiding" behind the sacraments). A priest may think, "The diocese doesn't have my back if a false report is made, so I need to protect myself." All of this contributes to fear and impacts our presbyterates' morale, well-being, and effectiveness. As the NSCP also highlighted, this is one reason for the erosion of trust between priests and bishops, which, sadly, affects every area of priestly well-being as well.

Impact of Findings and Steps We Have Taken

The findings of this research urgently call for the Church to face the reality of the state of our presbyterates with courage, prayer, sacrifice, and humility.

In the Diocese of Fall River, already sensing the urgent need to support our priests in new ways, we hired a full-time Director of Clergy Support in 2019 to directly oversee and implement individual and programmatic initiatives aimed at priestly flourishing. This was a necessary first step. However, upon seeing the results of the NSCP in 2022 and after consultation with leaders in our diocese, we determined that we needed to go a step further and begin the process of making the foundational changes necessary to gather the diocese around the central theme of supporting our priests.

For us, the first step in this new process was to understand our local presbyterate's state on a deeper level. Utilizing the NSCP as a catalyst and starting point, we undertook our own "in-house" study to analyze national and diocesan data and review other relevant research to understand the current landscape of our presbyterate clearly. We reviewed the current situation from the perspective of the priest himself and from the organization's perspective. As discussed, both perspectives—individual and organizational characteristics—are essential to form the complete foundation for any person's personal and professional success.

In short, the essential findings of that study include the following:

1. Deficiencies in three specific areas of priestly life: human wellness, understanding priestly identity/mission, and lack of a balanced contemplative/active priestly lifestyle.
2. Deficiencies in diocesan and parish organizational structures leading to a less-than-ideal environment for priests.

Even in the midst of many incredible priests, these findings are leading to a generally frustrated and underperforming presbyterate plagued by insecurity, cynicism, self-doubt, chronic fatigue, a felt lack of support, and isolationism, and thus, men who are stuck in a low-level depressive and survivalist mode of existence.

Unfortunately, these issues have led to a significant number of priests requiring some level of intervention and/or enhanced support. When priests struggle to a level that may require some form of absence from ministry, this often leads to three consequences: damaged faith life in the laity, lowered morale in the presbyterate, and significant temporal strain on the diocese.

Due to this "in-house" study, prompted by the NSCP, we concluded that doing nothing was no longer an option. We indeed have good priests who became priests out of love for the Lord and a desire to share that love with others; however, we came to see that many of our priests are hurting, and many of the damaging behaviors we have witnessed (such as addictions, mental health crises, or misconduct) are none other than cries for help to be welcomed, rescued, healed, and restored as the Father did for the Prodigal Son and as Pope Saint John Paul II did for the "beggar priest."

We fully realized that it was time to courageously and innovatively consider how to adapt our priesthood and our diocese to the current realities of the contemporary secular and ecclesial landscapes. At this critical juncture, both the priests and the diocese needed a "paradigm shift" toward a new and more effective way of operating so that priests could be happier, freer, holier, and as effective as possible in bringing souls to Christ.

The good news is that, upon learning this new information, there was still a 2 to 3-year window to make foundational changes before these changes were to be forced upon us. By God's grace, we were in a privileged position to plan and execute a process prayerfully, allowing the Holy Spirit to take the lead and to turn what seems calamitous by human eyes into the very avenue through which Christ renews and restores our priests and, consequently, those they shepherd. Such a process will hopefully result in a presbyterate set up for success for years to come and a new positive ministerial environment where Christ can more readily reach every soul in our diocese through the mediation of His priests.

The next step for our diocese was to formulate a plan for priestly renewal. We began planning a three-year priestly renewal and restructuring process. It was and continues to be imperative that this is not conceptualized as another "program" or "document." This must be a process of action. This is, in effect, the whole diocese working together to help our priests be holy and successful, the benefits of which include a priesthood and diocese unleashing its full evangelical potential with thriving parishes, happy and holy priests, and financial stability. This plan would also be predicated upon both the presbyterate and the bishop making a mutual commitment to work proactively towards a new model of priestly wellness, holiness, and effectiveness.

The vision for this plan of priestly renewal is to ensure that our priests have both the training and the organizational support to uninhibitedly exercise their priestly ministry. This vision requires a clear understanding of the priesthood's purpose so that this project can be fully aligned with the truths of our faith.[7] In some respects, the purpose of the priesthood is simple: "to bring Christ's redemptive gifts to His people."[8] Subsequently, this project is organized to comprehensively address systemic personal and organizational obstacles that hinder our priests from confidently achieving this divinely-mandated mission.

As we continue to emphasize in this reflection, the field of social psychology has established that both individual differences and the environment drive human behavior. Any person (priest or laity) requires both individual knowledge, skills, and abilities and an environment that yields to their efforts to succeed in a given task or mission. An organization—any organization—cannot expect its members to "muscle through" an unsupportive environment. Likewise, individuals cannot expect an organization to be solely responsible for their actions.

For our purposes, this means that our priestly renewal project is designed to address diocesan-centric (environmental) and priest-centric (individual) obstacles to priestly success. The diocese will commit to creating a ministerial environment where priests can most readily accomplish their priestly mission, and the presbyterate will commit to addressing their own personal and professional obstacles to the same mission. Both are required for success.

The three diocesan-centric goals include fast-tracking pastoral planning, invigorating parish ministry, and developing a strong presbyteral culture.

7 Editor's note: chapter 6 of this book by Bishop Fredrik Hansen provides such a perspective, integrating canon law and theology.

8 United States Conference of Catholic Bishops, *Program of Priestly Formation*, 6th ed (USCCB, 2022), no. 41.

The three priest-centric goals include enhancing priestly holiness, improving personal and ministerial training and standards, and increasing vocations while enhancing seminarian formation.

Diocesan-Centric Strategies

Fast-Track Pastoral Planning

In our diocese, 50% of our pastors have multiple full-time assignments. By 2026, it is estimated that we will no longer be able to backfill retiring pastors with new pastors. These unsustainable realities are causing multiple adverse downstream effects.

Consequently, pastoral planning efforts will be accelerated, and innovative measures will be utilized to bring relief to our priests who are overextended by too many assignments.

It is believed that reducing the number of assignments is one of the quickest ways to improve presbyteral morale.

Invigorate Parish Ministry

What would it take to design parish ministry so that parishes are exciting places to minister for our priests? That is to say, places where priests are not routinely hampered by bureaucracy but are instead incentivized to preach, evangelize, offer the sacraments much more regularly, visit the sick, and so on.

The current reality is that many parishes are not exciting places to minister. For example, one priest who is a pastor in a parish that clearly needs to be closed described his ministry as "hospice care." Not "hospice care" in the sense of visiting those close to death, but "hospice care" in the sense of accompanying his parish that is close to death. Priests are men, and men need the opportunity to build, innovate, take risks, and lead, so a priest in a "hospice care" parish assignment is being set up for failure.

Other priests feel that parish ministry is primarily about being a "caretaker" of an institution, as the US Bishops pointed out in the recent *Guide to Ongoing Formation* (2023).[9] These priests feel like keeping the "customer" happy is the

9 USCCB, *Guide to Ongoing Formation of Priests*, available at https://www.usccb.org/resources

whole job. They feel they should simply keep the peace and do the minimum to ensure that the parish as an institution remains unchanged before moving on to the next assignment. For priests in this category, a job well done is an assignment without complaints to the diocese and a parish that has maintained itself. This should not be the image of success in our pastor's hearts and minds.

Exciting and successful parish ministry is currently being stifled by various obstacles: too much administration, poor support staff, a lack of pastoral agency, entitled non-practicing parishioners, fear of making meaningful changes, a lack of individualized diocesan direction, and so on. The Church must address these realities in order to set up priests for success. Our pastoral plan will concentrate on re-energizing parish ministry with new initiatives to allow our priests to focus on evangelization, the spiritual life, pastoral care, and sacramental ministry.

Develop a Strong Presbyteral Culture

It is no secret that a positive culture is the most critical factor in any organization's ability to achieve its goals. As Peter Drucker, one of the foremost experts in organizational growth, famously said, culture trumps strategy. In other words, having a positive culture is much more important and productive than having a strategy for reaching organizational goals. The reason is that culture guides attitudes and behaviors in the absence of rules and policies.

Research indicates that the best organizational cultures marry high care with high accountability. The order of these two elements is important because people need to feel loved and valued before they can withstand high accountability. But both of these elements are essential.

Put simply, an organization cannot expect its members to muscle through the natural fear of being vulnerable with their true thoughts and feelings. The organization has to provide protection for their vulnerability. Those who feel that they are safe to be vulnerable will perform, while those who feel unsafe to be vulnerable will be in a state of fear. For these reasons, no team can be entirely successful without psychological safety, and no innovation can occur without psychological safety.

In addition to addressing psychological safety, among other things, this goal will also include concrete steps to improving the feeling of ministerial safety, whereby the diocese will work towards strengthening the relationship between the bishop and priests and communicating due process protections.

Knowing the importance of positive culture in any organization, our presbyteral culture will be strengthened to promote fraternity and stability.

Priest-Centric Strategies

Enhance Priestly Holiness

Parish and diocesan stability ultimately hinges on priestly holiness. This is because a priest's growth in holiness always produces greater pastoral charity,[10] which is his ability to most effectively minister in the image and likeness of Christ. For this reason, "The priest can give no greater gift to his people than his own resolve to grow in sanctity."[11]

However, we know that the spiritual life is often weak in our diocesan presbyterate. Many do not make time for the essentials, such as private contemplative prayer, spiritual direction, spiritual reading, and group support. To reach our goals, priests must re-commit to the holiness of life.

Improve Personal and Ministerial Training and Standards

It has been noted that growth in holiness does not happen at the expense of human development. Grace builds on nature. In other words, a thriving priest must first be a thriving man.[12] Consequently, all the known elements necessary for human and masculine growth to maturity and well-being apply especially to priests, without which the grace of orders cannot take root.

Likewise, today's ministerial environment is an increasingly complex place to minister. We will focus on enhanced training of our priests to help them thrive and successfully minister in an increasingly challenging world. These efforts will also extend to those who support our priests (such as diocesan and parish staff and the lay faithful). We will also include improvements to priest personnel decision-making and individualized guidance.

Increase Vocations and Enhance Seminarian Formation

The sixth and final priority is enhancements in the number, quality, and formation of vocations to the diocesan priesthood. There is an urgent need for more vocations in our diocese and a corresponding need to enhance seminarian formation with the skills and competencies needed for the

10 *Guide to Ongoing Formation of Priests*, no. 153.

11 *Guide to Ongoing Formation of Priests*, no. 153.

12 *Guide to Ongoing Formation of Priests*, no. 25.

current landscape. Of course, men can more easily discern a vocation when they encounter thriving priests, so all of the prior goals will also feed into this one.

Conclusion

The NSCP has become an invaluable source of reflection and a catalyst for implementing new concrete strategies to strengthen our presbyterate. As the Church in the United States concludes the grace-filled Eucharistic Revival, perhaps the work of The Catholic Project has provided an avenue for us to prayerfully discern the renewal of that sacrament of service, which is intrinsically linked to the Body and Blood of Christ—holy orders.

We hope and pray that this may be a call to each one of us—bishops, priests, deacons, religious, and laity alike—to re-commit to our priests above all through prayer and sacrifice because, while concrete action is necessary, the renewal of our priesthood requires faith in God, fervent prayer, and constant attention to the inspirations of the Holy Spirit, without Whom every program in the Church is without fruit.

May the intercession of the Blessed Mother and St. John Vianney lead us into this new phase of priestly holiness, stability, and success.

CHAPTER TEN

SUMMARY OF RECOMMENDATIONS: STRENGTHENING THE PRIESTHOOD FOR THE FUTURE

Rev. Anthony Stoeppel and Sara Perla

As has been observed many times in the course of this book, a strong and vibrant presbyterate is essential to the life of the Church. Priests serve as spiritual fathers and shepherds, sustaining the faith and vitality of parish communities. However, for the priesthood to flourish, both individual priests and the broader ecclesial environment must be strengthened. This chapter synthesizes key insights and recommendations from the National Study of Catholic Priests (NSCP) and the previous chapters, offering concrete steps for renewing the presbyterate. These recommendations focus on four critical areas: supporting individual priests, strengthening fraternity among clergy, enhancing the role of the bishop in supporting clergy, and institutional/structural reform (see Table 10.1). By implementing these reforms, dioceses can cultivate a priesthood that is spiritually vibrant, pastorally effective, and deeply united in its mission.

Supporting Individual Priests

The first way to support priests individually is to remind them that Jesus Christ must be the center of their lives; the NSCP showed that priests who are most devoted to the Eucharist also report being the happiest and most fulfilled

Table 10.1 Recommendations for strengthening the priesthood

Category	Recommendation
Supporting individual priests	1. Prioritize Christ-centered priestly life, with strong devotion to the Eucharist and accountability in spiritual disciplines 2. Encourage habits of self-care and resilience including rest, boundaries, friendships, hobbies, and access to mental health services 3. Expand ongoing formation to include spiritual fatherhood, emotional regulation, conscience formation, and relevant pastoral topics 4. Offer leadership and management training for priests becoming pastors, integrated into seminary or post-ordination formation
Strengthening priestly fraternity	1. Foster priestly camaraderie through small groups, retreats, informal gatherings, and attention to isolated assignments 2. Establish fellowship groups mindful of diversity in the presbyterate yet providing strong community
Strengthening the bishop's role	1. Cultivate trust through consistent presence, listening, reliability, and maintaining confidences; take first steps in relationship-building 2. Promote structured opportunities for feedback in large dioceses and ensure every priest feels known and cared for 3. Lead by example in holiness, humility, and fairness; affirm faithful priests and act against known violations of priestly conduct
Institutional and structural reforms	1. Extend role of episcopal vicar for clergy to include responsibility for priestly formation and well-being 2. Establish dedicated funds and regular opportunities for theological and pastoral education 3. Create clear, standardized processes for handling abuse allegations, including due process and transparency under *Vos estis lux mundi*

in their ministry. There is no reason to persevere as a priest if Christ is not with you at all times. To support men of prayer and service, bishops should seek to ensure, as well as is possible, that their priests are diligent in praying the Liturgy of the Hours, saying Mass, hearing confessions regularly, and visiting the poor and sick. Bishops are encouraged to ask about these things specifically, not to gloss over them. Priests need accountability.

Relatedly, bishops and dioceses should also try to ensure that the habits of self-care and resilience have been inculcated in their priests (whether early in life, through seminary, or after ordination). While self-care may be a secular phrase, the elements comprised in it are perennial and not incompatible with a holy life: knowing when to draw boundaries, saying "no," making time for rest and restoration, going on retreats or vacations, spending time with friends, delegating responsibilities, accepting human limitations, engaging in hobbies, and the like. Priests should have clear and easy ways of accessing mental health services whenever they are in need of them, and they should be encouraged to seek counseling particularly when they have been supporting others through trauma. "Help the helper" is a saying from the field of social work that is applicable here. The Church ought not to ask priests to carry the cross alone; sometimes a Simon of Cyrene must help them carry it.

As a more formal way to support priests, we encourage bishops and dioceses to enhance ongoing priestly formation by offering expanded seminary and continuing education programs. These programs should emphasize elements of the priesthood that we know matter for priestly well-being: a sense of being a spiritual father to their people; affective maturity and ability to regulate themselves emotionally; and pastoral charity, or giving themselves in service that they see as meaningful. Ongoing formation should also support and encourage the priests' prayer lives, offering them opportunities to learn from various spiritualities (Ignatian, Franciscan, and so on). Communion with the Church should be fostered in formation programs, possibly engaging in study of the most recent papal documents or Vatican initiatives. It would also be worthwhile for ongoing formation to offer space for discussions on accompaniment, human freedom, and conscience formation—issues that come up constantly in pastoral ministry even if they are not named. (A person may come for pastoral counseling who is engaging in an objectively wrong act but who is subjectively convinced of their rightness.) Priests may also appreciate periodic refreshers on hot-button topics, such as human sexuality or masculinity, especially as they come up in the culture and social media. Finally, the bishop/diocese would do well simply to ask priests themselves what type of formation they would be interested in and what topics are most relevant to them; this will vary according to diocese.

Finally, much of the stress of the priesthood comes from being asked to do things that these men have had no background or training in. Present or expected future pastors should be offered classes or training in essential leadership and management skills, as well as in areas such as budgeting and human resources. If an "apprenticeship" period is not possible due to a shortage of priests in the diocese, these skills should be incorporated into seminary training. A priest should be given many opportunities to observe things such as pastoral council meetings, finance council meetings, employee interviews, building assessments, donor meetings, and the like, before he is expected to lead them. This will give priests more confidence in the administrative and practical aspects of their role (which are nevertheless pastoral, due to their connection to his identity as a shepherd).

Even if these opportunities for training and enrichment are already available, it can be difficult for priests to step away from the many demands on their time and energy. Therefore, it is generally preferable to make "continuing education" required by the diocese rather than merely suggested, or to include graded assignments rather than merely passive listening; this will allow the class and its material to rise to the level of a priority despite a crowded to-do list. Of course, priests are likely to prefer a continuing education program that lets them choose areas of interest to focus on. If the training is well-designed, in the long run priests will find that it helps lighten their burdens, rather than simply adding one more requirement.

Strengthening Priestly Fraternity

The NSCP found that priestly fraternity is an important element in priestly well-being. As such, bishops and dioceses should seek to foster priestly camaraderie by creating intentional spaces for peer support. This could be establishing small groups (or encouraging priests to form their own), priestly convocations or retreats, pilgrimages, or regular informal gatherings for priests like hikes, sports (playing or watching), or dinners. This becomes especially important in dioceses with generational or ideological divides in the presbyterate, where priests need to be encouraged to get to know one another as human beings and not through any ideological lens. Particularly noteworthy in this section is for bishops to pay attention to priests who are in demanding or isolated assignments, such as rural parishes, hospitals, and chaplaincies. It is imperative that those under the most practical strain are offered structured opportunities for connection and support that they do not have to initiate and that they know are available.

A bishop or diocese may also want to consider establishing formal or informal priestly fellowship groups, taking into account individual needs and the diversity of the presbyterate. Since priests from religious communities reported higher levels of well-being in the NSCP than diocesan priests, it is possible that fostering a deeper sense of community in the diocesan presbyterate will have beneficial effects. Of course, correlation is not causation, so it is possible that men who choose the diocesan priesthood are less inclined to be part of a group! Nevertheless, we encourage experimenting with this in order to see what helps.

Strengthening the Role of the Bishop in Supporting Priests

The bishop is meant to be a spiritual father to his priests, and while that analogy may be difficult in particular circumstances (such as when the bishop is younger than the priest), many of the principles still apply: a bishop ought to be available to the priest, open to listening to his problems, counseling him, and offering guidance and accountability. Since bishops have been priests, they ought to consider what they learned about good leadership when they, too, were under a bishop's authority. What did they appreciate that their bishop did for them? What did they not? Bishops ought to reflect on their experiences as priests if that will help them see their priests with compassion.

While the relationship of bishop to priest is never one of equals due to the difference in authority, it is not meant to be a cold or distant relationship. The two should be known to each other, at least in so far as that is possible. We recognize that in large archdioceses, individual knowledge of every priest would be impossible for one man. In that latter case, when there are hundreds of priests in a diocese, it might be helpful for bishops to institute structured opportunities for priests to voice their concerns and offer feedback. Priests are not generally unreasonable; they understand that bishops have demands on their time and may not be able to support the priest in all circumstances, but they do want to know that the bishop *cares*.

Since we learned through the NSCP that priests who trust their bishops are also generally doing better in every area of well-being, it greatly behooves bishops to improve their priests' trust in them. Ultimately this comes down to personal relationships, which we recognize is a difficult answer for bishops to hear.[1] There is no magic bullet here; trust is earned by repeatedly demonstrating trustworthiness. The analogy of parenthood may be helpful: a child learns to trust (or not) by whether the parent responds well to their needs (or not). As adults, we are likewise attuned to other people's actions: Do they do what they said they would do, when they said they would do it? Do they keep my confidences? Do they tell the truth? If they make a mistake, do they apologize? Over time, if the answer is consistently "yes" to these questions, trust is engendered.

Priests in the NSCP, particularly in the qualitative interviews, reported various ways that their bishops had gained their trust over the years. A bishop's taking the first steps in demonstrating availability and interest in building relationships is important, as priests are often hesitant to initiate personal interactions with their superior. This could be as simple as a phone call on a priest's birthday or as involved as initiating a shared meal. Some bishops set aside designated hours each week for private meetings with priests or for a meal with any priests who want to join it. Some bishops make it a habit to reach out to priests by phone, paying special attention to those in exceptionally demanding assignments. Many bishops make their personal cell phone available to priests, and promptly respond to priests' communications, reinforcing a sense of connection and accessibility.

To demonstrate strong and fair leadership, which leads to trust, the bishop should first of all exhibit his own emotional maturity, interpersonal skills, and attentive listening. A bishop who gets defensive, seems to be vindictive, or lashes out at the slightest criticism will not be able to gain the trust of

1 The NSCP also shows that this trust comes more easily when bishop and priest share a similar theological outlook. This does not seem at first like an actionable item on the bishop's part—pretending to hold crowd-pleasing theological opinions seems likely to come across as inauthentic, not trustworthy. But perhaps it is possible for a bishop to choose not to stoke the fires of ideological division in the diocese without compromising his own integrity.

his priests. Priests want to be treated as collaborators and know that their perspectives are valued in decision-making for the diocese. A bishop who applies policies consistently and fairly, avoiding favoritism, will be trusted, while one who seems to have his own "clique" will not. A bishop must keep his promises and honor commitments he makes. He ought to affirm and recognize priests who serve faithfully, reinforcing a culture of encouragement among the clergy in the diocese. He can lead the way in service by eschewing special treatment or exorbitant displays of wealth or prestige, and staying "down to earth" and demonstrating a willingness to share the "smell of the sheep" as Pope Francis put it. On the other hand, a bishop must hold priests accountable if they are violating the standards they pledged to live by. For example, if a priest is leading a "double life" and this is known among his brothers, a bishop who fails to act will likely lose other priests' respect.

Finally, and most importantly, the bishop should be the first in holiness in his diocese. He should be striving to be as close to Christ crucified as he can be. Priests will follow a holy man, even if they personally dislike him or disagree with his decisions. A prayerful, humble bishop will always have his detractors, but the priests who are likewise striving for perfection will trust and follow him.

Institutional and Structural Reforms

We know from the NSCP that priests thrive in situations where governance is consistent and clear, and where priests feel connected to the Church as a whole. Priests know that they are ordained for the sake of the whole world, not just their own parish, but the parish and the faithful in it are their primary responsibility. Doctrinal clarity and faithfulness to tradition at the top (whether from the Vatican or the chancery) helps priests by reinforcing the reasons they became priests in the first place. As the saying goes, no one gives their life for a question mark. Priests appreciate stability and clarity in the Church's vision, giving them an anchor of faith amidst the world.

At the institutional level, extending the role of the episcopal vicar for clergy to oversee continuing formation is one practical step that could help implement some of the suggestions above. In a larger archdiocese, the auxiliary bishop(s) could play a role. However it is instituted, someone at the chancery should have as their primary concern the well-being of the presbyterate. A diocese could establish a dedicated fund to support theological and pastoral study days for clergy, and/or structuring regular academic and formation opportunities for priests.

Finally, in regards to the implementation of the *Charter for the Protection of Children and Young People* (a primary concern of the NSCP), we strongly recommend a national standard by which dioceses evaluate sexual abuse or misconduct allegations. There are currently different definitions being used around the country, and different rules being applied particularly in cases with adults. Words such as "credible," "substantiated," and "vulnerable" must be defined more clearly in order to avoid any semblance of arbitrary enforcement of the Charter, Essential Norms, or other abuse policies. Priests ought to be educated by the diocese on what happens if an allegation is made against them, what the due process protections are in such a case, how the canonical process will proceed, and so on. Robust protection for victims must be maintained while avoiding a presumption of guilt on the part of the priest. Due process must be maintained, and there must be accountability for bishops to follow the protocols established. This is meant to be provided for by Pope Francis's *Vos estis lux mundi*, so the reporting mechanism for bishops should be just as public and clear as the one for priests.

Conclusion

By implementing these recommendations, the Church can renew and strengthen the priesthood, ensuring that priests are spiritually grounded, well-supported, and pastorally effective. A bishop who fosters fraternity, invests in ongoing formation, and cultivates trust within his presbyterate will not only empower his priests but also enhance the vitality of the entire diocese. More broadly, dioceses should recognize that many priests experience the current structure of ecclesial governance as opaque and unjust. Priests in the NSCP expressed a strong desire for clearer processes, consistent application of policies, and meaningful input into decisions that affect their lives and ministry—as well as being treated with respect rather than in a depersonalized way. Renewing trust will require not only pastoral attentiveness, but structural reforms grounded in justice, transparency, and shared responsibility. Ultimately, the renewal of the priesthood is essential for the future of the Church. A thriving presbyterate is the "center of gravity" of a diocese; it leads to thriving parishes, flourishing clergy, and a faithful Church that is both steadfast in mission and resilient in the face of challenges.

APPENDIX A: METHODOLOGY

The National Study of Catholic Priests included three components: (1) a national survey of US Catholic priests, carried out by Gallup, (2) in-depth interviews with priests, conducted by a team of experienced interviewers led by Dr. Tricia Bruce at the University of Notre Dame, and (3) a census of US Catholic Bishops conducted by CARA.

1. National Survey (Gallup)

The national survey of US Catholic priests was conducted by Gallup between February 15 and June 30, 2022.[1]

Sampling Frame

The Official Catholic Directory provided by P. J. Kenedy and Sons is a commercially available database of US priests and served as the sampling frame for this study. The Official Catholic Directory is thought to be the most complete listing of US priests. The directory includes affiliations, addresses, and, when available, emails for priests. Gallup added a limited number of emails to its sampling frame in a review of church websites and other online sources. Twenty-five percent of priests in the sample had an email listed.

Pilot Study

A pilot study using a random sample of 500 priests with email addresses was conducted in December 2021. A total of 84 priests completed the pilot survey. Each priest received a $25 incentive upon completing the survey. The pilot survey was conducted by web only. Sampled priests were contacted by email. The pilot survey was used to refine the final survey questionnaire based on the results of the pilot survey as well as feedback obtained from pilot survey respondents.

1 The details in this section are prepared by Gallup in their final methodology report.

Sampling Approach: Main Study

The study used a random sample of 10,000 US priests from the 26,807 unique priests listed in the Official Catholic Directory (minus the 500 sampled for the pilot survey).

The sampling approach used a stratified sampling design. In the current study, Gallup sorted priests according to the size of their diocese (based on number of priests within the diocese) and the region of the country in which they work. Random samples were drawn within each strata to ensure adequate representation of priests across regions and dioceses. Strata were defined as follows, similar to those used in the 1970 Andrew Greeley and Richard Schoenherr study of priests:[2]

- Diocese size: Very large (More than 500 priests), large (201–500 priests), medium (101–200 priests), small (100 or fewer priests)
- Census region: Northeast, Midwest, South, West

Random samples of priests were drawn from each strata (proportionate to size) in the following quantities.

Table A1 Quantities by strata in US priest sample frame

Size of Diocese	Census Region				
	Northwest	Midwest	South	West	Total
Small (100 or fewer priests	255	763	869	426	**2313**
Medium (101–200)	899	785	634	420	**2738**
Large (201–500)	473	974	754	646	**2847**
Very large (501+ priests)	1241	373	200	288	**2102**
Total	**2868**	**2895**	**2457**	**1780**	**10000**

2 National Opinion Research Center and United States Catholic Conference, *American Priests: A Report* (NORC, 1971).

Outreach

Letters and/or emails were addressed and sent to the sampled priests in English language only. Priests without an email were mailed a letter and reminder postcards directing them to a website to take the survey. The letter included a website URL and access code to enter the survey, as well as a QR code respondents could scan to be taken directly to the web survey. Priests who had an email listed were contacted by email which included a hyperlink to the survey.

Table A2 Scheduling of mailings for priest survey

Send	Material—Mail sample	Sample Group	Date
1	Pre-notification Letter + Letter from President	Mail + Web	February 15
2	Postcard 1	Mail	March 1
2a	Remediation letter*	Mail	March 11
3	Postcard 2	Mail + Web	March 25
4	Mail survey + Cover letter	Mail	April 15
5	Postcard 3	Mail + Web	May 2

Send	Material—Web sample	Sample Group	Date
1	Invitation email	Web	February 15
2	Reminder email 1	Web	March 1
3	Reminder email 2	Web	March 15
4	Reminder email 3	Web	April 18
5	Final reminder email	Web	May 2

* A printing error in the first postcard resulted in priests who were in the mail portion of the sample being given the wrong access code for their survey. Gallup sent a letter to all priests notifying them of the error and sending them a new access code with which to take the survey.

The prenotification letter announcing the survey included a letter from the president of The Catholic University describing the purpose of the study. The fourth contact attempt included a hard copy survey mailed to all respondents (mail and web samples) who had not yet completed a survey. The mail survey was slightly shorter than the web survey, omitting a subset of questions near the end of the web survey. Priests in the email sample whose emails were returned as undeliverable were converted to mail survey respondents. Email respondents received reminder postcards #2 and #3 in addition to the reminder emails. Priests received a $25 incentive paid upon completion of the survey.

Data Collection

Field dates were February 15 through June 30, 2022. Web and mail data collection was done in English language only. Of the 10,000 sampled cases, 153 were returned by the US Postal Service as undeliverable. Another 27 were removed from the sample at the request of the sampled priest or the institution listed on the address.

A total of 3,794 surveys were completed or returned. Of these, 278 surveys were excluded from the final sample for the following reasons:

1. The priest did not answer the informed consent item at the beginning the survey.
2. A priest took the survey more than once. If respondents completed a web survey and mailed back a mail survey, the web survey data was kept and the mail survey data discarded. If respondents completed multiple web surveys, the more complete survey was retained. If both web surveys had the same number of items answered, the first survey completed was retained.
3. The respondent answered less than half of the survey items.
4. The priest moved and indicated in the survey that they are serving in a diocese outside of the United States. Since these priests are outside of the target sample of US priests, in addition to removing their completed survey from the final obtained sample, they were also removed from the base (starting) sample count for computing the response rate.

The final count of usable surveys was 3,516, of which 3,033 were completed by web and 483 completed by mail. The final response rate for the final sample was 36%, based on the total number of usable surveys (3,516) divided by the total number of eligible sample records (9,797).

Weighting

The obtained sample was weighted to adjust for selection probability, nonresponse, and eligibility status by sample strata (diocese size by census region), comparing the obtained sample for each strata with the target strata size from the priest database/original sample. The target size for each stratum was derived by multiplying the stratum size in the original priest database by the stratum level eligibility rates. The eligibility rate for each stratum was estimated based on eligibility rate observed in the sample from the corresponding stratum.

Table A3 Quantities by strata in US priest obtained sample

Size of Diocese	Census Region				
	Northwest	Midwest	South	West	Total
Small (100 or fewer priests)	89	297	262	145	793
Medium (101–200)	319	334	207	142	**1002**
Large (201–500)	173	427	257	241	**1098**
Very large (501+ priests)	366	109	67	81	**623**
Total	**947**	**1167**	**793**	**609**	**3516**

Priests from strata underrepresented in the final sample received a weight of greater than 1.00 and priests from strata overrepresented in the final sample received a weight of less than 1.00. The sample weights range from a low of .81 to a high of 1.28, with the average weight of 1.00. The weight should be applied when analyzing the data to ensure the sample is representative of US priests. Projected targets are based on the Official Catholic Directory information at the time of the sampling. Priests who indicated on the survey that they were affiliated with a different diocese than listed in the sample were updated in the data file. However, the weighting targets were based on the original sample information given the small number of cases that required updated information on diocese.

Margin of Error

The margin of sampling error for the final sample is ±2 percentage points at the 95% confidence level. This margin of error considers the design effect from weighting the sample. In addition to sampling error, question wording and practical difficulties in conducting surveys can introduce error or bias into the findings of public opinion polls.

Nonresponse Bias Assessment

To assess potential nonresponse bias, Gallup compared the unweighted distributions of geographic region, diocese-size stratum, and diocesan vs. religious order affiliation in the sampling frame with those same distributions in the obtained sample. Absolute differences for each category were all under three percentage points, and chi-square tests indicated no statistically significant divergences (all $p > 0.05$). Finally, post-stratification weights were applied to adjust the sample exactly to the known population margins for region and diocese size, thereby minimizing any remaining bias related to these characteristics. Given these analyses and the small magnitude of the observed differences, we are confident that nonresponse has not materially affected the representativeness of the sample.

Respondent Privacy

Gallup removed priests from the sample if they did not answer affirmatively when asked for their consent to take the survey. Additionally, in the final dataset, Gallup has removed any information it used to contact priests that could be used to identify a priest and link their responses to them, such as their address, institution, or name. The dataset does include information on the priest's diocese and/or religious order. However, because priests with unique demographic characteristics in smaller dioceses or smaller religious orders could potentially be identified using a combination of information about the priest, the dataset does not include diocese information for priests from dioceses with 50 or fewer priests and for priests from religious orders that contain 50 or fewer members, based on counts from the Official Catholic Directory.

Web Survey Questionnaire, National Survey of Catholic Priests

PSTATUS. Status as Diocesan or Religious priest

1. Which of the following characterizes your situation?

1 Diocesan priest
2 Religious priest

2. Are you affiliated with [**IF '1' IN Q1:** the **INSERT "DIO_NAME" FROM SAMPLE / IF '2' IN Q1:** the **INSERT "R_ORDER_NAME" "R_ORDER" FROM SAMPLE** religious order]?

1 Yes
2 No

[IF '2' IN Q.2, ASK Q.2A; OTHERWISE SKIP TO TEXT BEFORE Q.3]

2A. With which [**IF '1' IN Q1:** diocese / **IF '2' IN Q.1:** religious order] are you currently affiliated?

INSERT TEXT BOX

--------------- INSERT PAGE BREAK ---------------

WELLBEING

We would like to ask you a series of questions about your life.

FLOURISH. Harvard Flourishing Index

3. Overall, how satisfied are you with life as a whole these days?

0 Not satisfied at all
1
2
3
4
5
6
7
8
9
10 Completely satisfied

Programmer: DISPLAY Q.4–12 IN RANDOM ORDER Programmer: DISPLAY Q.3 AND NEXT FOUR SELECTED QUESTIONS ON ONE SCREEN, THEN THE NEXT FIVE SELECTED QUESTIONS ON THE NEXT SCREEN

--------------- INSERT PAGE BREAK ---------------

4. In general, how happy or unhappy do you usually feel?

0 Extremely unhappy
1
2
3
4
5
6
7
8
9
10 Extremely happy

5. In general, how would you rate your physical health?

0 Poor
1
2
3
4
5
6
7
8
9
10 Excellent

6. How would you rate your overall mental health?

0 Poor
1
2
3
4
5
6
7
8
9
10 Excellent

7. Overall, to what extent do you feel the things you do in your life are worthwhile?

0 Not at all worthwhile
1
2
3
4
5
6
7
8
9
10 Completely worthwhile

8. I understand my purpose in life.

0 Strongly disagree
1
2
3
4
5
6
7
8
9
10 Strongly agree

9. I always act to promote good in all circumstances, even in difficult and challenging situations.

0 Not true of me
1
2
3
4
5
6
7
8
9
10 Completely true of me

10. I am always able to give up some happiness now for greater happiness later.

0 Not true of me
1
2
3
4
5
6
7
8
9
10 Completely true of me

11. I am content with my friendships and relationships.

0 Strongly disagree
1
2
3
4
5
6
7
8
9
10 Strongly agree

12. My relationships are as satisfying as I would want them to be.

0 Strongly disagree
1
2
3
4
5
6
7
8
9
10 Strongly agree

SUPPORT. Support network

13. We would like to ask you about your support network. In your priestly ministry, how much support do you experience from:

1 Strong support
2 Somewhat strong support
3 Mixed or inconsistent support
4 Little to no support

PROGRAMMER: DISPLAY A–G IN RANDOM ORDER AS APPROPRIATE

A. Your fellow priests
B. The bishop of your diocese
C. [**IF '2' IN Q.1, DISPLAY:**] The leader of your religious institute
D. Parishioners
E. Lay friends
F. Your family
G. [**IF '1' IN Q.1, DISPLAY:** The USCCB] / [**IF '2' IN Q.1, DISPLAY:** The Conference of Major Superiors of Men]

-------------- INSERT PAGE BREAK --------------

SUPPORT3. Spiritual support

14. Do you belong to a support group for priests?

Yes
No

15. Do you meet regularly with a spiritual director?

Yes
No

MORALE

In the next set of questions, we would like to learn about you as a priest in your diocese or religious community.

MORALE. Morale as a priest

Please indicate your level of agreement or disagreement with each of the following statements:

PROGRAMMER: DISPLAY Q.16–22 IN RANDOM ORDER

16. My morale as a priest is good.

1 Strongly agree
2 Agree
3 Neither agree nor disagree
4 Disagree
5 Strongly disagree

17. The Eucharist is the center of my life.

1 Strongly agree
2 Agree
3 Neither agree nor disagree
4 Disagree
5 Strongly disagree

18. I actively encourage men to become priests.

1 Strongly agree
2 Agree
3 Neither agree nor disagree
4 Disagree
5 Strongly disagree

19. In general, I feel respected as a priest.

1 Strongly agree
2 Agree
3 Neither agree nor disagree
4 Disagree
5 Strongly disagree

20. I believe God has called me to live a celibate life.

1 Strongly agree
2 Agree
3 Neither agree nor disagree
4 Disagree
5 Strongly disagree

21. I am expected to do too many things that go beyond my calling as a priest.

1 Strongly agree
2 Agree
3 Neither agree nor disagree
4 Disagree
5 Strongly disagree

22. I am thinking of leaving **[IF '1' IN Q.1, DISPLAY:** the priesthood / **IF '2' IN Q.1, DISPLAY:** religious life].

1 Strongly agree
2 Agree
3 Neither agree nor disagree
4 Disagree
5 Strongly disagree

DISTRESS. Psychological distress

23. During the past 30 days, about how often did you feel each of the following?

1 All of the time
2 Most of the time
3 Some of the time
4 A little of the time
5 None of the time

PROGRAMMER: DISPLAY A–H IN RANDOM ORDER

A. Joyful
B. Nervous
C. Hopeless
D. A sense of wonder
E. Restless or fidgety
F. So depressed that nothing could cheer you up
G. That everything was an effort
H. Worthless

-------------- INSERT PAGE BREAK --------------

CONFIDENCE IN LEADERSHIP

[**IF '1' IN Q.1, DISPLAY:** In the following section, we would like to ask you about your opinions of your bishop and US bishops more generally.]

[**IF '1' IN Q.2, DISPLAY:** In the following section, we would like to ask you about your opinions of your bishop and major superior, as well as bishops and major superiors more generally.]

BISHOP. Confidence in bishop's leadership

24. How much confidence do you, yourself, have in the decision-making and leadership of your diocesan bishop?

1 A great deal
2 Quite a lot
3 Some
4 Very little

PROGRAMMER: DISPLAY Q.25 IF Q.1=2 INSTLDRS.

25. How much confidence do you, yourself, have in the decision-making and leadership of the superiors of your religious order/institute?

1 A great deal
2 Quite a lot
3 Some
4 Very little

BISHOPG. Confidence in bishops' leadership in general

26. How much confidence do you, yourself, have in the decision-making and leadership of US bishops in general?

1 A great deal
2 Quite a lot
3 Some
4 Very little

-------------- INSERT PAGE BREAK --------------

BTYPES. Typologies of leadership styles

27. Which of these images best describe your current **[IF '1' IN Q.1, DISPLAY: bishop / IF '2' IN Q.1, DISPLAY: major superior]**? ***Please select all that apply***

PROGRAMMER: DISPLAY 1–11 IN RANDOM ORDER, THEN DISPLAY 12

1 Administrator
2 Brother
3 Co-worker
4 Father
5 Friend
6 Human Resources manager
7 Policeman
8 Role-model
9 Servant
10 Shepherd
11 Theologian
12 None of the above **(Programmer: Exclusive)**

BISHOPREL. Relationship with bishop/ms

For the next questions, please reflect upon your relationship with your [IF '1' IN Q.1, DISPLAY: bishop / IF '2' IN Q.1, DISPLAY: major superior]

28. How well do you and your **[IF '1' IN Q.1, DISPLAY:** bishop / **IF '2' IN Q.1, DISPLAY:** major superior] know each other?

1 Very well
2 Moderately well
3 Not very well
4 Not well at all

PROGRAMMER: DISPLAY Q.29–32 IN RANDOM ORDER

29. How well does your **[IF '1' IN Q.1, DISPLAY:** bishop / **IF '2' IN Q.1, DISPLAY:** major superior] take criticism from priests?

1 Very well
2 Moderately well
3 Not very well
4 Not well at all

30. How well do you and your **[IF '1' IN Q.1, DISPLAY:** bishop / **IF '2' IN Q.1, DISPLAY:** major superior] align on theological matters?

1 Very well
2 Moderately well
3 Not very well
4 Not well at all

31. How well do you and your **[IF '1' IN Q.1, DISPLAY:** bishop / **IF '2' IN Q.1, DISPLAY:** major superior] align on political matters?

1 Very well
2 Moderately well
3 Not very well
4 Not well at all

32. How well would your **[IF '1' IN Q.1, DISPLAY:** bishop / **IF '2' IN Q.1, DISPLAY:** major superior] help you with your personal struggles if you asked for help?

1 Very well
2 Moderately well
3 Not very well
4 Not well at all

--------------- INSERT PAGE BREAK ---------------

SEMVIEWS. Views of seminary experience

We would like to learn about some aspects of your experience at seminary or at your house of formation. To what extent do you agree or disagree with the following statements?

33. Adequate counseling or mental health resources were available at my seminary while I was there.

1 Strongly agree
2 Agree
3 Neither agree nor disagree
4 Disagree
5 Strongly disagree

34. Struggles with sexuality were a taboo topic at my seminary while I was there.

1 Strongly agree
2 Agree
3 Neither agree nor disagree
4 Disagree
5 Strongly disagree

35. Sexual harassment, abuse, and/or misconduct by seminarians, priests or instructors were a problem in my seminary while I was there.

1 Strongly agree
2 Agree
3 Neither agree nor disagree
4 Disagree
5 Strongly disagree

36. I personally experienced sexual harassment or abuse or suffered sexual misconduct during my formation or seminary.

1 Yes
2 No
3 Unsure/Prefer not to answer

-------------- INSERT PAGE BREAK --------------

The following questions address different aspects of what has come to be known as "the crisis" in the Catholic Church, and the policies implemented in response to it.

ZEROTOL. Zero-tolerance policy

37. In 2002, the USCCB introduced its zero-tolerance policy in response to the clergy sex abuse crisis. The policy demands the permanent removal from ministry, and, in most cases, laicization, for a justified allegation of sexual abuse of a minor.

To what extent do you agree or disagree with the following statements about the zero-tolerance policy?

1 Strongly agree
2 Agree
3 Neither agree nor disagree
4 Disagree
5 Strongly disagree

PROGRAMMER: RANDOMIZE ORDER OF A–C

A. The zero-tolerance policy positively demonstrates the Church's values (e.g., protecting the weak).
B. The zero-tolerance policy is helpful to regain the Church's trust with the wider public.
C. The zero-tolerance policy is harsher than is necessary.

38. How effective do you think the **[IF '1' IN Q.1, DISPLAY:** USCCB's policy has / **IF '2' IN Q.1, DISPLAY:** Standards of the Conference of Major Superiors of Men have] been in dealing with the problem of sexual abuse committed by priests?

1 Very effective
2 Somewhat effective
3 Not too effective
4 Not at all effective

BISHOPSRES. Bishops' response to the clergy sex abuse crisis

39. To what extent do you agree or disagree with the following statements concerning US bishops and their handling of the crisis?

1 Strongly agree
2 Agree
3 Neither agree nor disagree
4 Disagree
5 Strongly disagree

PROGRAMMER: DISPLAY A–E IN RANDOM ORDER

A. Bishops have unfairly placed the blame for the crisis on priests.
B. Bishops should have been subject to the same anti-abuse protocols as priests.
C. Bishops should be forced to step down if they failed to act on a single case of clergy sex abuse.
D. I feel betrayed by US bishops in general for their mismanagement of the crisis.
E. Bishops who actively covered up clergy sex abuse should be laicized.

--------------- INSERT PAGE BREAK ---------------

BCRISIS: View of bishop's response to crisis

40. How would you rate the job your diocesan bishop has done in responding to the crisis?

1 Excellent
2 Good
3 Fair
4 Poor

POLICYVIEWS. Attitudes towards safety policies

41. To what extent do you disagree or agree with the following statements about your [IF '1' IN Q.1, DISPLAY: diocese / IF '2' IN Q.1, DISPLAY: local religious community]?

1 Strongly agree
2 Agree
3 Neither agree nor disagree
4 Disagree
5 Strongly disagree

PROGRAMMER: DISPLAY A–H IN RANDOM ORDER

A. My **[IF '1' IN Q.1, DISPLAY:** diocese / **IF '2' IN Q.1, DISPLAY:** local religious community] has a strong culture of child safety and protection.
B. My **[IF '1' IN Q.1, DISPLAY:** diocese / **IF '2' IN Q.1, DISPLAY:** local religious community] has a strong culture of protecting vulnerable adults from abuse.
C. Anti-abuse policies have reduced priests' trust in the **[IF '1' IN Q.1, DISPLAY:** diocese / **IF '2' IN Q.1, DISPLAY:** local religious community].
D. Anti-abuse policies do not address the main causes of the abuse problem.
E. Anti-abuse policies leave too much room for interpretation in their application.
F. I regularly fear being falsely accused of sexual abuse.
G. Church compliance with the call for transparency (e.g., the extent of publicizing priestly failures) has gone too far.
H. In my **[IF '1' IN Q.1, DISPLAY:** diocese / **IF '2' IN Q.1, DISPLAY:** local religious community], legal or financial concerns take precedence over the well-being of priests/religious.

CRISUPPORT. Support of innocent priests in times of crisis

42. If an accusation of sexual abuse was falsely made against you, how confident are you that . . .

1 Very confident
2 Moderately confident
3 Not very confident
4 Not at all confident

PROGRAMMER: DISPLAY A–D IN RANDOM ORDER

A. Your brother priests would support you?
B. Your **[IF '1' IN Q.1, DISPLAY:** bishop / **IF '2' IN Q.1, DISPLAY:** major superior] would support you?
C. You would be provided with sufficient resources by your **[IF '1' IN Q.1, DISPLAY:** diocese / **IF '2' IN Q.1, DISPLAY:** local religious community] to defend yourself (e.g., in court)?
D. The legal process would prove your innocence?

Thank you for answering those questions. This next set of questions concerns your personal experiences of and response to the crisis.

CRISIMPACT. Impact of the crisis

43. Please indicate the extent to which you agree or disagree with the following questions

1 Strongly agree
2 Agree
3 Neither agree nor disagree
4 Disagree
5 Strongly disagree

PROGRAMMER: DISPLAY A-H IN RANDOM ORDER

A. The clergy sexual abuse crisis (including the response by bishops and major superiors) has negatively impacted my faith.
B. The clergy sexual abuse crisis (including the response by bishops and major superiors) has deepened my commitment to the priesthood.
C. The clergy sexual abuse crisis (including the response by bishops and major superiors) has made me feel ashamed of being a priest.
D. The revelations in the McCarrick Report were unsurprising to me.
E. The revelations in the McCarrick Report made me angry at the US bishops.
F. I think that there are still many unrevealed abuse cases in the Church.
G. I think that there is still wide-scale corruption in the Church.
H. I think the sexual abuse crisis in the Church is basically over.

CRISISCAUSE. Beliefs about causes of crisis

44. Which of the following do you think played an important role in causing "the crisis" in the Catholic Church? ***Please select all that apply.***

PROGRAMMER: DISPLAY A–L IN RANDOM ORDER, THEN DISPLAY M

A. Increased consumption of pornography by priests
B. The requirement of priestly celibacy
C. Clericalism (e.g., priests' sense of superiority over the people of God)
D. Excessive concern about the Church's image and reputation
E. Belief that perpetrators of child sexual abuse could be cured by psychological treatment
F. Homosexual inclinations of individual priests
G. Homosexual sub-cultures in some seminaries, dioceses, and religious institutes
H. Lack of transparency on the part of bishops or major superiors
I. Poor seminary formation regarding sexuality
J. Poor psychological screening of seminarians
K. Seduction or grooming by other priests into sexual abuse
L. The Devil and his minions
M. None of the above **(Programmer: Exclusive)**

-------------- INSERT PAGE BREAK --------------

CONTACTVIC. Contact with victims of abuse

For the next four questions, please respond with Yes or No:

45. I have been approached by someone who believes they have been a victim of child sexual abuse.

1 Yes
2 No

46. I have personally done outreach to, or otherwise supported, victims.

1 Yes
2 No

47. I feel reasonably well-prepared to support victims of clergy sexual abuse.

1 Yes
2 No

48. I regularly pray for victims of clergy sexual abuse.

1 Yes
2 No

-------------- INSERT PAGE BREAK --------------

COUNTS. Personal knowledge of certain categories of people

49. Please indicate how many people (including casual acquaintances) you personally know in the following categories.

1 None
2 One to two
3 Three to five
4 More than five

PROGRAMMER: DISPLAY A–F IN RANDOM ORDER

A. People who were victims of clergy sexual abuse
B. Priests who were falsely accused of sexual abuse
C. Priests who were accused of sexual abuse and found guilty
D. Priests who are sexually active
E. Priests who have a homosexual orientation
F. Priests who watch pornography

-------------- INSERT PAGE BREAK --------------

ACCOUNT. Accountability

Please indicate which of the following you agree with.

50. "As a priest, I value being accountable to . . ."

1 Strongly agree
2 Agree
3 Neither agree nor disagree
4 Disagree
5 Strongly disagree

PROGRAMMER: DISPLAY A–G IN ORDER

A. God
B. Pope Francis
C. My **[IF '1' IN Q.1, DISPLAY:** bishop / **IF '2' IN Q.1, DISPLAY:** major superior**]**
D. My brother priests
E. My parishioners
F. The laity
G. The general public

-------------- INSERT PAGE BREAK --------------

POSITION

51. What is your current position? *Select all that apply*

1 Pastor with special work outside the parish
2 Pastor without special work outside the parish
3 Full-time diocesan or religious community administration
4 Full-time parochial vicar
5 Parochial vicar with special work outside the parish
6 Educational apostolate
7 Hospital chaplaincy
8 Prison chaplaincy
9 Ministry with a special group
10 Social service apostolate
11 Fully retired
12 Retired, but still in active ministry.
13 Other (Please specify)

-------------- INSERT PAGE BREAK --------------

PRAY. Prayer

52. How much time do you typically spend in private prayer daily?

1 0–15 minutes
2 16–30 minutes
3 31–60 minutes
4 More than 60 minutes

--------------- INSERT PAGE BREAK ---------------

BURNOUT. Burnout in ministry.

53. To what extent do you agree or disagree with the following statements?

1 Strongly agree
2 Agree
3 Neither agree nor disagree
4 Disagree
5 Strongly disagree

PROGRAMMER: DISPLAY A–C IN RANDOM ORDER

A. It happens more and more often that I talk about my ministry work in a negative way.
B. During my ministry work, I often feel emotionally drained.
C. I usually feel worn out and weary after my ministry work.

--------------- INSERT PAGE BREAK ---------------

COVID-19. Effects of COVID-19

54. Considering all of the various vital aspects of a person's life (mental health, physical health, relationships with others, etc.), which statement below best represents your personal experience?

The changes to my life stemming from the COVID-19 pandemic have been overall . . .

1 Very positive
2 Positive
3 Neither positive nor negative
4 Negative
5 Very negative

--------------- INSERT PAGE BREAK ---------------

ORGCYN. Organizational cynicism and citizenship among priests/religious

In my [IF '1' IN Q.1, DISPLAY: diocese / IF '2' IN Q.1, DISPLAY: local religious community] . . .

PROGRAMMER: DISPLAY Q.55–60 IN RANDOM ORDER

55. Priests seem stressed out when they talk about our **[IF '1' IN Q.1, DISPLAY:** bishop / **IF '2' IN Q.1, DISPLAY:** major superior].

1 Strongly agree
2 Agree
3 Neither agree nor disagree
4 Disagree
5 Strongly disagree

56. Priests believe that our **[IF '1' IN Q.1, DISPLAY:** bishop / **IF '2' IN Q.1, DISPLAY:** major superior] says one thing and does another.

1 Strongly agree
2 Agree
3 Neither agree nor disagree
4 Disagree
5 Strongly disagree

57. Priests feel a sense of pride when talking about the **[IF '1' IN Q.1, DISPLAY:** diocese / **IF '2' IN Q.1, DISPLAY:** religious community].

1 Strongly agree
2 Agree
3 Neither agree nor disagree
4 Disagree
5 Strongly disagree

58. Priests criticize the policies or practices of the **[IF '1' IN Q.1, DISPLAY:** diocese / **IF '2' IN Q.1, DISPLAY:** religious community].

1 Strongly agree
2 Agree
3 Neither agree nor disagree
4 Disagree
5 Strongly disagree

59. Priests feel they will be seen as a liability if they approach the **[IF '1' IN Q.1, DISPLAY:** bishop / **IF '2' IN Q.1, DISPLAY:** major superior] with their personal struggles.

1 Strongly agree
2 Agree
3 Neither agree nor disagree
4 Disagree
5 Strongly disagree

60. Priests in my **[IF '1' IN Q.1, DISPLAY:** diocese / **IF '2' IN Q.1, DISPLAY:** religious community] are supportive of each other.

1 Strongly agree
2 Agree
3 Neither agree nor disagree
4 Disagree
5 Strongly disagree

-------------- INSERT PAGE BREAK --------------

MINISTRYHELP. Supports needed in ministry

61. Which of the following would you find valuable in your ministry as a priest? **Please select up all that apply.**

PROGRAMMER: DISPLAY 1–6 IN RANDOM ORDER, THEN DISPLAY 7

1 The opportunity for greater participation in decision-making in my diocese or religious institute
2 The opportunity to be free from involvement in diocesan or religious institute affairs, so I can concentrate on my own ministry
3 More opportunity for training in leadership and organizational skills (for example, conflict management, communications, budgeting, investing, and insurance)
4 More opportunity to discuss the clergy sex abuse crisis with other priests
5 More opportunity for training in mental health and self-care
6 More opportunity for spiritual formation or direction
7 Other (Specify)

INSERT TEXT BOX

62. In your opinion, what is one step that should be taken to improve priests' trust in **[IF '1' IN Q.1, DISPLAY:** bishops / **IF '2' IN Q.1, DISPLAY:** major superiors]? Please do not identify yourself in your response, so that we can maintain confidentiality

INSERT TEXT BOX

-------------- INSERT PAGE BREAK --------------

DEMOGRAPHICS AND GENERAL INFORMATION

The last few questions are about your personal background. The responses will only be used to analyze how groups of priests with similar characteristics answer questions compared with groups of priests with different characteristics.

AGE. Age

63. What is your current age?

PROGRAMMER: DROP DOWN MENU

1 18–24
2 25–29
3 30–34
4 35–39
5 40–44
6 45–49
7 50–54
8 55–59
9 60–64
10 65–69
11 70–74
12 75–79
13 80–84
14 85–89
15 90 or older

YORD. Year of ordination

64. In what year were you ordained as a priest?

PROGRAMMER: DROP DOWN MENU

1 Before 1960
2 1960–1964
3 1965–1969
4 1970–1974
5 1975–1979
6 1980–1984
7 1985–1989
8 1990–1994
9 1995–1999
10 2000–2004
11 2005–2009
12 2010–2014
13 2015–2019
14 2020 or later

YCOMM. Years in diocese or community

65. How many years have you served as a priest in your current diocese/religious community?

PROGRAMMER: DROP DOWN MENU

1 Less than one year
2 One year
3 Two years
4 Three–five years
5 Six–nine years
6 Ten–14 years
7 Fifteen–20 years
8 More than 20 years

-------------- INSERT PAGE BREAK --------------

PEDUC. Parental education

66. What is the highest level of education completed by either of your parents?

1 High school or less
2 Some college, no degree
3 Associate degree
4 Bachelor's degree
5 Master's or professional degree
6 Doctorate

-------------- INSERT PAGE BREAK --------------

RACE. Race/ethnicity

67. Are you of Hispanic, Latino, or Spanish origin—such as Mexican, Puerto Rican, Cuban, or other Spanish origin?

1 Yes
2 No

68. Which of the following describes your race? You can select as many as apply.

1 White
2 Black or African American
3 Asian
4 American Indian or Alaska Native
5 Native Hawaiian or Pacific Islander

-------------- INSERT PAGE BREAK --------------

USBORN. Born in the US

69. Were you born in the US or another country?

1 US
2 Another country

[IF '2' IN Q.70, DISPLAY]
USMOVE

70. In what year did you move to the US?

PROGRAMMER: DROP DOWN MENU

1 Before 1960
2 1960–1964
3 1965–1969
4 1970–1974
5 1975–1979
6 1980–1984
7 1985–1989
8 1990–1994
9 1995–1999
10 2000–2004
11 2005–2009
12 2010–2014
13 2015–2019
14 2020 or later

USORD. Ordained in the US

71. Were you ordained as a priest in the US?

1 Yes
2 No

SOCMEDIA. Social media use

72. Please select the most representative choice regarding your use of social media (e.g., Facebook, Twitter, etc.).

1 An hour or more a day
2 Daily but less than an hour
3 A few times a week
4 Once a week
5 Less than once a week
6 Rarely
7 I do not use social media.

--------------- INSERT PAGE BREAK ---------------

TVIEWS. Theological views

73. Would you describe your views on most matters having to do with theology and doctrines as?

PROGRAMMER: IF FORM=1, DISPLAY 1–5 IN ORDER; IF FORM=2, DISPLAY 5–1 IN ORDER

1 Very progressive
2 Somewhat progressive
3 Middle-of-the-road
4 Conservative/orthodox
5 Very conservative/orthodox

PVIEWS. Political views

74. Would you describe your views on most matters having to do with political issues as?

PROGRAMMER: IF FORM=1, DISPLAY 1–5 IN ORDER; IF FORM=2, DISPLAY 5–1 IN ORDER

1 Very liberal
2 Somewhat liberal
3 Moderate
4 Conservative
5 Very conservative

--------------- INSERT PAGE BREAK ---------------

Next, we would like to gauge your interest in additional opportunities to participate in this research or to learn about the findings of it:

Follow-up interviews (Gallup National Survey of Catholic Priest Recontact):

To further expand on our understanding of the survey themes, the research team from the Catholic University of America will be conducting follow-up interviews with a portion of survey participants. If you are interested in participating in a follow-up interview, your contact information will need to be shared with the researchers.

Your participation in these interviews would be completely voluntary and would in no way affect your participation in the current survey. If you are interested in participating in a follow-up interview, please select the "Yes" option as an indication of your consent for Gallup to share your contact information with the Catholic University of America researchers.

RECONTACT 1

R1. Do you agree to be contacted for the follow-up interview and to have Gallup share your contact information with the Catholic University of America research team?

1 Yes
2 No

-------------- INSERT PAGE BREAK ---------------

Follow-up events (Gallup National Survey of Catholic Priest Webinars, Workshops, and Other Events):

The research team from the Catholic University of America will be conducting a series of events such as workshops and webinars informed by the results of the survey. The research team can contact you to let you know when those events will occur. In order to be recontacted about these events, your contact information will need to be shared with the researchers.

RECONTACT 2

R2. Do you agree to be contacted to learn about special events tied to the results of this survey and to have your contact information shared with the Catholic University of America research team?

1 Yes
2 No

-------------- INSERT PAGE BREAK --------------

Summary of Results:

The research team from the Catholic University of America will share results of the study with any interested participants. In order to receive the results, your contact information will need to be shared with the Catholic University of America research team.

RECONTACT 3

R3. Do you agree to share your contact information with the Catholic University of America research team so they can send you a summary of the results of this survey by email?

1 Yes
2 No

-------------- INSERT PAGE BREAK --------------

R4. Please provide your preferred email address at which Gallup can email you a code for the $25 incentive. **[IF R1, R2 AND R3 '2' OR BLANK, DISPLAY:** If you prefer not to receive the incentive, leave the question blank.

[IF R1 =1 OR R2 =2 OR R3 =1, DISPLAY: Gallup will provide the same email address to the Catholic University research team so they can contact you for any of the follow-up opportunities you consented to.

Catholic University will only use your email for the specific activities you have chosen on the preceding screens, and no others.]

Please enter in your email using the following format: address@organization.org

INSERT TEXT BOX

IF R4 BLANK, SKIP TO CLOSING; OTHERWISE, CONTINUE

-------------- INSERT PAGE BREAK --------------

R5. Please confirm that your email is correct:

[INSERT TEXT ENTERED IN R4]

1 Yes, correct
2 No, not correct

[IF '1' IN R5, SKIP TO CLOSING; IF '2' IN SKIP BACK TO R4]

-------------- INSERT PAGE BREAK --------------

CLOSING

Thank you for participating in this survey. Your responses have been submitted.

If you or anyone you know would like more information about protective services or abuse survivor resources, here is a list below of a few resources that can provide support:

USCCB—CHILD AND YOUTH PROTECTION RESOURCES

https://www.usccb.org/offices/child-and-youth-protection/diocesan-resources

SNAP—SURVIVORS NETWORK OF THOSE ABUSED BY PRIESTS
https://www.snapnetwork.org/

Child Welfare Information Gateway

https://www.childwelfare.gov/topics/systemwide/laws-policies/statutes/clergymandated/

Childhelp
1-800-4ACHILD

As a reminder, you may also reach out to local authorities, including local law enforcement officers, your state's department of social and health services, social workers, health-care workers, mental health professionals, teachers, principals, school personnel and childcare providers to report any instances of sexual abuse.

2. In-depth Interviews

The second phase of data collection involved in-depth interviews with a "purposive" or strategically selected sample of 104 priests, designed to explore their experiences and views on well-being, burnout, relationships, and trust. The NSCP Qualitative Research Team (which was responsible for interviewing, transcript editing, and coding of qualitative data) was led by Dr. Tricia Bruce and included Caitlin Fitzgerald, David Flores, Christopher Jacobi, Kate Middleton, Christina Martinez, Cella Masso-Rivetti, Gabrielle Poma, Judith Ramon, Lucas Sharma, Jennifer Sherman, Brandon Vaidyanathan, and Lori Vien.[3]

Interviewees were selected from among survey respondents who indicated their willingness to be contacted for a follow-up interview. This produced a sampling frame of 1,543 potential participants—representing 44% of all survey respondents and 15% of the total pool of priests initially invited to take the survey. From this list, 104 priests were selected using a stratified quota sampling approach designed to ensure diversity and representation across a range of demographic characteristics and key survey responses.

Sampling decisions were based on self-reported survey data and considered the following variables: age, ordination cohort, race, nativity, geographic region, diocese size, diocesan versus religious affiliation, current ministerial role, political orientation, and theological orientation. In addition, we sought variation in priests' responses to several key survey items, including:

- "My morale as a priest is good."
- "How much confidence do you, yourself, have in the decision-making and leadership of your diocesan bishop?"
- "How much confidence do you, yourself, have in the decision-making and leadership of the superiors of your religious order/institute?"
- "Sexual harassment, abuse, and/or misconduct by seminarians, priests, or instructors were a problem in my seminary while I was there."
- "How would you rate the job your diocesan bishop has done in responding to the crisis?"
- "If an accusation of sexual abuse was falsely made against you, how confident are you that your brother priests would support you?"
- "If an accusation of sexual abuse was falsely made against you, how confident are you that your bishop/major superior would support you?"

3 This section reflects the methodology report for the interview component of the study, prepared by Dr. Tricia Bruce.

Table A4 Key descriptive statistics, National Survey of Catholic Priests (2022, N=3,516)

Category	Subgroup	%
Type of Priest		
	Diocesan priest	66%
	Religious priest	34%
Current Age		
	Under age 45	22%
	Age 45 to 64	39%
	Age 65 to 74	23%
	Age 75 or older	17%
Year Ordained		
	Before 1980	25%
	1980–1999	34%
	2000 or later	41%
Race/Ethnicity		
	White	76%
	Hispanic	10%
	Asian	8%
	Black or African American	5%
	American Indian or Alaska Native	1%
	Native Hawaiian or Pacific Islander	1%
	Foreign-born	24%

Table A4 *continued*

Category	Subgroup	%
Census Region		
	Northeast	29%
	Midwest	29%
	South	25%
	West	18%
Diocese Size		
	Small (100 or fewer)	23%
	Medium (101–200)	27%
	Large (201–500)	28%
	Very large (501+)	21%
Theological Orientation		
	Very progressive	7%
	Somewhat progressive	21%
	Middle-of-the-road	31%
	Conservative/orthodox	35%
	Very conservative/orthodox	6%
Political Orientation		
	Very liberal	5%
	Somewhat liberal	19%
	Moderate	37%
	Conservative	33%
	Very conservative	5%

Although the interview sample (n = 104) does not perfectly represent every demographic or attitudinal subgroup, it reflects a wide range and thoughtful balance of perspectives, selected with the aim of deepening understanding. Interviewees were drawn in waves as additional survey responses came in, minimizing bias toward early respondents. In total, priests from 34 states and 58 (arch)dioceses or eparchies are represented in the final sample. The interviews aimed to provide a more in-depth look at themes that emerged in the survey, including the experience, hopes, and fears of priests, their understandings of the causes and implications of the sex abuse crisis, and their relationships with their bishops and superiors. Table A5 below details the profile of interviewees.

All interviewers completed online training covering interview techniques, human subject protections (including the University of Notre Dame's Institutional Review Board protocols for human subjects research), safety considerations, and the interview guide. Each held relevant academic or professional expertise, language skills, and familiarity with research on US Catholicism. All team members submitted CITI certification for human subjects research. The team met regularly via videoconference throughout the project. Interviewers contacted selected participants by email using a standardized script, often with a calendaring link, and followed up to three times if there was no response. Interviews were conducted in person (22%), by videoconference (63%), or by phone (14%), depending on geographic location and interviewee preference. Consent was obtained before each interview, which was audio recorded and averaged 90 minutes. Participants received a $40 gift card in appreciation for their time. Upon transcription, all interviews were coded and analyzed using the ATLAS.ti qualitative data analysis software.

Table A5 Demographic profile of interview respondents

		# of Interviewees	% of Interviewees
Type of Priest			
	Diocesan	70	67%
	Religious Order	34	33%
Age			
	Under age 40	16	15%
	41–49	21	20%
	50–59	21	20%
	60–69	24	23%
	70+	22	21%
Nativity			
	US-born	89	86%
	International	15	14%
Race			
	Non-Hispanic White	71	67%
	Black [inc. Black Hispanic]	9	8%
	Hispanic [inc. Black Hispanic]	19	18%
	Asian	5	5%
	American Indian or Alaska Native	2	2%
Year Ordained			
	1960–1979	19	18%
	1980–1989	20	18%
	1990–1999	16	15%
	2000–2009	20	19%
	2010 or later	29	28%

Table A5 *continued*

	# of Interviewees	% of Interviewees
"Would you describe your views on most matters having to do with theology and doctrines as…?"		
Very progressive	13	13%
Somewhat progressive	23	22%
Middle-of-the-road	20	19%
Conservative/orthodox	41	39%
Very conservative/orthodox	7	7%
"Would you describe your views on most matters having to do with political issues as…?"		
Very liberal	7	7%
Somewhat liberal	23	22%
Moderate	32	31%
Conservative	35	34%
Very conservative	7	7%
"How much confidence do you, yourself, have in the decision-making and leadership of your diocesan bishop?"		
A great deal	18	17%
Quite a lot	23	22%
Some	31	30%
Very little	31	30%
"My morale as a priest is good"		
(Strongly) Agree	69	66%
Neither Agree or Disagree	13	13%
(Strongly) Disagree	22	21%

Table A5 *continued*

	# of Interviewees	% of Interviewees
"How would you rate the job your diocesan bishop has done in responding to the crisis?"		
Excellent	32	31%
Good	35	34%
Fair	22	21%
Poor	14	14%
"If an accusation of sexual abuse was falsely made against you, how confident are you that your bishop/major superior would support you?"		
Moderately Confident or Very Confident	52	50%
Not Very Confident or Not at All Confident	52	50%
"If an accusation of sexual abuse was falsely made against you, how confident are you that your brother priests would support you?"		
Moderately Confident or Very Confident	71	68%
Not Very Confident or Not at All Confident	33	32%
"Sexual harassment, abuse, and/or misconduct by seminarians, priests or instructors were a problem in my seminary while I was there."		
(Strongly) Agree	23	22%
Neither Agree or Disagree	17	16%
(Strongly) Disagree	64	62%

National Study of Catholic Priests Interview Protocol[4]

I. Consent to participate, record

Email consent form in advance of the interview; confirm receipt.

Request verbal consent to participate in the interview and record (signed, if in-person).

II. Introduction

Thank you again for agreeing to do this interview. Before we begin, I want to remind you that your participation is voluntary and that your answers are **totally confidential.** We won't share your name or identifying information about you. Please share your honest opinions. Also, you can skip any questions or end the interview at any time.

I'll be recording so that I don't miss things you say—is that okay? ***(Begin recording)***. Great, now I'm going to ask one more time just to get it on record: Is it okay to record? Thank you.

Getting started, I'll ask you about what your day-to-day life as a priest looks like these days. From there, I'll want to ask you some things about the "crisis" in the Church and how it has impacted you, your ministry, your diocese, your relationship with bishops, and the Church as a whole. Lastly, I'd love to hear your thoughts about the future. Sound good?

[Nb. Below, "Q" stands for question and "P" for prompt or probe].

III. Background and Professional Identity

Q: Great. So, to start, can you tell me a bit about when/how you knew you wanted to be a priest?

- **P:** What is it about your personality, do you think, that led you into the priesthood?

4 Given the nature of qualitative research, interview questions evolved modestly based upon interactions in the field. Interviewers generally followed this script (including prompts), but were asked to also probe for depth/clarity as the conversation unfolded in real time.

Q: What does your life as a priest look like these days? For example, how does a typical week unfold for you?

P: Can you tell me what some of your favorite things are about being a priest (or, what makes for a "good day" in your life and work as a priest?)?

P: (Where) do you encounter beauty in your work as a priest?

P: What about the other side of the coin—least favorite thing(s) about being a priest, or what makes for a "bad" day?

Q: I'm curious—what do you think is the greatest challenge or problem that priests today face?

P: We are living in a "Covid" age—what has this meant for your work as a priest?

IV. The Crisis—Origins and Personal Impacts

Now, I want to talk to you about the "crisis" in the Church. *[+ Reminder of confidentiality and no "right" or "wrong" answers]*

Q: And, before I even ask you anything more specific about it—what comes to mind with that phrase, "crisis in the Church?"

P: Why does that come to mind?

Q: Thinking specifically about the crisis of clergy sexual abuse: In your own words, how has the crisis impacted you

P: . . . personally / as a Catholic?

P: . . . as a priest?

P: . . . in your work as a priest?

Q: Do you think the crisis has changed how others see you as a priest? If so, how?

P: . . . or how others see the priesthood, in general?

P: How do you feel about that?

Q: How hard is it to minister as a priest in the current climate of the Church?

P: Has the crisis changed your own behavior? How?

P: Has "burnout," fatigue, or exhaustion been an issue for you?

P: What about for other priests in your diocese/community (impacts/ burnout)?

Q: Thinking about some of the roots of the crisis of abuse in the Church, some people talk about _______ *[probe, prompt as needed from list below if not already mentioned].* What are your thoughts on that?

P1: "rotten apples" (just a few bad individuals)

P2: the culture of the priesthood (e.g., clericalism, a culture of silence, too much concern or reputation, "yes" men)

P3: some point to homosexuality as a cause, either among individual priests or gay subcultures

P4: policies (e.g., poor psychological screening of priests, lack of transparency)

P5: structural issues (e.g., mandatory celibacy; role of Vatican II)

P6: broader society (e.g., secularization, promiscuity, pornography.)

P7: spiritual causes (e.g., devil, lack of prayer)

Q: Thinking about victims or survivors of abuse—can you tell me what kinds of interactions you have had with this group?

P: What do you think holds most promise for survivors' healing vis-a-vis the Church?

V. The Crisis—Diocesan Impacts

Thank you so much for sharing. Now, I want to ask you some questions about your diocese [religious community] and relationship with your bishop [Major Superior].

Q: Let's start with a more general question. How would you describe the overall climate [culture] in your diocese at this time?

P: What issues are on the front-burner?

P: What is changing now in your diocese?

(**P:** priest shortage; alternative leadership models inc. women's roles; parish closures; supersized parishes)

Q: Thinking again about the crisis, what changes have transpired in your diocese as a result of the crisis (whether positive or negative)?

Q: I want to better understand your relationship with your bishop [Major Superior]. Can you tell me about a recent interaction you had with your bishop?

P: What made that interaction positive, negative, or neutral?

Q: Can you recall the last informal, perhaps social event you shared with your bishop? Tell me about it.

P: How often do informal, social events happen with your bishop?

P: Do you think your bishop enjoys spending time with priests?

P: Do you feel as though you could bring a personal problem to your bishop?

Q: What about other priests in your diocese/community—do you spend time together?

- **P:** How would you describe the level of trust and camaraderie among priests in your diocese/community?

Q: How much would you say that you agree or disagree with your bishop on matters related to the Church or Church in the world?

- **P:** Where have you disagreed?
- **P:** How does your bishop handle disagreement (your own or that of others)?

Q: How much trust would you say that you have in your own bishop when it comes to managing the abuse crisis?

- **P:** What about trust in your bishop when it comes to other matters, or overall?
- **P:** (If applicable) How does your bishop's response to the crisis compare to that of prior bishop(s) in your diocese?

VI. The Crisis—Church Response

That's really helpful, thank you. I'm also curious to hear more about what you think regarding the Church's response to the crisis.

Q: You've told me some about your own bishop . . . what about other bishops [including any former bishops]? Would you say that you trust them?

Q: How do you feel about the ways that the bishops overall have responded to the crisis of abuse in the Church?

P: What do you think has "worked" / been effective in the ways that bishops (individually or on the whole) have responded to the crisis?

P: What about what's <u>not</u> worked—are there things you'd point to that have "failed" in responding to the crisis?

Q: I want to ask you more specifically about policies. For example, in 2002, the USCCB introduced its "zero-tolerance policy," demanding permanent removal from ministry, and, in most cases, laicization, for a justified allegation of sexual abuse of a minor.

P: Can you tell me some of your own thoughts about this policy?

P: Do you agree with this approach, or not?

P: How effective (or how effectively implemented) do you think it is?

P: Do you know any priests who have been accused of abuse?

P: How do you think through concerns regarding credibility or degree of allegations?

Q: Are there any other policies that come to mind that you want to mention or react to?

(**P:** e.g., holding bishops accountable; extending concern to vulnerable and nonvulnerable adults; boundary violations; addressing child pornography; papal statements)

3. Census of Catholic Bishops[5]

In June 2021, The Catholic University of America (CUA) commissioned the Center for Applied Research in Apostolate (CARA) to conduct a survey of bishops in the United States.

The questionnaire (attached below) contains 115 questions (including three open-ended questions). The questionnaire was developed based on questions provided by CUA and by CARA. CARA prepared two instruments: a paper survey and an online survey. CARA also assisted CUA in drafting a cover letter explaining the research project and inviting the bishops to complete the survey.

In October 2021, CARA mailed a cover letter of explanation and invitation to the census of Catholic dioceses and eparchies in the United States. Each of these letters was personalized to the bishop. The letter provided a short web link and QR code for completing the survey online for those who prefer to do so. Included in the mailing was a paper copy of the survey, a return envelope, and a return postcard indicating that the survey was completed. CARA monitored the data collection and conducted two follow-ups with non-respondents (in November 2021 and January 2022) to produce the highest possible response rate. The survey was conducted anonymously with an option for bishops to self-identify if they wish. To preserve bishops'

5 Prepared by CARA

anonymity and be able to track their participation, bishops were provided with a return postcard to mail to CARA once they completed the survey.

In February 2022, CARA closed the survey and entered all paper responses into the electronic dataset. After removing metadata (such as IP addresses of respondents to protect their anonymity), CARA handed the dataset to CUA. Overall, 131 US arch/bishops responded to the survey (out of a total of 196 for a final response rate of 67%). Assuming random distribution of the sample, if all respondents answered all the questions, then in nineteen out of twenty cases (i.e., 95% confidence level), the amounts for the entire studied population would fall within ±5.1% range of the values derived from univariate analysis (i.e., the margin of error is 5.1%). All survey responses were 100% finished except for one. The median time to finish the survey was 15 minutes 20 seconds.

SURVEY OF U.S. CATHOLIC BISHOPS
CENTER POR APPLIED RESEARCH IN THE APOSTOLATE AT GEORGETOWN UNIVERSITY

DIRECTIONS: Please fill out this questionnaire and return it in the envelope provided. To maintain the confidentiality of your response, return the postcard separately to let us know that you have completed the survey. **If a question does not apply to yon or yon do not know how to respond, please leave it blank.** Please note that "Diocese" is used here as a generie reference to both Archdiocese, Archeparchy, Diocese, and Eparchy.

For questions 1-10 please enter a number from 0 to 10.

__ 1. Overall, how satisfied are you with life as a whole these days? (0=Not Satisfied at All, 10=Completely Satisfied)
__ 2. In general, how happy or unhappy do you usually feel? (0=Extremely Unhappy, 10=Extremely Happy)
__ 3. In general, how would you rate your physical health? (0=Poor, 10=Excellent)
__ 4. How would you rate your overall mental health? (0=Poor, 10=Excellent)
__ 5. Overall, to what extent do you feel the things you do in your life are worthwhile? (0=Not at All Worthwhile, 10=Completely Worthwhile)

__ 6. I understand my purpose in life. (0=Strongly Disagree, 10=Strongly Agree)
__ 7. I always act to promote gond in all circumstances, even in difficult and challenging situations. (0=Not True of Me, 10=Completely True of Me)
__ 8. I am always able to give up some happiness now for greater happiness later. (0=Not True of Me, 10=Completely True of Me)
__ 9. I am content with my friendships and relationships. (0=Strongly Disagree, 10=Strongly Agree)
__ 10. My relationsbips are as satisfying as I would want them to be. (0=Strongly Disagree, 10=Strongly Agree)

For questions 11-29 please use the responses below.
1=No problem at all 3=Somewhat of a problem
2=Very little problem 4=A great problem
How much are each of the following a problem to you on a day-to-day basis?
1 2 3 4
□ □ □ □ 11. Theological divisions among my priests.
□ □ □ □ 12. Political divisions among my priests.
□ □ □ □ 13. Unrealistie demands and expectations of lay people.
□ □ □ □ 14. Conflict with parishioners or laity about issues of the day.
□ □ □ □ 15. Loneliness of priestly/episcopal life.
□ □ □ □ 16. Too much work.
□ □ □ □ 17. The way authority is exercised in the Church.
□ □ □ □ 18. The image of the priesthood today.
□ □ □ □ 19. The image of bishops today.

1 2 3 4
□ □ □ □ 20. Criticism from priests.
□ □ □ □ 21. Criticism from laity about priests.
□ □ □ □ 22. Criticism in the secular press or media.

How much of a problem are these administrative issues to you on a day-to-day basis?
1 2 3 4
□ □ □ □ 23. Limited number of available priests.
□ □ □ □ 24. Parish restructuring in the Diocese.
□ □ □ □ 25. The diocesan financial situation.
□ □ □ □ 26. Diocesan legal issues.
□ □ □ □ 27. Priest morale.
□ □ □ □ 28. Priest personnel issues.
□ □ □ □ 29. Non-priest diocesan personnel issues.

For questions 30-36 please use the responses below.
1=Disagree strongly 4=Agree somewhat
2=Disagree somewhat 5=Agree strongly
3=Neither agree nor disagree
Please indicate the extent to which you agree or disagree with the following statements: "As a bishop, I value being accountable to..."
1 2 3 4 5
□ □ □ □ □ 30. God
□ □ □ □ □ 31. The Pope
□ □ □ □ □ 32. My priests
□ □ □ □ □ 33. The laity
□ □ □ □ □ 34. The geueral public

Please indicate the extent to which you agree or disagree with the following statements:
1 2 3 4 5
□ □ □ □ □ 35. I take great efforts to know each of my priests personally (e.g., by having dinner with each priest of my Diocese or small groups of priests at least once a year),
□ □ □ □ □ 36. It is not possible for a bishop to know each priest personally.

Yes No
□ □ 37. Are you personally aetive on social media?
□ □ 38. Do you think bishops should be active on social media?
□ □ 39. Do you think priests should be active on social media?

For questions 40-45, please use the responses below.
1=Not well at all 3=Moderately well
2=Not very well 4=Very well
Reflecting upon your relationship with your priests, how well…
1 2 3 4
□ □ □ □ 40. do you and your priests know each other?
□ □ □ □ 41. do you support your priests?
□ □ □ □ 42. do you take criticism from your priests?
□ □ □ □ 43. do you and your priests align on theological matters?
□ □ □ □ 44. do you and your priests align on political matters?
□ □ □ □ 45. would you help your priests with their personal struggles if they asked for help?

For statements 46-62, please use the responses below.
1=Disagree strongly 3=Agree somewhat
2=Disagree somewhat 4=Agree strongly
1 2 3 4
□ □ □ □ 46. I am too busy to pray as much as I would like.
□ □ □ □ 47. I would be happier if I could focus on my pastoral ministry and let others do administrative work.
□ □ □ □ 48. I frequently feel burned out.
□ □ □ □ 49. I wish to spend more time with other priests in the Diocese.
□ □ □ □ 50. I am too busy to personally counsel and pastor all the priests of my Diocese.
□ □ □ □ 51. I feel my current Diocese is my home.
□ □ □ □ 52. I feel accepted by most priests of my current Diocese.
□ □ □ □ 53. Most of my closest priest friends are priests of my current Diocese.
□ □ □ □ 54. Other bishops are among my closest friends.
□ □ □ □ 55. I support bringing more international priests into my Diocese.
□ □ □ □ 56. It is essential to uphold the distinction between priests and laity in the Church.
□ □ □ □ 57. Catholic laity are sufficiently respectful of the priest's authority in my Diocese.
□ □ □ □ 58. Priests are sufficiently respectful of the voice of the laity in my Diocese.
□ □ □ □ 59. Priests in a Diocese should be able to elect their bishop.
□ □ □ □ 60. The Catholic Church's right to religious freedom faces increasing threat from the government.
□ □ □ □ 61. Women should have more leadership roles in my Diocese.
□ □ □ □ 62. Media coverage of clergy sexual abuse has made it challenging to present or defend Church teachings in my Diocese.

For questions 63-68, please use the responses below.
1= No diocesan policy 4= Detailed/highly standardized
2= General guidelines 5=Don't know
3= Specific guidelines in key areas
How would you describe diocesan-wide policies related to parish operations in the following areas?
1 2 3 4 5
□ □ □ □ □ 63. Liturgy.
□ □ □ □ □ 64. Sacramental preparation.
□ □ □ □ □ 65. Finances.
□ □ □ □ □ 66. Personnel management.
□ □ □ □ □ 67. Religious education.
□ □ □ □ □ 68. Sexual abuse prevention.

For questions 69-76, please use the responses below.
1=Never 3=Often
2=Occasionally 4=On a regular basis
In the last five years, how often have you written to Catholics (e.g., a pastoral letter or column in the diocesan newspaper) on these topics?
1 2 3 4
□ □ □ □ 69. Spiritual or Biblical reflection.
□ □ □ □ 70. Catholic theology.
□ □ □ □ 71. Catholic teaching on the family.
□ □ □ □ 72. Catholic teaching on sexual morality.
□ □ □ □ 73. Catholic teaching on sanctity of life.
□ □ □ □ 74. Catholic social teaching.
□ □ □ □ 75. Religious freedom issues.
□ □ □ □ 76. Clergy sexual abuse crisis

77. Which of these images reflect how you see your relationship to your priests? (*Select all that apply)*
□ Administrator □ HR manager
□ Brother □ Policeman
□ Co-worker □ Role-model
□ Father □ Servant
□ Friend □ Shepherd

78. In what USCCB region is your current Diocese?
______

79. What is the name of your current Diocese? (Optional)
______

80. How much media coverage, either local or national, was directed at your current Diocese in the wake of the revelations of clergy sexual abuse in the Church?
□ Little or no coverage.
□ Some coverage.
□ A large amount of coverage.
□ Extensive coverage.

81. What is your age?
□ <60 □ 65-69 □ 75 or more
□ 60-64 □ 70-74

82. How many active diocesan and religious priests are in your diocese?
□ <100 □ 200-299 □ 400 or more
□ 100-199 □ 300-399

For questions 83-86, please use the responses below.
1=Disagree strongly 3=Agree somewhat
2=Disagree somewhat 4=Agree strongly
In 2019, Pope Francis issued the Motu Proprio "Vos Estis Lux Mundi". To what extent do you agree or disagree with the following aspects as they pertain to the US?
1 2 3 4
□ □ □ □ 83. The emphasis on bishops' responsibility in handling sexual abuse accusations.
□ □ □ □ 84. The mandatory reporting requirement.
□ □ □ □ 85. Expanding the category of vulnerable persons to include more than minors.
□ □ □ □ 86. The recommendation to involve lay people in the process of handling sexual abuse accusations

87. How effective do you think the Dallas Charter has been in dealing with the problem of sexual abuse committed by priests?
☐ Very effective
☐ Somewhat effective
☐ Not too effective
☐ Not at all effective

For questions 88-94, please use the responses below.
1=Disagree strongly 4=Agree Somewhat
2=Disagree somewhat 5=Agree Strongly
3= Neither agree nor disagree
To what extent do you agree/disagree with the following?
1 2 3 4 5
□ □ □ □ □ 88. Bishops should have been subject to the same anti-abuse protocols as priests.
□ □ □ □ □ 89. Anti-abuse policies have reduced priests' trust in bishops.
□ □ □ □ □ 90. The clergy sexual abuse crisis has negatively impacted my faith.
□ □ □ □ □ 91. The McCarrick revelations and Report were not surprising to me.
□ □ □ □ □ 92. I think there are still many unrevealed abuse cases in the Church.
□ □ □ □ □ 93. I think there is still wide scale corruption in the Church.
□ □ □ □ □ 94. I think the sexual abuse crisis in the Church is basically over.

Yes No
□ □ 95. Were you born in the United States?
□ □ 96. Did you grow up in your current Diocese?
□ □ 97. Are you a member of a religious order?
□ □ 98. Did you attend a high school seminary?
□ □ 99. Do you currently have a spiritual director?
□ □ 100. Did you make a personal retreat last year?

101. Which best describes your current role in the Chureh?
☐ Archbishop with (an) auxiliary bishop(s).
☐ Archbishop without an auxiliary bishop.
☐ Bishop with (an) auxiliary bishop(s).
☐ Bishop without an auxiliary bishop.

102. What kind of undergraduate college did you attend? *(Select all that apply)*
□ Diocesan Seminary. □ Other Private.
□ Catholic college. □ Public.

103. When were you ordained to the episcopacy?
□ <2000 □ 2005-2009 □ 2015-2019
□ 2000-2004 □ 2010-2014 □ 2020+

104. When were you appointed to your current position?
□ <2000 □ 2005-2009 □ 2015-2019
□ 2000-2004 □ 2010-2014 □ 2020+

105. Which one category best describes your primary racial or ethnic background?
☐ African / African-American / black.
☐ Native American / Alaska Native.
☐ Asian / Pacific Islander / Native Hawaiian.
☐ Caucasian / European American / white.
☐ Hispanic / Latino.
☐ Other (describe:)____________________________

106. Your priot experience as a bishop: *(Select all that apply)*
☐ Auxiliary in current Diocese.
☐ Auxiliary in a different Diocese.
☐ Ordinary in a different Diocese.
☐ No prior experience as bishop.

107. Typical number of hours you work each week. ______

108. Describe your general theological orientation:
☐ Very traditional.
☐ Moderately traditional.
☐ Moderate.
☐ Moderately progressive.
☐ Very progressive.

109. Considering all of the various vital aspects of a person's life (mental health, physical health, relatioships with others, etc.), which statement below best represents your personal experience? "The changes to my life stemming from the COVID-19 pandemic have been overall…"
- ☐ Very negative
- ☐ Negative
- ☐ Not significant
- ☐ Positive
- ☐ Very positive

110. Do you follow a regular routine of physical exercise?
- ☐ Yes
- ☐ No

111. Overall, how healthy would you say your diet is?
- ☐ Not at all healthy
- ☐ Not too healthy
- ☐ Somewhat healthy
- ☐ Very healthy

112. In general, how can the priests of your Diocese reach you?
- ☐ Through my personal email address.
- ☐ Through my office email address.
- ☐ Through my secretary's email address.
- ☐ They call or text my personal cell phone.
- ☐ They call the secretary at my office.
- ☐ Other:________________________________.

113. What aspect of the Church in the U.S. today gives you the greatest amount of hope?

114. What do you perceive as the greatest challenge to the Church in the U.S. today?

115. In your opinion, what is one step that needs to be taken to improve priests' trust in bishops?

Thank you for completing this survey.

Center for Applied Research in the Apostolate (CARA)
2300 Wisconsin Ave NW, Suite 400A, Washington, DC 20007
Phone: (202) 687-8080 Fax: (202) 687-8083

APPENDIX B: LONGITUDINAL FOLLOW-UP TO THE NATIONAL STUDY OF CATHOLIC PRIESTS

Stephen Cranney and Brandon Vaidyanathan

In 2025, The Catholic Project conducted a brief longitudinal follow-up survey of priests to assess changes over time in priests' well-being and institutional trust. Gallup re-contacted every diocesan and religious priest who completed the 2022 NSCP survey and had provided an email address (N = 3,063). They then fielded a secure, online questionnaire between May 12 and June 30, 2025. The survey yielded a 38 percent response rate (1,164 usable responses). In what follows, we summarize key highlights from the follow-up results using weighted data.

These results are not discussed elsewhere in this book, which had already been written before these new results were available. However, while there are some signs of small improvements in the three years between studies, the overall picture remains largely the same in terms of both positives and negatives, helping to confirm the results of the NSCP in 2022.

Flourishing and Morale

Priests' overall well-being remains strikingly robust in the follow-up data. The mean Harvard Flourishing Index score in 2025 is 82, identical to the baseline recorded three years earlier and well above the US adult population norm. Fully 81 percent of follow-up respondents affirm that their "morale as a priest is good," while only 10% disagreed. Only about 3 percent report that they are "thinking about leaving the priesthood/religious life," virtually unchanged since 2022 (4%).

Satisfaction in priestly life, however, co-exists with pressure: 35 percent feel they are "expected to do too many things that go beyond [their] calling as a priest," echoing qualitative complaints of being "stretched thin" reported in the initial study (see Figure B1).

Figure B1. Priestly morale and expectations

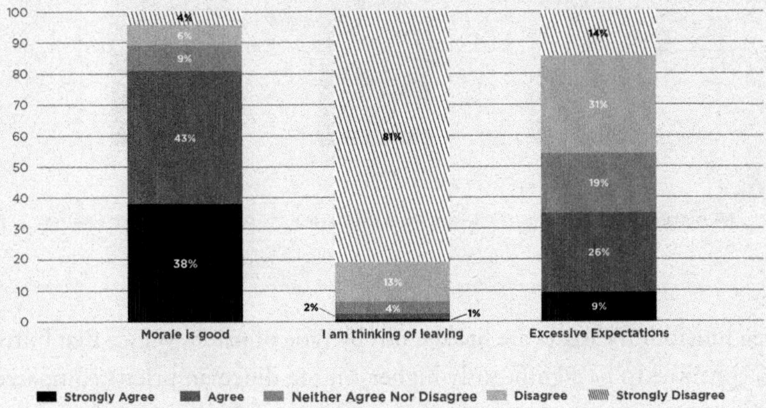

Psychological Distress, Burnout, and Loneliness

We measured psychological distress using a widely used validated measure called the Kessler scale. Using this measure, we find that only 2 percent of priests in 2025 can be classified as experiencing severe psychological distress, which is lower than the first wave (3.5 percent), and considerably lower than the US population (6 percent).[1]

Nonetheless, symptoms of ministerial burnout persist. As in the first wave, we asked the following items: "It happens more and more often that I talk about my ministry work in a negative way"; "During my ministry work, I often feel emotionally drained"; and "I usually feel worn out and weary after my ministry work." We found again that approximately 39 percent agree with at least one of three burnout items, and 5 percent register "high burnout," or agreement with all three (see Figure B2).

1 Judith J. Prochaska et al., "Validity Study of the K6 Scale as a Measure of Moderate Mental Distress Based on Mental Health Treatment Need and Utilization." *International Journal of Methods in Psychiatric Research* 21, no. 2 (2012): 88–97.

Figure B2. Burnout among priests

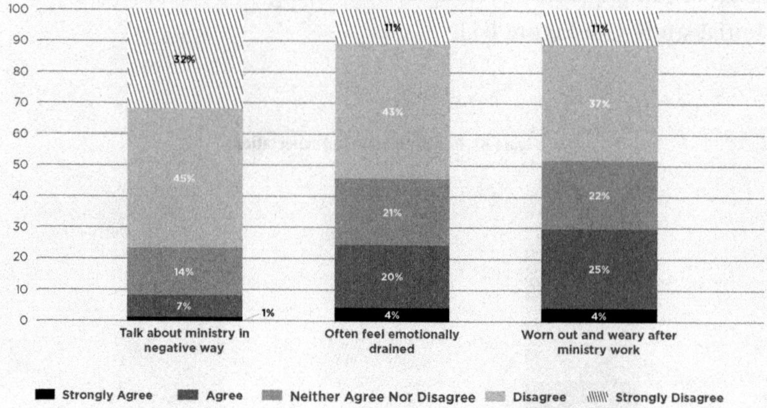

When burnout measures are broken out by type of priest, we see that burnout rates continue to be significantly higher among diocesan priests compared to religious.

Figure B3. Burnout among diocesan and religious priests

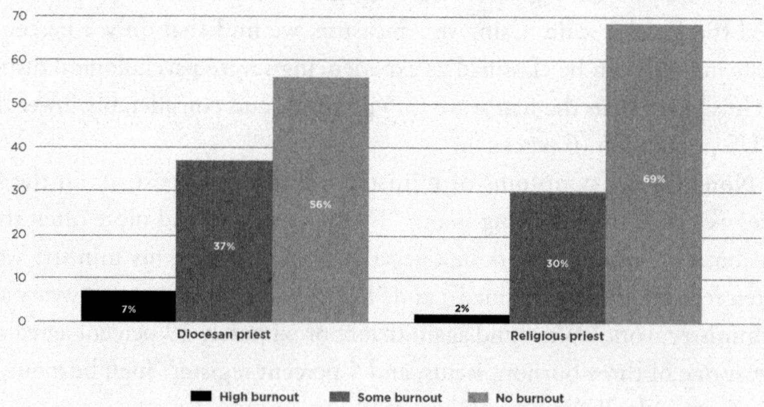

We also find that despite their high flourishing scores, priests are no strangers to loneliness. Again, while it is rare to have chronic loneliness—only about 8 percent of priests experience loneliness "often," about half feel it at least some of the time.

Figure B4. Priests' experiences of loneliness

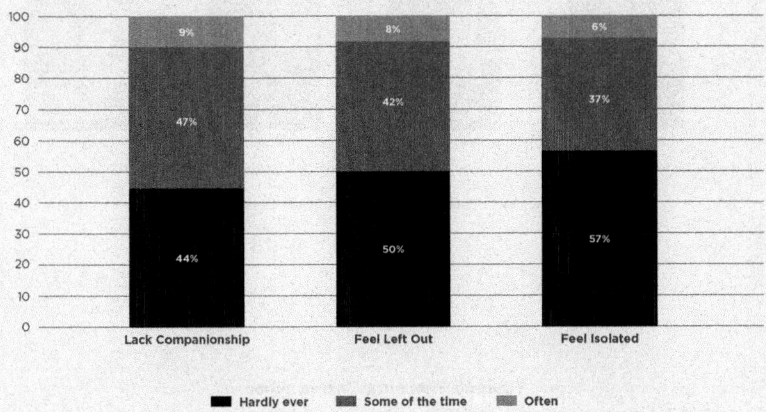

Confidence in Ecclesial Leadership

In what is perhaps a Catholic version of Fenno's Paradox, where everybody hates Congress but many love their own congressperson, priests continue to report much higher levels confidence in their own bishop compared to confidence in the US bishops in general. Specifically, while only 15 percent of diocesan priests and 8 percent of religious priests have "very little" confidence in the leadership and decision-making of their superior, more than a quarter of priests feel the same about US bishops in general (see Figure B5).

Trust in one's bishop as well as trust in US bishops in general have, however, both increased over the past couple of years. In 2025, 52 percent of diocesan priests answered that they had "a great deal" or "quite a lot of" confidence in their own bishop, up from 49 percent in 2022 (see Figure B6). We also find that 27 percent of priests now express either "a great deal" or "quite a lot of" confidence in US bishops in general, compared to 24 percent in 2022.

Figure B5. Priests' confidence in their leaders

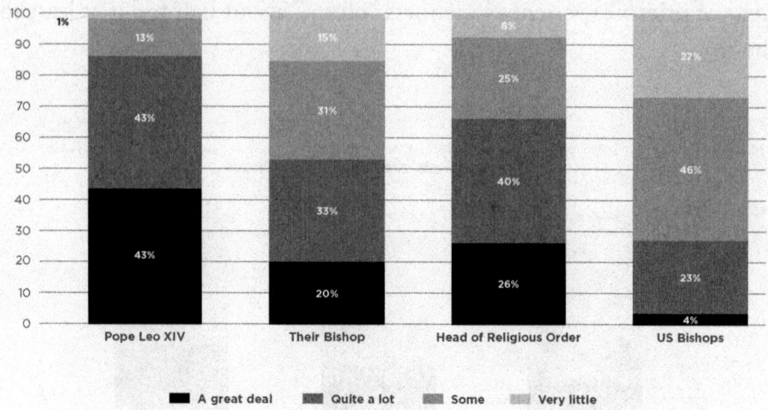

Figure B6. Priests' trust in their bishop

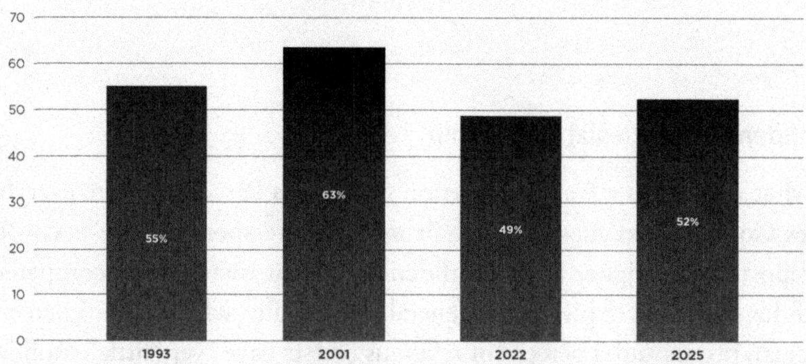

The election of Pope Leo XIV appears to have lifted papal sentiment among priests; scarcely 1 percent register minimal confidence in the Holy Father, while the vast majority (around 86 percent) report "quite a lot" or "a great deal" of confidence. As the survey period roughly coincided with Leo's first two months in office, this result shows that the first American pope made a widely positive impression to begin his reign.

Perceived Theological and Political Alignment

Priests' theological and political views do not show significant change since 2022. In the 2025 survey, we introduced a question asking whether priests perceived their bishops and major superiors to be more or less conservative than themselves on theological and political issues (see Figure B7).

Figure B7. Priests' perceptions of theological and political alignment with their bishop/major superior

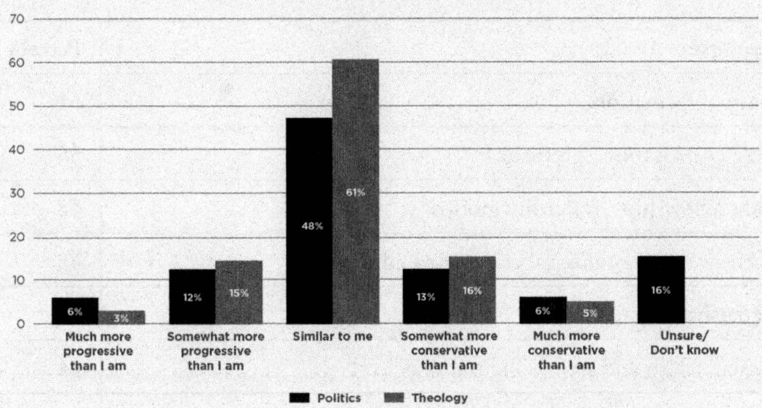

Our results demonstrate that the modal priest sees his bishop or major superior as broadly aligned with his own views. More than half perceive theological concord; those who perceive a gap are evenly split between viewing their bishop as more conservative or as more liberal than themselves. The pattern remains generally similar when analyzed separately for diocesan priests' perceptions of their bishops and religious priests' perceptions of their major superiors. Overall, there is no consistent perception among priests that bishops or major superiors lean systematically more conservative or liberal relative to their own views.

Ongoing Formation Needs

We also asked the priests which opportunities for additional formation they were interested in (Table B1). We find that appetite for continuing formation remains high. Major interests include spiritual formation (61 percent), convocations/retreats (55 percent), and priest-fellowship initiatives (48 percent). Surprisingly, given the degree that priests in the interviews talked about the difficulties of doing administrative tasks for which they were not trained, only 24 percent mentioned business and administrative training. Only one priest in ten feels no current need for additional formation, underscoring the value of sustained investment in collegial, fraternal, and theological development.

Table B1 Priests' interests in ongoing formation

Response	Percent
Spiritual formation	61
Priest convocations / retreats	55
Priest fellowship / fraternity groups	48
Doctrinal and theological continuing education	48
Leadership training	36
Mental health and well-being training	34
Business and administrative training	24
Intercultural ministry training	21
Formal education (higher degree studies)	20
Do not feel need for continuing formation at this time	10
Other	8

Conclusion

These highlights from our longitudinal data analysis paint a picture of stable flourishing coupled with persistent stressors. Priests continue to exhibit high morale, low psychological distress, and enduring vocational commitment. Nevertheless, one priest in four reports burnout symptoms, and skepticism toward the episcopate (especially in general) remains pronounced.

Ongoing analyses of our data, presently underway, will probe cohort effects, diocesan context, predictors of change since 2022, as well as attitudes around timely topics like synodality and the Traditional Latin Mass (TLM). We anticipate that this continued research will deepen the Church's understanding of the presbyterate's lived experience and inform concrete strategies to support their spiritual, emotional, and pastoral health.

BIBLIOGRAPHY

Adams, C. J., H. Hough, R. J. Proeschold-Bell, J. Yao, and M. Kolkin. "Clergy Burnout: A Comparison Study with Other Helping Professions." *Pastoral Psychology* 66, no. 2 (2016): 147–75.

Adamsons, Kary, and Pasley, Kay. "Parents' Fathering Identity Standards and Later Father Involvement." *Journal of Family Issues* 37 (2016): 221–44.

Armstrong, Regis J., J. A. Wayne Hellman, and William J. Short, eds. *Francis of Assisi: Early Documents, vol. I: The Saint.* New City Press, 1999.

Barrera, Angelica Y. "Educational Attainment and Growth Among Individuals with Absent Fathers." PhD diss., Walden University, 2021.

Benedict XVI, Pope. *Jesus of Nazareth: From the Baptism in the Jordan to the Transfiguration.* Doubleday, 2007.

Benedict XVI, Pope. *Omnium in mentem.* Apostolic Letter. October 26, 2009.

Berry, Jason. *Lead Us Not Into Temptation: Catholic Priests and the Sexual Abuse of Children.* Doubleday, 1992.

Bohr, David. *The Diocesan Priest: Consecrated and Sent.* Liturgical Press, 2009.

Boren, Justin P. "The Relationships Between Co-Rumination, Social Support, Stress, and Burnout Among Working Adults." *Management Communication Quarterly* 28 (2014): 3–25.

Blankenhorn, David. *Fatherless America: Confronting Our Most Urgent Social Problem.* Basic Books, 1995.

Bradshaw, M., C. G. Ellison, and K. J. Flannelly. "Prayer, God Imagery, and Symptoms of Psychopathology." *Journal for the Scientific Study of Religion* 47, no. 4 (2008): 644–59.

Bradshaw, M., and B. V. Kent. "Prayer, Attachment to God, and Changes in Psychological Well-Being in Later Life." *Journal of Aging and Health* 30, no. 5 (2018): 667–91.

Byrd-Craven, J., D. Geary, A. Rose, and D. Ponzi. "Co-Ruminating Increases Stress Hormone Levels in Women." *Hormones and Behavior* 53, no. 3 (2008): 489–92.

Cahill, Lisa Sowle. "Accent on the Masculine." In *Understanding Veritatis Splendor: The Encyclical Letter of Pope John Paul II on the Church's Moral Teaching*, edited by John Wilkins. SPCK, 1994.

Cairo, Michael F. *The Gulf: The Bush Presidencies and the Middle East.* University Press of Kentucky, 2012.

Cajka, Peter. *Follow Your Conscience: The Catholic Church and the Spirit of the Sixties*. University of Chicago Press, 2021.

Castelli, Jim. *The Bishops and the Bomb: Waging Peace in a Nuclear Age.* 1st ed. Image Books, 1983.

Castellucci, Erio. "La *Presbyterorum Ordinis* cinquant'anni dopo: Genesi, sviluppo, attualità." In *Una vocazione, una formazione, una missione*, edited by Congregazione per il Clero. Libreria Editrice Vaticana, 2016.

Casto, Lucio. *La Direzione spirituale come paternità*. Effatà Editrice, 2003.

Catechism of the Catholic Church. Libreria Editrice Vaticana, 1994.

Center for Applied Research in the Apostolate (CARA). "New Seminarians Bring Graces and Challenges." *The CARA Report* 5, no. 4 (2000): 1, 11.

Code of Canon Law. Latin-English Edition. Canon Law Society of America, 1999.

Congregation for Bishops. *Directory for the Pastoral Ministry of Bishops: Apostolorum successores*. Libreria Editrice Vaticana, 2004.

Congregation for the Clergy. *The Gift of the Priestly Vocation: Ratio Fundamentalis Institutionis Sacerdotalis.* Libreria Editrice Vaticana, 2016.

Congregation for the Clergy. *The Priest, Pastor, and Leader of the Parish Community*. August 4, 2002. All Vatican documents available at vatican.va unless otherwise noted.

Council of Trent. *Decree of Reform of the 23rd Session*, July 15, 1563. In *Decrees of the Ecumenical Councils*, vol. 2, edited by Norman Tanner. Georgetown University Press, 1990.

Cranney, Stephen. "Conservatism, Prayer, and Flourishing Among Catholic Priests." *Review of Religious Research* 66, no. 4 (2024): 388–98.

Donohue, William. *The Truth About Clergy Sexual Abuse: Clarifying the Facts and the Causes*. Ignatius Press, 2021.

Doyle, Thomas, Michael Peterson, and Ray Mouton. "The Problem of Sexual Molestation by Roman Catholic Clergy: Meeting the Problem in a Comprehensive and Responsible Manner." Confidential report, 1985. https://www.bishop-accountability.org/reports/1985_06_09_Doyle_Manual/DoyleManual_NCR_combined.pdf

Dulles, Avery Cardinal. *Church and Society: The Laurence J. McGinley Lectures, 1988–2007*. Fordham University Press, 2009.

Dulles, Avery. "Rights of Accused Priests: Toward a Revision of the Dallas Charter and the Essential Norms." *America* 190. June 21–28, 2004: 19–23.

Dulles, Avery, and Germain Grisez. "Sin, Grace, and Zero Tolerance: An Exchange." *First Things* 151. March 2005: 27–36.

Ellison, C. G., M. Bradshaw, K. J. Flannelly, and K. C. Galek. "Prayer, Attachment to God, and Symptoms of Anxiety-Related Disorders Among US Adults." *Sociology of Religion* 75, no. 2 (2014): 208–33.

Fenton, Joseph C. *The Diocesan Priest in the Church of Christ*. Cluny Media, 2018.

Fichter, Joseph H., SJ. *America's Forgotten Priests: What They Are Saying*. Harper and Row, 1968.

Fichter, Joseph H., SJ. *Religion as an Occupation: A Study in the Sociology of Professions*. University of Notre Dame Press, 1961.

Fichter, Stephen J., Thomas P. Gaunt, Catherine Hoegeman, and Paul M. Perl. *Catholic Bishops in the United States: Church Leadership in the Third Millennium*. Oxford University Press, 2019.

Fornés, Juan. "Part I: Christian Faithful." In *Exegetical Commentary on the Code of Canon Law*, edited by Ernest Caparros, vol. 2/1. Wilson & Lafleur; Midwest Theological Forum, 2004.

Foss, Richard W. "Burnout Among Clergy and Helping Professionals: Situational and Personality Correlates." PhD diss., Fuller Theological Seminary, 2002.

Francis, Pope. "Address to the Community of the Pontifical Lombard Seminary." February 7, 2022.

Francis, Pope. *Disciples Together on the Road: Words of Pope Francis for Priests*. Libreria Editrice Vaticana, 2016.

Francis, Pope. *Patris Corde: An Apostolic Letter on the 150th Anniversary of the Proclamation of St. Joseph as Patron of the Universal Church*. December 8, 2020.

Francis, Pope. *Vos estis lux mundi*. Apostolic Letter Issued Motu Proprio. May 7, 2019.

Francis of Assisi. "A Letter to a Minister (1221–1223)." In *Francis of Assisi: Early Documents,* vol. I, edited by Regis J. Armstrong, J. A. Wayne Hellman, and William J. Short. New City Press, 1999.

Fredrickson, Barbara L. "The Role of Positive Emotions in Positive Psychology: The Broaden-and-Build Theory of Positive Emotions." *American Psychologist* 56, no. 3 (2001): 218–26.

Froehle, Bryan T. "Research on Catholic Priests in the United States, Since the Council: Modeling the Dialogue Between Theology and Social Science." *U.S. Catholic Historian* 29, no. 4 (2011): 19–46.

Gati, Charles. *Zbig: The Strategy and Statecraft of Zbigniew Brzezinski*. Johns Hopkins University Press, 2013.

Gautier, Mary L., Paul M. Perl, and Stephen J. Fichter. *Same Call, Different Men: The Evolution of the Priesthood Since Vatican II*. Liturgical Press, 2012.

Gottman, J. M., and R. W. Levenson. "Marital Processes Predictive of Later Dissolution: Behavior, Psychology and Health." *Journal of Personality and Social Psychology* 63 (1992): 221–33.

Gottman, J. M., J. Coan, S. Carrere, and C. Swanson. "Predicting Marital Happiness and Stability from Newlywed Interactions." *Journal of Marriage and the Family* 60 (1998): 5–22.

Granados, José. "Priesthood: A Sacrament of the Father." *Communio: International Catholic Review* 36, no. 2 (2009): 186–218.

Greeley, Andrew. *Priests in the United States: Reflections on a Survey*. Doubleday, 1972.

Greeley, Andrew, and National Opinion Research Center. *The Catholic Priest in the United States: Sociological Investigations*. United States Catholic Conference, Publications Office, 1972.

Griffin, Carter. *Why Celibacy? Reclaiming the Fatherhood of the Priest*. Emmaus Road Publishing, 2019.

Grosch, William N., and David C. Olsen. "Clergy Burnout: An Integrative Approach." *Journal of Clinical Psychology* 56, no. 5 (2000): 619–32.

Gula, Richard M. *The Call to Holiness: Embracing a Fully Christian Life*. Paulist Press, 2003.

Gula, Richard M. *Reason Informed by Faith: Foundations of Catholic Morality*. Paulist Press, 1989.

Hansen, Fredrik. "Sound Decentralization and Institutional Synodality." *The Jurist* 79 (2023): 375–92.

Hentoff, Nat. *John Cardinal O'Connor: At the Storm Center of a Changing American Catholic Church*. Scribner, 1988.

Hochschild, Arlie Russell with Anne Machung. *The Second Shift*. Penguin Books, 2003.

Hoge, Dean R., and Jacqueline E. Wenger. *Evolving Visions of the Priesthood: Changes from Vatican II to the Turn of the New Century*. Liturgical Press, 2003. 2nd ed., 2017.

Hoge, Dean R., and Jacqueline E. Wenger. "Survey of American Catholic Priests," 2001. https://www.thearda.com/data-archive?fid=PRIEST01

Hoge, Dean R., Joseph J. Shields, and Douglas L. Griffin. "Changes in Satisfaction and Institutional Attitudes of Catholic Priests, 1970–1993." *Sociology of Religion* 56, no. 2 (1995): 195–214.

Hoge, Dean R., Joseph J. Shields, and Mary Jeanne Verdieck. "Changing Age Distribution and Theological Attitudes of Catholic Priests, 1970–1985." *Sociological Analysis* 49, no. 3 (1988): 264–80.

Hünermann, Peter. "Theologischer Kommentar zur dogmatischen Konstitution über die Kirche, *Lumen Gentium*." In *Herders Theologischer Kommentar zum Zweiten Vatikanischen Konzil*, vol. 2, edited by Peter Hünermann and Bernd Jochen Hilberath. Herder, 2009.

Ignatius of Antioch. "Letter to the Ephesians." In *The Apostolic Fathers in English*, edited by Michael W. Holmes. 3rd ed. Baker Academic, 2006.

Isacco, Anthony. "A Developmental Model of Evidence-Based Interventions for Catholic Clergy." Paper presented at the *Catholic Psychotherapy Association Annual Conference*. Scottsdale, AZ, May 2020.

Isacco, Anthony, and David Songy. "Spiritual Fatherhood of Catholic Priests: Conceptualization and Practical Applications." *Spirituality in Clinical Practice* 9 (2022): 114–26.

Isacco, Anthony, and Jay C. Wade. *Religion, Spirituality, and Masculinity: New Insights for Counselors*. Routledge, 2019.

Jacobi, Christopher Justin, Brandon Vaidyanathan, and Maria Andronicou. "Mental Health Correlates of Sharing Private Problems in Congregations During the COVID-19 Pandemic." *Journal for the Scientific Study of Religion* 61 (2002): 553–63.

Jiang, Lixin, and Tahira M. Probst. "Do Your Employees (Collectively) Trust You? The Importance of Trust Climate Beyond Individual Trust." *Scandinavian Journal of Management* 31, no. 4 (2015): 526–35.

John Jay College of Criminal Justice. *The Causes and Context of Sexual Abuse of Minors by Catholic Priests in the United States, 1950–2010*. USCCB, 2011.

John Jay College of Criminal Justice. *The Nature and Scope of the Problem of Sexual Abuse of Minors by Catholic Priests and Deacons in the United States, 1950–2002*. USCCB, 2004.

John Paul II, Pope. "Address to CELAM" (Opening Address of the 19th General Assembly of CELAM, March 9, 1983, Port-au Prince, Haiti). *L'Osservatore Romano* English Edition 16, no. 780 (April 18, 1983).

John Paul II, Pope. *Christifideles laici*. Post-Synodal Apostolic Exhortation. December 30, 1988.

John Paul II, Pope. *Crossing the Threshold of Hope*. Knopf, 1994.

John Paul II, Pope. *Evangelium Vitae*. Encyclical Letter. March 25, 1995.

John Paul II, Pope. *Letter to Families Gratissimam Sane*. February 2, 1994.

John Paul II, Pope. *Pastores dabo vobis*. Post-Synodal Apostolic Exhortation. March 15, 1992.

John Paul II, Pope. *Pastores gregis*. Post-Synodal Apostolic Exhortation. October 16, 2003.

Kane, Michael N. "A Qualitative Survey of the Attitudes of Catholic Priests Toward Bishops and Ministry Following the Sexual Abuse Revelations of 2002." *Pastoral Psychology* 57 (2008): 183–98.

Kengor, Paul. *A Pope and a President: John Paul II, Ronald Reagan, and the Extraordinary Untold Story of the 20th Century*. Regnery Publishing, 2017.

Kereszty, Roch A. *The Church of God in Jesus Christ: A Catholic Ecclesiology*. The Catholic University of America Press, 2019.

King, Autumn P. "The National Fatherhood League: Increasing Father Involvement in the Black American Community." DSW diss., California Baptist University, 2022.

Kiselica, Mark S., Sheila Benton-Wright, and Matt Englar-Carlson. "Accentuating Positive Masculinity: A New Foundation for the Psychology of Boys, Men, and Masculinity." In *APA Handbooks in Psychology: APA Handbook of Men and Masculinities*, edited by Y. Joel Wong and Stephen R. Wester. American Psychological Association, 2016.

Konieczny, Mary Ellen, Charles C. Camosy, and Tricia C. Bruce, eds. *Polarization in the US Catholic Church: Naming the Wounds, Beginning to Heal*. Liturgical Press, 2016.

Lacey, Michael J., and Francis Oakley, eds. *The Crisis of Authority in Catholic Modernity*. Oxford University Press, 2011.

Lamb, Matthew L., and Matthew Levering, eds. *The Reception of Vatican II.* Oxford University Press, 2017.

Lamb, Michael E. "How Do Fathers Influence Children's Development? Let Me Count the Ways." In *The Role of the Father in Child Development, 5th ed.,* edited by Michael E. Lamb. Wiley & Sons, 2010.

Langan, John P., ed. *Catholic Universities in Church and Society: A Dialogue on Ex Corde Ecclesiae.* Georgetown University Press, 1993.

Lee, Matthew T., Laura D. Kubzansky, and Tyler J. VanderWeele, eds. *Measuring Well-Being: Interdisciplinary Perspectives from the Social Sciences and the Humanities.* Oxford University Press, 2021.

Lockwood, Christopher. "Spiritual Fatherhood After the Model of Christ in the Gospel According to John." *Greek Orthodox Theological Review* 59 (2010): 81–127.

Maher, Joseph R., and David A. Shaneyfelt. "When the Church Defames Her Priests." *Homiletic and Pastoral Review.* July 21, 2017. https://www.hprweb.com/2017/07/when-the-church-defames-her-priests/

Mankowski, Paul V., SJ. *Jesuit at Large: Essays and Reviews.* Edited by George Weigel. Ignatius Press, 2021.

Marlin, George J., and Brad Miner. *Sons of Saint Patrick: A History of the Archbishops of New York, from Dagger John to Timmytown.* Ignatius Press, 2017.

Maslach, Christina, and Michael P. Leiter. "Burnout and Engagement in the Workplace: A Contextual Analysis." In *Advances in Motivation and Achievement*, vol. 11, edited by Timothy C. Urdan. JAI Press, 1999.

Maslach, Christina, and Michael P. Leiter. "Understanding the Burnout Experience: Recent Research and Its Implications for Psychiatry." *World Psychiatry* 15, no. 2 (2016): 103–11. https://doi.org/10.1002/wps.20311

Mazza, Michael J. "*Bona Fama* in an Age of 'Transparency': Publishing Lists of 'Credibly Accused' Clerics." *The Jurist: Studies in Church Law and Ministry* 78 (2022): 445–76.

Mazza, Michael J. "Moral Certainty in Uncertain Times: The Importance of Standards of Proof When Responding to Accusations of Clerical Misconduct." *The Jurist: Studies in Church Law and Ministry* 79 (2023): 285–323.

McChesney, Kathleen. "What Caused the Crisis? Key Findings of the John Jay College Study on Clergy Sexual Abuse." *America.* June 6, 2011.

McCormick, Richard A., SJ. "Some Early Reactions to 'Veritatis Splendor.'" *Theological Studies* 55, no. 3 (1994): 481–507.

McCoy, John A. *A Still and Quiet Conscience: The Archbishop Who Challenged a Pope, a President, and a Church.* Orbis Books, 2015.

Newman, David Benjamin. "Within-Person Relationships Among Prayer, Well-Being, and Daily Events." MA thesis, College of William and Mary, 2014.

Newman, John Henry. *The Via Media of the Anglican Church.* 3rd ed. London: Longmans, Green, 1877.

Nichols, Aidan. *Holy Order: Apostolic Priesthood from the New Testament to the Second Vatican Council.* Wipf and Stock Publishers, 1990.

Parke, Ross D. *Fatherhood.* Harvard University Press, 1996.

Pennsylvania Office of Attorney General. *Report I of the 40th Statewide Investigating Grand Jury: The Sexual Abuse of Children in the Roman Catholic Church.* Harrisburg, PA: Office of Attorney General, 2018. https://www.attorneygeneral.gov/report/

Perone Seidel, Flory L. "The Proclivity of Juvenile Crime in Fatherless Homes: An Urban Perspective." PsyD diss., University of Arizona, 2021.

Philippe, Jacques. *Priestly Fatherhood: Treasure in Earthen Vessels.* Scepter Publishers, 2021.

Pius XII, Pope. *Sacramentum Ordinis.* Apostolic Constitution, November 13, 1947. *AAS* 40 (1948): 5–7.

Plante, Thomas G., and Kathleen L. McChesney, eds. *Sexual Abuse in the Catholic Church: A Decade of Crisis, 2002–2012.* Praeger, 2012.

Pleck, Joseph. "Paternal Involvement: Revised Conceptualization and Theoretical Linkages with Child Outcomes." In *The Role of the Father in Child Development,* 5th ed., edited by Michael E. Lamb. Wiley, 2010.

Rahner, Karl. "Chapter III. The Hierarchical Structure of the Church, with Special Reference to the Episcopate." In *Commentary on the Documents of Vatican II,* vol. 1, edited by Herbert Vorgrimler. Burns and Oates, 1967.

Ratzinger, Joseph. *The God of Jesus Christ: Meditations on God in the Trinity.* Franciscan Herald Press, 1979.

Reese, Thomas J., SJ. *A Flock of Shepherds: The National Conference of Catholic Bishops.* Rowman & Littlefield, 1992.

Richi Alberti, Gabriel. "L'episcopato: Pienezza del sacramento dell'ordine." In *L'esercizio dell'autorità nella Chiesa: Riflessioni a partire dell'esortazione apostolica 'Pastores gregis'*, edited by Arturo Cattaneo. Marcianum Press, 2005.

Rossetti, Stephen J. *Priesthood in a Time of Crisis: A New Study of the Psychological and Spiritual Health of Priests*. Ave Maria Press, 2023.

Rossetti, Stephen J. *Why Priests Are Happy: A Study of the Psychological and Spiritual Health of Priests*. Ave Maria Press, 2011.

Rossetti, Stephen. J., and Colin J. Rhoades. "Burnout in Catholic Clergy: A Predictive Model Using Psychological and Spiritual Variables." *Psychology of Religion and Spirituality* 5, no. 4 (2013): 335–41.

Saint Luke Institute Clergy & Religious Health Monitor. https://sli.org/health-monitor/, accessed July 27, 2024.

Second Vatican Council. *Gaudium et spes*. Pastoral Constitution on the Church in the Modern World. December 7, 1965. In *Vatican Council II: The Conciliar and Post Conciliar Documents*, new rev. ed., vol. 1, edited by Austin Flannery. Costello, 1996.

Schuth, Katarina. *Seminaries, Theologates, and the Future of Church Ministry: An Analysis of Trends and Transitions*. Liturgical Press, 1999.

Scott, Hannah K., Ankit Jain, and Mark Cogburn. "Behavior Modification." In *StatPearls*. StatPearls Publishing, 2023. Last modified July 10, 2023. https://pubmed.ncbi.nlm.nih.gov/29083709/

Secretariat of the Holy See. *Report on the Holy See's Institutional Knowledge and Decision-Making Related to Former Cardinal Theodore Edgar McCarrick (1930–2017)*. November 10, 2020.

Serrianne, Nina Esperanza. *America in the Nineties*. Syracuse University Press, 2015.

Skolnick, Arlene. "Grounds for Marriage: How Relationships Succeed or Fail." In *Family in Transition*, 15th ed., edited by Arlene S. Skolnick and Jerome H. Skolnick. Pearson, 2009.

Skolnick, Arlene. "Married Lives: Longitudinal Perspectives on Marriage." In *Present and Past in Middle Life*, edited by Dorothy H. Eichorn, John A. Clausen, Norma Haan, Marjorie P. Honzik, and Paul H. Mussen. Academic Press, 1981.

Songy, David G. *Spiritual Direction for Priestly Celibacy.* Capuchin Province of Mid-America, 2012.

Steinfels, Peter. *A People Adrift: The Crisis of the Roman Catholic Church in America.* Simon and Schuster, 2013.

Tanner, Norman, ed. *Decrees of the Ecumenical Councils.* 2 vols. Georgetown University Press, 1990.

Tertullian. *The Prescription Against Heretics.* Translated by Peter Holmes. In *Ante-Nicene Fathers,* vol. 3, edited by Alexander Roberts and James Donaldson. Christian Literature Publishing Co., 1885. Revised and edited for New Advent by Kevin Knight. http://www.newadvent.org/fathers/0311.htm

Tremblay, Sandra, and Tamarha Pierce. "Perceptions of Fatherhood: Longitudinal Reciprocal Associations Within the Couple." *Canadian Journal of Behavioural Science* 43, no. 2 (2011): 99–110.

Toups, David L. *Reclaiming Our Priestly Character.* Rev. ed. IPF Publications, 2010.

United States Conference of Catholic Bishops. *Charter for the Protection of Children and Young People.* USCCB, 2002. Revised 2018. https://www.usccb.org/offices/child-and-youth-protection/charter-protection-children-and-young-people

United States Conference of Catholic Bishops. *Guide to Ongoing Formation of Priests.* USCCB, 2023.

United States Conference of Catholic Bishops. *The Program of Priestly Formation in the United States of America.* 6th ed. USCCB, 2022.

United States Conference of Catholic Bishops. *The Roman Pontifical: Ordination of a Bishop, of Priests, and of Deacons.* USCCB, 2021.

Upenieks, Laura. "Occupational Stressors and Flourishing Among Roman Catholic Priests: The Eucharist as the 'Source and Summit.'" *Review of Religious Research* 66, no. 4 (2024): 305–31.

Upenieks, Laura. "Unpacking the Relationship Between Prayer and Anxiety: A Consideration of Prayer Types and Expectations in the United States." *Journal of Religion and Health* 62 (2023): 1810–31.

Upenieks, Laura, and David E. Eagle. "Divine Struggles Among Those Doing God's Work: A Longitudinal Assessment Predicting Depression and Burnout and the Role of Social Support in United Methodist Clergy." *Sociology of Religion* 85, no. 1 (2024): 83–111.

Vaidyanathan, Brandon, Christopher Jacobi, Chelsea Rae Kelly, Tricia Bruce, Stephen White, and Sara Perla. "Polarization, Generational Dynamics, and the Ongoing Impact of the Abuse Crisis: Further

Insights from the National Study of Catholic Priests." The Catholic University of America, November 2023.

Vaidyanathan, Brandon, Christopher Jacobi, Chelsea Rae Kelly, Stephen White, and Sara Perla. "Well-Being, Trust, and Policy in a Time of Crisis: Highlights from the National Study of Catholic Priests." The Catholic Project. The Catholic University of America, 2022.

VanderWeele, Tyler J. "On the Promotion of Human Flourishing." *Proceedings of the National Academy of Sciences* 114, no. 31 (2017): 8148–56.

VanderWeele, Tyler J., Ying Chen, and Matthew T. Lee. "Measuring Well-Being: A Review of the Flourishing Index and the Secure Flourishing Index." *Social Science & Medicine* 266 (2020): 113302.

Vermurlen, Brad, Stephen Cranney, and Mark Regnerus. *Introducing the 2021 Survey of American Catholic Priests: Overview and Selected Findings.* SSRN, October 28, 2021. https://ssrn.com/abstract=3951931

Vermurlen, Brad, Stephen Cranney, and Mark Regnerus. "The Ongoing Conservative Turn in the American Catholic Priesthood." *Sociological Spectrum* 43, no. 2–3 (2023): 72–88.

Weigel, George. *The End and the Beginning: Pope John Paul II—The Victory of Freedom, the Last Years, the Legacy.* Random House Publishing Group, 2011.

Weigel, George. *Witness to Hope: The Biography of Pope John Paul II.* 1st Perennial ed. Harper Perennial, 2001.

Wiggins, Jonathan L., and Mary L. Gautier. *Summary of 20 Years of Data Collected Annually for the CARA Survey of Allegations and Costs for U.S. Catholic Dioceses, Eparchies, and Religious Communities of Men.* Center for Applied Research in the Apostolate, January 2025.

LIST OF CONTRIBUTORS

Stephen Cranney, PhD, has a data science business in the Washington, DC area; he is a non-resident fellow at Baylor's Institute for the Studies of Religion and teaches at The Catholic University of America.

Most Rev. Edgar M. da Cunha, SDV, DD, is Bishop of Fall River, Massachusetts.

Maureen K. Day, PhD, is a visiting research fellow at Villanova University's Center for Church Management and award-winning author of *Cultural Catholics: Who They Are, How to Respond* (Liturgical Press 2024).

Rev. Msgr. Thomas G. Guarino, STD, is professor emeritus of systematic theology at Seton Hall University, South Orange, NJ.

Most Rev. Fredrik Hansen, JCD, is the Diocesan Bishop of Oslo, Norway.

Christopher Jacobi, PhD, serves as the executive director of the independent Expert Council for the Protection from Sexual Abuse and Experiences of Violence, which was established and is funded by the German Bishops' Conference.

Sara Perla (editor) is the communications manager for The Catholic Project at The Catholic University of America.

Matthew S. Robinson is Director of Clergy Support at the Diocese of Fall River, Massachusetts, and founder of The Shepherd Within LLC.

Fr. David Songy, OFMCap., STD, PsyD, is a clinical psychologist and former President and CEO of Saint Luke Institute, and presently serves as Provincial Minister of the Capuchin Province of St. Conrad.

Rev. Anthony Stoeppel, STD, a bi-ritual Latin-Byzantine priest, serves as Associate Professor of Church Management at The Catholic University of America's Busch School of Business.

Brooke Tranten, PhD, holds a doctorate in American History from Marquette University and is a staff member at the de Nicola Center for Ethics and Culture at the University of Notre Dame.

Brandon Vaidyanathan, PhD (editor), is Professor of Sociology and Director of the Institutional Flourishing Lab at The Catholic University of America.

Stephen P. White (editor) is executive director of The Catholic Project at The Catholic University of America and a fellow in Catholic Studies at the Ethics and Public Policy Center.

INDEX